MODERN ECONOMICS

Jan Pen was born in 1921. He studied economics at Amsterdam University, where he received a doctorate in 1950. Until 1956 he worked in the Ministry of Economic Affairs, finally as Director of General Economic Policy. Since 1956 he has been Professor of Economics at Groningen University, and from 1960 until 1967 he was Visiting Professor of Macro-economics at the Free University of Brussels. He is a Fellow of the Royal Netherlands Academy of Sciences.

He has published several books in D... *The Joy of Economics* ... *Economic Actualities* (... *gaining*, written in 1949 ... the Harvard University ... not sure why. *Harmony* ... (1966), which contains a ... ...gy than the present volume, *A Pri... ...national Trade* (1967) and *Income Distribution* (Penguin, 1971) have also been published in English. His most recent works are *Those Stupid Economists and Their Holy Cows* (1976) and (with Jan Tinbergen) *Towards a More Equitable Income Distribution* (1977). In 1979 he published a book which tries to visualize economic life and economic theory, *Look, Economics.*

J. PEN

MODERN ECONOMICS

TRANSLATED FROM THE DUTCH
BY
TREVOR S. PRESTON

Second Edition

PENGUIN BOOKS

Penguin Books Ltd, Harmondsworth, Middlesex, England
Penguin Books, 625 Madison Avenue, New York, New York 10022, U.S.A.
Penguin Books Australia Ltd, Ringwood, Victoria, Australia
Penguin Books Canada Ltd, 2801 John Street, Markham, Ontario, Canada L3R 1B4
Penguin Books (N.Z.) Ltd, 182–190 Wairau Road, Auckland 10, New Zealand

—

Moderne Economie first published by Uitgeverij Het Spectrum Utrecht 1958
Published in Pelican Books 1965
Reprinted 1966, 1967
Reprinted with revisions 1969
Reprinted 1970, 1972
Reprinted with revisions 1974, 1976
Reprinted 1978
Second edition 1980
Reprinted 1982

—

—

Made and printed in Great Britain by
Hazell Watson & Viney Ltd, Aylesbury, Bucks
Set in Monotype Times

Contents

CONTENTS

CHAPTER IV

How do we Build a Model?

CHAPTER V

The Impact of International Trade

CHAPTER VI

The Role of the Budget

CHAPTER VII

The World of Money

CONTENTS

CHAPTER VIII

The Price Level

CHAPTER IX

The Wage Level and Unemployment

CHAPTER X

Economic Growth

CHAPTER XI

Fitting the Jigsaw Together

CONTENTS

CHAPTER XII

Economic Steersmanship

Preface to the Second Edition

A PORTRAIT OF THE AUTHOR AS A WISER MAN

The first edition of *Modern Economics* was written in the fifties. The little book reflected the spirit of the decade; post-war Europe was young and on its way to greater prosperity. So was the author. Insight into economic relationships was growing – model-building and econometric techniques, invented in the thirties, were making conspicuous progress. Government control of economic development, though still highly imperfect, was supposed to improve as long as politicians would heed the advice of economists. Keynesian economics seemed to be the key to a deeper understanding and more efficient control of economic life. The author, though a sceptic by nature, stressed the things he knew. The text radiated confidence. Perhaps this explains part of its commercial success.

The sixties did not dash the economist's hopes. Economic growth in the Western world accelerated to unprecedented rates. Income distribution became less unequal. The welfare state was expanded. We had full employment. There were a few disquieting signs: inflation grew, incomes policies did not really get started, and the balance of payments kept some countries worried, in particular Britain. But the intellectual scene was most lively. Both classical theory and the monetary school made a vigorous comeback. The theory of economic growth acquired new and fascinating dimensions. The wage–price spiral received a good deal of attention. The model-builders integrated these various approaches into their impressive set-ups. Models grew in number and scope. Econometric techniques improved. Even the Treasury got into the act and produced, in 1968, a formidable, fully computerized, set of equations (discussed later on in this book).

In addition, a new school of antigrowth men came to the fore: those who believe that the world will be smothered by the

9

by-products of industrial production. The discussions on the future of Western civilization were tinged with slight alarm. But the debate was an intense one; from the intellectual point of view Europe was a pleasant and stimulating place to live in. The new editions of *Modern Economics* were perhaps less positive in their pronouncements than the original text, but they were selling well. The book was translated into exotic languages (like Polish and Japanese). Hundreds of thousands of copies found their way to the consumer.

The seventies brought economic turbulence of a less pleasant kind. The international monetary system broke down; rates of exchange lost their reassuring semi-constancy. Import prices started to contribute to the wage–price spiral. Unemployment crept up. The profit squeeze made itself felt. The oil crisis precipitated a recession which, in some countries, notably Britain, worsened into a minor depression. Growth rates fell to almost zero, or even became negative. Keynesian recipes did not seem to work. A good deal of bitter criticism was heard. The blame fell on a variety of parties: governments for not governing, trade unions for the 'wage grab', the welfare state for creating excessive tax rates that stifled enterprise. Economists were blamed for failing to understand the situation. This is the Crisis of the Seventies. Confidence in economic steersmanship, democracy, free enterprise and economic science ebbed away.

This new edition of *Modern Economics* has certainly been marked by the events of the seventies. The author is not the same person as the eager young man of the fifties. His approach to the fundamental issues is somewhat different. In three respects the argument has shifted. Firstly, I now believe that the manageability of the economy should not be depicted in overly optimistic tones. The world is somewhat more chaotic than young liberals would have us believe. In particular, the international economy is extremely difficult to keep under control. Of course, economists have always been aware of the fact that national governments have no power over the monetary behaviour of other nations, but in the fifties there was a general belief in international co-operation under the benevolent supervision of organizations like the International Monetary Fund. It was also felt that a reasonable national policy could restore temporary deficits on the balance of payments. The sixties undermined this kind of confidence, and the seventies brought great disappointment – to the author of this book, too – which will be described in Chapter V.

The limits of national policies also came more clearly to the fore. An incomes policy is rejected by the parties that have to consent to it – they usually react to the invitation to observe income moderation by saying: after you. Keynesian demand management is jeopardized by deficits on the balance of payments – that *damned* consequence of international trade. This may easily lead to stop–go. The present edition of this book gives a list of reasons why economic policies of various kinds are likely to meet with limited success.

My second reaction to the Crisis of the Seventies is to stress an old distinction: that between insight and remedy. This distinction is often blurred in popular discussion; the older writings of the present author are guilty of spreading the blur. Economics as a science aims at understanding the world – it has no desire to change it, nor does it supply clear-cut recipes for the politician. The individual economist may feel that steps should be taken towards full employment, higher growth rates, less inflation – but when he makes this type of statement it is the citizen taking over from the scientist. Full employment and price stability are not economic goals. The goal of economics is to explain why Britain experienced 5 per cent unemployment and 24 per cent price inflation in 1975. Or why output per head in manufacturing industry rose during the period 1955–73 by 3·2 per cent in the U.K., and by 5 per cent in France, Italy, Belgium, the Federal Republic of Germany and the Netherlands. What caused the difference? Above all, economics should give the answer in such a form as to shed light on the future.

Of course, insight into the workings of the economy may be helpful to the politician; that is why economics is not a mere intellectual exercise. Indeed, this book contains a section on planning. But in some cases, insight into an undesirable situation may be quite satisfactory without a remedy following from it. If a person dies of old age, the medical profession may have a perfect explanation of the course of events without being able to suggest a therapy. If the volume of world trade shrinks and people in Britain become unemployed (while, at the same time, asking for higher money wages) the economist may have a perfect explanation for the internal situation in the U.K. – but perhaps there is no obvious remedy. Economics as a science should be judged on its powers of explanation, not by the successes or failures of government policy. This point will be taken up in Chapter XII where I shall defend the viewpoint that we do not lack explanations for what happened in the seventies. Indeed, both Keynesian and classical theory predict rather more unemployment than actually occurred in Britain.

These two points – the limited manageability of the economy and the separation between scientific and political responsibility – have little to do with the performance of economics as a science. However, the Crisis of the Seventies also led to a crisis in scientific confidence. This is nothing new. Economics is subject to recurrent crises of this type and they have never discouraged mainstream economists from continuing with their work. But this time the shock was greater than before. Anyway, it changed my personal view of our understanding of the world and this is reflected in the present edition which sees something of a break with my earlier ideas. It is not just caused by a confrontation with unpleasant events like the oil crisis and rising unemployment; it is also a result of spelling out the implications of the methodological insights associated with the name of Karl Popper.* If the reader is interested in an economist's confessions, he should read the following reflections with some attention.

Economics, and in particular macro-economics, is strong in building formal models. Simple theory suggests, for instance, that national income is determined by a three-equation system, saying (1) that national income equals consumption plus investment, (2) that consumption depends on income while (3) investment may be autonomously given. This can be written down in simple algebra: the Keynesian model. It can be extended and refined. The classical model, which says that income depends on labour and capital inputs, can also be defined in a rigorous and elegant manner.

* K. Popper, *Conjectures and Refutations*, 1963.

Textbooks are very good at explaining how this works, and that is how it should be. But the next step is the econometric specification: equations should be given a definite form – relationships should be pinned down in a quantitative way. Here we meet a vast number of uncertainties, difficulties and unsolved problems. They are not just technical ones; these problems have to do with a fundamental gap in our knowledge.

Our ignorance relates in particular to the value of the coefficients that determine the relationship between variables. The coefficients constitute the constant element in a changing world. In the language of mathematics they are called *parameters*, and they are usually represented by Greek letters. Taken together, they determine the structure of the economy. This is what economics is looking for: the structure of the economic interdependencies, defined as the specification of the model and the numerical value of its parameters. Economic science *à la* Popper starts from the idea that the parameters will stay constant with time and that we are able to quantify them.

This idea is not new in itself; it was set forth in earlier editions of *Modern Economics* where the tone was one of self-assurance. Take for instance the first chapter. There the concept of a regression equation is explained: $Z = aX + bY$. I quote (p. 28): 'The connection is given by the theory. The statisticians have collected time series of X, Y and Z. The econometricians have correlated, studied correlation coefficients with a critical eye, and found everything in order.' If I had to write this anew, I would put it as follows: 'More often than not the econometricians found that things were *not* in order: correlation coefficients were rather unsatisfactory for past periods. In times of fast change not only do variables like prices display violent movements, but parameters too sometimes lose their constancy. So the econometricians had to seek new theories. They did so sometimes because they were still confident that they would find a solid relationship, sometimes because they had been at it for a long time, and sometimes because they did not like the possible outcome of a mental process in which the weaknesses of econometric model-building were fully considered.' It cannot be denied that unreliable models unfortunately characterize the state of the art. Some parameters have the highly disagreeable property of changing with time: models turn soft under our hands – sometimes as soft as butter – and relationships between crucial variables are *not* stable. This is particularly true of the factors that determine investment and profits – strategic elements in any model.

The human mind can react to this fact in various ways.* My former reaction would have been as follows: '*Of course* parameters are not really constant with time, it would be most naïve to believe the contrary. In the eighteenth century the relationship between British consumption and British national income – the propensity to consume – was probably different from that in the twentieth century. The velocity of circulation of money was probably different. Investment incentives were different. *Of course* models hold water over only relatively short periods – say twenty years – and even then there is always room for doubt; correlation is never perfect. But this is just one more reason for devising better theories and better models. A lack of insight into quantitative relationships is a perpetual incentive to do better.' I could point to various paragraphs in my earlier publications that are written in this slightly sceptical but still confident spirit. Our knowledge of economic life is still full of holes, but we should try to fill them as soon as possible, and I still believe that the attitude of perseverance is basically the right one.

Yes, but with a change of mood. If economics cannot supply a list of solid parameters, we cannot predict the future. External shocks to the economy – and the seventies were full of them – may have quite unforeseen effects. Nor can we predict the consequences of policy measures. A stern scientist in the spirit of Popper would say: if that is so, economics has no true theory of the economy. We have many unproven hypotheses, sometimes of a highly stimulating nature; we have at our disposal some bits of insight that have stood the test of falsification; we trust that

---

*One possible reaction is that stable parameters do not exist in economic life and that the search for them is a waste of time. In this view, events are unique. They may be analysed but they do not repeat themselves; prediction becomes utterly tenuous. This denial of economic structure means that economic theory goes down the drain and economic history takes its place.

our research will provide us with some more of these results; *but the structure of the economy as a whole is still unknown.* It is subject to speculation and belief.

This in fact is a much more faithful reflection of my present frame of mind than the casual optimism of the earlier editions.

Of course, this does not mean to say that we should abandon the search for the structure of economic life. I do believe that such a thing exists – that is, I do believe that in the course of change, even violent change, some strategic relationships remain the same. If I didn't, I'd be looking for another job. The denial of any kind of constancy implies the end of economics, and this utter agnosticism is certainly not mine.

What, then, is the practical difference between my old and my new frame of mind? Let me stress two points, one negative, one positive. The negative point is that economic textbooks, including the earlier editions of *Modern Economics*, may create a false mood of self-assurance. The elegant models may tempt the reader into believing that he or she understands the real world. That real world is much more chaotic than the smooth, clockwork operation of the models. The Greek alphabet may conceal the fact that many parameters are constant in the textbooks but not in reality. Illustrative numbers take the place of research results, which means that speculation takes the place of empirical science. Moreover, the would-be parameters are given *names* like 'propensity to consume', 'multiplier' ,'capital–output ratio' – this again unconsciously suggests that they are constant. The linguistic pressure on the mind is very great. The formal model is absolutely necessary to provide the mind with coherent ideas, but the reader of the traditional textbook is insufficiently warned against the pitfalls of formal reasoning. The economist's prestige is enhanced by a kind of algebra that is just algebra, and a language that is mere language, not knowledge of the economy.

The more positive point is that, after all, empirical economics has found a limited number of rather stable relationships. We should handle them with cautious pride, and we should try to separate these relationships from the weak and the soft ones. It is one of the duties of the scholar to specify the things that we don't know, even if this specification does away with some of the goodwill which the profession has accumulated by its formal model-building and its technical language.

The reader will find in this new edition a fresh emphasis on the things we don't know. This makes the present book somewhat different from other simple tracts on economics and I hope it will not give rise to the barren feeling that we know nothing at all.

CHAPTER I

The Necessity of Macro-Economics

1·ORDERING YOUR MIND

Most people are economists. They think and talk about incomes, employment, prices, taxes. They are aware of the fact that these key elements of the economy influence each other and that they influence people's lives. But the exact nature of these relationships often remains difficult to grasp; the world is so complex that parts of the whole are easily overlooked. Sometimes rather obvious connections are ignored; for instance, if prices go up, incomes go up – incomes *are* prices, as a matter of fact. Moreover, if we apply the experience of daily life to the national economy, we may arrive at the wrong kind of conclusion. Whilst private debt reduces a person's future income – he has to pay interest on it – public debt does not reduce a nation's future wealth; future generations inherit the obligation to pay interest, but they also inherit the bonds. Finally, strategic figures are often wrongly estimated. There seems to be something about the capitalist system that leads people to overrate the part of national income that goes to the owners of stocks and shares, land and other forms of capital. In most Western countries these capitalists get less than 10 per cent of national income; some casual observers think it may be 50 per cent. Also, the rate of increase of real wages is often underrated. Everybody knows that the seventies have been lean years: external conditions (world trade, import prices) have been adverse, economic policy has failed, the depression has made itself felt. But real disposable income in 1976 was almost 10 per cent higher than in 1970. The latter fact will be denied by many housewives who will say that the loot must have gone to somebody else.*

*But the percentage of households having a washing machine went up from something over 60 per cent to well over 70 per cent and those with central heating from less than a third to almost half.

17

In all these cases professional economics may be helpful. It provides basic facts. More important, it can boast of a tradition, starting with the eighteenth-century *tableau économique*, in which the various economic relationships are ordered in such a way that the whole looks like a system. Economics has developed a language which is particularly suited to discovering these systematic relationships. It has invented special forms of logic, leading to surprising conclusions like the following: given certain conditions, the growth of real income per head equals the quotient of technical progress and the share of labour in national income. Model-building, which is an effective way of creating order in a person's mind, has assumed impressive proportions. The availability of figures has increased enormously, and so have econometric techniques.

The aim of this book is to provide a simple account of how modern economics tries to make the world understandable. The word 'modern' implies that the science is changing. Half in jest it has been said that 'it's all in Marshall'* but this is no longer true. In particular the theory of the economy as a whole – and that is what this book is about – is changing continually. Its vocabulary is growing all the time (Marshall had never heard of stagflation); new results of research are continuously becoming available; schools are waging scientific warfare, with varying success. The reader of this book is free to choose his own ideas. One thing is certain: modern economics is strongly influenced by the Keynesian ideas that originated in the thirties; but the neo-classical comeback has also produced fascinating ideas. What are we to think, for instance, of the proposition that consumption can be maximized if the growth rate of national income equals the rate of interest? Such glittering little intellectual gems are neo-classical, but they are not in Marshall.

Opinions may differ as to which schools we should single out. A Marxist will say: the most illuminating distinction is that between Marxism and bourgeois economics – the latter being an instrument in the hands of the ruling class, a very useful trick for concealing the real situation under capitalism, whilst the former is a powerful analysis of the laws of accumulation and a mighty

* Referring to Alfred Marshall's famous *Principles of Economics*, 1890.

weapon in the class struggle. This is not my opinion – Marxist macro-economics is a poor show, mainly consisting in labelling non-labour incomes as exploitation and predicting things that don't happen (the decreasing share of labour in national income and the breakdown of capitalism). It does not even explain income distribution. The members of the institutionalist school hold that their own loving attention to historical detail should be confronted with the cold abstraction of economic theory; in this debate my view is that both approaches, the institutionalist and the theoretical, should exist side by side, but this little book happens to deal with rather abstract theory – as will be explained below, I am looking for structures, not for events.

The main distinction dominating this book is that between classical and Keynesian economics, sometimes labelled 'the old' and 'the new' approach. However, here and there a third school pops up: the monetary view. In section 5 a preliminary overview of these three schools will be given.

One peculiar aspect of macro-economics should be stressed: things are not what they seem. If a small group of people increase their money incomes, their real income also goes up; but if a large group of people – say all wage and salary earners – get a higher income, it may well be that their real income does not increase as a consequence. Real incomes are determined by other factors (viz. productivity) than prices and money incomes. The introduction of machines is often bad for employment on a small scale, but it has proved to be good for employment on a large scale. When a person increases the part of his income that is saved, more savings will be the result, but if everybody tries to save more, total savings may decrease. These paradoxes, to be discussed in later chapters, illustrate that sound micro-economic views may be quite misleading if applied to the key relationships of the big variables. The examples also show that systematic macro-economics is a discipline in itself which cannot be entirely ignored by anyone interested in the workings of modern society. If you want to discuss Britain's present predicament, if you worry about the country's future, or if you just want to understand current events, a bit of macro-economics is a necessary part of your mental equipment.

2 · MACRO VERSUS MICRO

This book deals with the 'great variables' or 'aggregates', such as national income, total production, total consumption, the price level, government expenditure. Micro-economics, on the other hand, studies the behaviour of small entities: business firms, households and branches of industry, and considers their interrelation. It is important briefly to describe here the relation between micro- and macro-economics, so that the reader knows what he can count on and what not.

It was already suspected in the eighteenth century that there had to be a meaningful connection between the decisions of entrepreneurs and consumers; the French physiocrats supposed that the 'natural order' would attend to the coordination of individual behaviour. This somewhat metaphysical idea was later defined by Adam Smith in *An Inquiry into the Nature and Causes of the Wealth of Nations* (1776), which indicated the market mechanism as the establisher of equilibrium between micro-economic units. Supply and demand, or in other words the price mechanism, thus became the central subject of classical economics. Economic life was regarded not as a chaos but as a price-regulated system.

This is the basic idea of micro-economics and it is still accepted, though with certain restrictions. At the end of the last century Alfred Marshall stated the ideas of Adam Smith more explicitly. For instance, he cast supply and demand in the form of curves; the quantity demanded depends on the price, and the same applies to the quantity supplied. The equilibrium price is located at the point of intersection of both curves. In addition Marshall made a clear-cut distinction between competition and monopoly. This is of importance to the allocation problem: the assignment of factors of production to branches of industry. Some (for instance Vilfredo Pareto) believed that perfect competition would lead to an allocation in perfect agreement with the consumer's wishes. This is the classical idea of harmony, which consequently does not hold good in the case of monopoly. This distinction between the market forms was elaborated in the thirties: concepts such as monopolistic competition and oligopoly (few suppliers) put in an appearance. It came to be doubted whether the market mechanism also operated perfectly in the absence of monopoly, and the answer was: sometimes it does, sometimes it doesn't. There is a lot of literature on this, but we shall not bother with it.

All this is micro-economics. It dominated economics textbooks up to and including the thirties. Of course, some attention was paid to national income and its fluctuations, and to money theory, but this was more of an afterthought. In this book the opposite applies – micro-economics stays in the background. The allocation of the factors of production to the various uses (i.e. cars against bicycles, butter against plastics), and the distribution of income among individual recipients are not discussed.* All 'small' things are compressed into large aggregates.

There is an obvious difference in atmosphere and habits of thought between micro- and macro-economics. The typical supply and demand curves barely occur in macro-economics. And, come to that, there is much less said about prices. Why?

The reason is that the regulating effect of prices in macro-economics is swamped by the consequences of changes in national income. By the way, these changes in income are not independent of the changes in price; they are systematically bound up with them, for incomes *are* prices. The reader can best see this truth by seeking a case in which a price increases without anyone's income having risen – he will not find one (if at least he is prepared to accept that taxes form the income of the State and that increased prices of imported goods point to increased incomes abroad). For this reason it is not correct to say: suppose that all prices rise while incomes remain the same. That is impossible. A general price increase is a macro-problem.

We can also put it this way. In micro-economics the effect of supply and demand is studied within a given framework of 'large variables'. Marshall looked at what happened when people wanted more butter, assuming their income remained the same. That is a legitimate question if the branch of industry concerned is small. But if the market that we have in mind becomes too great, the question is no longer correct. In a small oil-producing country

---

*The latter subject, though, is close to my heart, which is why I have written a separate book about it: *Income Distribution*, Pelican, 1974.

income is not independent of the volume of oil production. A feedback occurs from production to income. If we ignore this feedback we make a mistake. This mistake is also made by those who believe that a country becomes poorer through a general price increase. They then tacitly assume that incomes remain the same, but that cannot be correct.

Macro-economics concerns itself precisely with these income effects. That gives it a different nature from micro-economics, where the causalities operate more in one direction. No wonder that in macro-economics so much stress is laid on the circulation of income: incomes become expenditure, and expenditure in turn becomes incomes. Complications occur to which micro-economics deliberately turns a blind eye.

In fact these income effects provide a way of making a sharp distinction between micro- and macro-economics or, in other words, of answering the question: when is small small? The answer is that an aspect of the overall economy is small when the feedback to national income (or to total production, or to the price level) may be ignored. In some countries agriculture is a micro-problem (Britain), in others (Australia) a macro-problem. The total government sector (roughly 20 per cent of national income) has a perceptible effect on national income, but this may be ignored for the building of an individual school. In general, care must be taken that the macro-effect is not too easily overlooked; as already mentioned, this can also lead to mistakes with regard to economic policy. A well-known example is the false idea that a depression could be combated by slashing wages. This may be good for the firm because its costs then fall, but at the same time bad because purchasing power and thus sales may also fall as a result. Anyone who forgets the latter point gives the wrong advice to governments. (We shall return to this subject in Chapter IX.)

It will appear from the following chapters that older economics occasionally lapsed into the error of applying micro-economic reasonings to macro-problems. This leads to an exaggerated importance being attached to the equilibrium effect of the price mechanism, even where this effect is thwarted by movements in national income. It was Keynes's particular significance that he cast a clear light on income effects.* In this sense he may be regarded as the father of modern macro-economics, although he himself never used this word.

3 · THE CONTROVERSIAL NATIONAL INCOME

It follows from the last section that national income is one of our central concepts. It is often used in international comparisons (Britain's national income per head is about 50 per cent higher than that of Italy) and in measuring economic growth (between 1970 and 1976 Britain's real national income rose by almost 10 per cent). Recently the concept came under heavy fire. Some radical observers deny its relevance – they say that human happiness does not depend on it, nor does it measure a nation's performance. Others do not go as far but criticize the way in which the statisticians calculate the figure.

To come to grips with these issues we should first of all make a distinction between money (or nominal) income, which we shall call Y, and real national income or national product Q. In its most simple form, Y is the sum of all money incomes.† These accrue essentially to working people, to a small extent to the owners of capital, and in part the incomes stay behind in business (company reserves). In addition, some of the flow of incomes is immediately drained off by the tax people; it goes to the government before the income recipients have even seen it (Pay As You Earn).

The money incomes that we add together in this way must have been earned in production. Transferred incomes, such as

*Some neo-classicists and neo-monetarists accuse the Keynesians of having gone too far with this, and of ignoring the influence of prices and wages. Unemployment is explained by the Keynesians without considering the wage level – wrong, say some classicists. According to the Keynesians a general price cut does not lead to an increasing demand for goods and services – wrong, say some adherents of the monetary school. The latter question (the Pigou effect) is discussed in Chapter VIII, section 1.

† The figure for Britain in 1976 was £110,000 million. There is no point in memorizing such a number: it changes with the years, and thus hardly has any direct significance. What do count are movements with time and relationships.

old age pensions and unemployment benefit, are no part of the sum. On the other hand, the incomes earned by civil servants are. National income money is the least problematic concept. Statistically speaking, it is more or less known, among other things from tax figures; however, part of it remains out of the latter's reach: 'black money'. (This is not only the money earned in heroin dealing and prostitution – it also covers some medical services, repair work by building trade operatives, and a wide range of services and deals, large and small, in which cash changes hands without the benefit of taxation.) It has on occasion been estimated at 10 per cent, but this is just a wild guess. Since black money grows in volume as the burden of taxation weighs more heavily, it is probable that the percentage increases in the course of time. Actual money income may well grow more quickly than the official money income.

Things again become more difficult if we consider real national income, indicated by Q and also known as national product. This is presented in popular terms as a flow of goods emerging from production: the universal chewing gum that beats as it sweeps as it cleans; you can live in it and you can make machines with it. Macro-economists do not find it so difficult to imagine such a product. Statisticians calculate Q by dividing Y by an index P, representing the price level of goods. By definition $Y = PQ$. We will set aside for a while the complications concealed in the calculation of P, which might lead a sceptic to the sombre conclusion that there is no such thing as macro-economics. At present what interests us is that Q is really the sum of those various micro flows of goods. We must therefore take care here to avoid double counting.

There are two forms of this. First of all we must not include wheat and flour and bread, for that would be double – indeed treble – counting. To avoid that, in each stage of production we pay attention only to the value added – the increase in value brought about in production – and not to the supply of semi-manufactures, etc. The sum of the values added is the value of the end-product, and these products together form net national product. But what are end-products?

We take for these the goods that are ultimately consumed plus the durable means of production produced: investment goods or capital goods. We then have gross national product. The danger now occurs of a second double counting: capital goods are used in part to replace worn-out machinery and the like. However, that replacing part, the writing-off for depreciation by business, is already incorporated in the value of consumer goods. Now if it is also included in investment goods, we have counted it twice. This is the reason why depreciation has to be deducted from gross national product to get net national product, the latter corresponding to the value added and (net) national income. This procedure is clear in principle, but the statisticians often have difficulty in establishing depreciation exactly. Often they just make a guess. Sometimes, therefore, gross national product is preferred and it is referred to as GNP.

A hotly debated possibility of double counting occurs in determining the value added. That is the value of the end-products less what other firms contributed to this. In other words, intermediate products (also known as inter-industry supplies) must be deducted when we measure the flow of production from the firms. Awkward problems pop up here. What is an intermediate product? There are observers who give a very generous interpretation to this concept, as a result of which real national income works out at a lower level. The question is particularly apposite when we consider growth situations.

An example. A factory switches to a new product that presents a fire hazard. The local fire service has to be expanded. Under the traditional approach to national income the salaries of the firemen are added to national income. The critical approach considers this wrong; it prefers to regard expansion of the fire service as an intermediate supply that is left out of consideration (or, once the salaries have been added to the government sector, they must be deducted from the value added to the new industrial product). This example is open to an enormous number of extensions. Small, compact towns grow and give birth to suburbs. Residents of the latter have to have cars. Traffic requires more roads, traffic lights, policemen and hospitals. Crime flourishes; though this is no part of national income, crime prevention *is*. Activity increases visibly, but whether real income grows as much is open to doubt. It could be maintained that it is above all the intermediate supplies that grow and flourish, not the final consumption. A similar viewpoint has been eloquently defended by E. J. Mishan in *The Costs of Economic Growth* (1968). Behind this way of thinking lies criticism of the use made of the traditional concept of national income. Sometimes it was thoughtlessly used in the past as a criterion of welfare. Welfare is the satisfaction of human wants by scarce goods, that is to say, a form of happiness.

The thesis that more income causes welfare to grow is understandable and certainly permissible as long as society is poor. Increasing production then leads to decreasing poverty. But in the later stages of economic development the relationship becomes uncertain. The assumption has sometimes been made that a person has to have at his disposal four times as many goods to be twice as happy. This factor of four indicates roughly what real income has done between 1900 and now. Moreover, our wants are apt to drift along with the means of satisfying them – ambitions grow and this acts as a brake on happiness. Little can be said for certain about the numbers involved as economists are pretty ignorant when it comes to human happiness.*

But one thing that is certain is that in modern society products come on the market that cause ethicists to wonder anxiously whether they do in fact serve to satisfy real wants. It is also an established fact that the by-products of industrial society are increasing at the same time. These have then to be discharged again (waste) or compensated for (danger on the roads). This underlines the problem of intermediate products, and provides a typical problem for the economist. How must national income be calculated?

The matter acquires a very sharp edge as soon as we start thinking about environmental pollution. According to some the harm done to nature must be deducted from the growth of real

---

*Dutch research workers (B. M. S. van Praag and A. Kapteyn) have calculated that the loss of satisfaction through the preference drift can be put at 50 per cent. An interesting but highly experimental figure; not one to go out on a limb for.

THE NECESSITY OF MACRO-ECONOMICS

national income: air and water pollution, noise, the disappearance of forests. Such calculations have occasionally been made – for instance, for the United States* it was revealed that the growth of income between 1950 and 1970 was about half that indicated by the traditional arrangements of figures. More pessimistic observers believe that the real growth rate is about zero or even negative.

However, in the quantifications of the cost of growth two very awkward difficulties appear. In the first place the prices of the pieces of environment that have been lost are tricky to determine, and yet that has to happen if we want to reach a quantitative conclusion.† In the second place, the question is how far we are prepared to go. Which part of the inter-industry supplies must be left out of consideration? Only the traffic police, or also the CID? Which part of the medical sector has been affected by economic growth? A sombre mind can go very far and condemn modern life because it makes people very unhappy; we then retain only a very small income, which corresponds to the 'genuine needs of the people' – a highly elastic notion.

I doubt the feasibility of these calculations. Instead of correcting the national income, what we could do is compile welfare indices – these indicate what people eat, how they live, how much they travel, how many concerts they attend, how life expectancy is developing. There are also negative indices: use of drugs, crime.‡

I am not against experimental calculations of national income

* W. Nordhaus and J. Tobin, *Is Growth Obsolete*? National Bureau of Economic Research, 1972.

† The problem becomes completely insoluble when human lives are lost as a result of modern life – as for instance happens daily in traffic. Very different figures can be entered for the value of a human life – from nil (for an old person no longer earning anything) to infinity (every human being is unique and irreplaceable). Moreover, nowadays human lives are saved that would once have been lost (penicillin used to cure pneumonia, for example). If we carry on like this *every* number is feasible. Conclusion: such calculations must be kept quite separate from national income.

‡ These are sometimes called social indicators. Cf. OECD, *Measuring Social Wellbeing, A Progress Report on the Development of Social Indicators*, 1976.

being made that can give something of an impression of the difference between the traditional and critical view. Thus we can perhaps say something about economic progress in the sense of growing welfare. But at the same time I would advocate that, in addition, the traditional method of calculating national income and national product be maintained. The reason is that these figures are of importance to the activity in a country, to employment and to the interplay of macro-economic variables in general. Keynesian theory in particular utilizes this kind of variable; admittedly, that is its weakness as a theory of human happiness, but Keynesian macro-economics was never meant to be that.

So far we have been speaking of deductions: national income might well be smaller than it seems, but in some respects the 'genuine' national product is much greater than the traditional way of measuring it indicates. The latter only takes into account activities for which a money income is paid; but very large parts of production take place without payment. The work of the housewife and the househusband is the most striking example. If we wish to calculate a welfare index, this work must of course also be counted. That is quite possible from a statistical point of view, and in any case much easier than deducting damage to the environment. We assign to a mother with children the paper salary of a female teacher, or, during the time that she is cooking, the salary of a cook. Along these lines a Dutch economist, M. Bruyn-Hundt, has calculated that national income is 12 per cent to 40 per cent higher than it seems. Her estimate was a modest one. Housewives do managerial work, which is highly valued in business, and they perform amorous services that command a good deal of money on the market. A schoolteacher's wage is poor remuneration for that. Moreover, more and more men occasionally help around the house in their leisure time. If we carry on with our calculations, and regard all kinds of leisure-time activity as production (shopping, taking the children to the beach, making tea), we arrive at still higher corrections than 40 per cent. A doubling of Y does not seem inconceivable. I simply mean that in this way national income becomes a highly arbitrary quantity.

My solution would therefore be that we stick to the traditional calculation of Y, P and Q while at the same time being aware of the conventional content of these figures. They are not empty, misleading data, but certainly no supreme standard and guide either. Human happiness depends on many other things. Moreover, there are situations in which a lower national income is preferable to a higher one. This is particularly so if the growth of national product threatens the natural environment or too quickly depletes the sources of energy. We shall return to these current problems when we discuss the limits to growth.

4 · THERE'S NO SUCH THING AS MACRO-ECONOMICS

So far we have been discussing the criticism of the traditional way of calculating national income – the critics find the figure too high, or too low, or they consider that it does not tell us enough about human happiness. But one can go further and argue that in principle it is impermissible to calculate macro-economic quantities.

Nobody denies that we can add money incomes together. The sum Y exists. But what do we mean by Q – national product? Heterogeneous goods cannot be added up: milk+fish and chips +cars+education does not make sense. Not to worry, the statistician says, we'll value everything in terms of money, and divide Y by P, a price index number.

All right, but P is calculated by investigating the prices of a package of goods. This package does not remain constant in the course of time. In 1950 it contained no TV sets, and far fewer cars than today. In 1950 Britain did not use natural gas; now one sixth of our total energy consumption consists of this source. We can calculate P on the basis of an old package, which is the Laspeyres method. In that case air travel counts for less than it should. We can also take the most recent package, the Paasche method. In that case air travel for old years counts for more than it should. We can also take the Paasche and the Laspeyres index numbers, multiply them and extract the square root (the Fisher method). Now that is *completely* artificial. A sceptic would say that these are all tricks. P doesn't exist, nor does Q. Macro-economics is a philosophy 'as if' – much ado about nothing.

Some critics apply this reasoning above all to the stock of capital goods, K. They say that machines installed in successive years embody a different technology. The vintages have a different productivity. It is strictly forbidden to add them together. The quantity K, which plays a strategic role in classical theory, is meaningless. Down with K, and down with classical theory. (Mrs Joan Robinson is a particular proponent of this view.) But if this reasoning holds good, we may not add different kinds of labour together. L, employment, is meaningless too. And so, down with macro-economics.

It is clear that this is carrying things too far for me, as otherwise this book would not have been written. But we must be well aware of the limited importance possessed by the big aggregates. They are rough estimates of something – what that 'something' is is difficult to say as soon as the package of goods undergoes a change, and it does so. Our models that endeavour to explain a growing Q suggest a precision which does not exist if only because of the aggregation problem.

Matters become even more complicated if we try to construct macro-*relations* from given micro-*relations*. Here we can slip up badly. Suppose there are two people, John and Bill, each of whom maintains a linear relationship between his consumption C and his income Y. For John, whose money burns a hole in his pocket, $C_j = Y_j$. (The letter j here means that we're discussing John.) Bill is a thrifty soul, and for him $C_b = 20 + 0.2Y_b$. The sum of two linear micro-functions must of course yield a linear macro-function. But watch what happens in the following case. In period one John and Bill both have an income of 100. John consumes 100, and Bill 40; national income is 200 and consumption is 140. In period two John has an income of 50 and Bill has an income of 250. National income has risen from 200 to 300, but total consumption has fallen to 120. We find a negative influence of Y on C, but that is of course misleading. The cause of this confusion lies in the shift in personal income distribution that occurs simultaneously with the growth of Y. This case again illustrates that aggregation is permitted only if the parts continue to occupy the same place in the whole. In reality they do not do so – personal income distribution becomes gradually less unequal. In this sense as well macro-economics is a precarious business.

But, once again, we can't manage without it. Whoever takes the critics completely seriously becomes speechless. It is more respectable to make do with what we have.

5 · THREE SCHOOLS

Because interrelationships are complex, one observer discovers different strategic influences from another observer – this is how schools come about. As I have said before, the most useful distinction is that between neo-classical macro-economics, the neo-Keynesian version and the monetary school. In this section a short characterization follows of these three views; in the chapters to come, these ideas are developed. The three points of view do not entirely exclude one another. On some points a synthesis is possible, but to see that we must first put all three side by side.

It is usually considered that classical economics, and therefore also classical macro-economics, started with Adam Smith (1723–90), whose book was mentioned in section 2 of this chapter. It contains numerous ideas, of which one is probably the most important: in society a steering mechanism operates in the form of the price system. This 'invisible hand' ensures that the individual decisions of producers and consumers are co-ordinated into one meaningful whole and this idea can be applied not only to allocation, but also to the total volume of production. The application is called after the Frenchman J.-B. Say (1767–1832). In 1803 he formulated the 'law of markets', later also known as Say's Law, which states that the total production of a country can always be purchased by the consumers. General overproduction is excluded by this 'law', and therefore general unemployment as well. If unemployment occurs, that is because too much is made of a certain good and too little of another good; the allocation must change and the workers must have themselves re-trained. (It is on this point that Keynesian macro-economics differs strongly from classical thought; we shall come back to this later.)

Owing to the fact that classical macro-economics does not acknowledge the existence of general unemployment (and also, as we shall see later, general overspending and inflation), classical economists can bend their minds to other problems. These are above all production problems. Classical macro-economics in its modern form has as a central element a production function, $Q = F(L, K)$, in which Q represents the volume of production (or real national income), and L and K the amounts of labour and capital. By writing the relation in such a way it is emphasized that Q depends in a systematic manner on K and L. If the amount of capital increases, so does Q, and if the function is known we know by exactly how much. This is a simple trick, but it is incredible what we can do with it. The compelling feature of classical economics is the formidable intellectual productivity of this production function. To mention just one thing: it leads to the idea of marginal productivity – the increment of Q that is the result of a small increment of L or K. Classical macro-economics has been utilizing this concept of marginal productivity since the beginning of the present century, and the adherents of this school use it to explain income distribution and economic growth. It results in small, radiant propositions. It can be easily forgotten that from the empirical point of view our knowledge of the production function is very limited indeed. We shall of course be coming back to these things.*

Keynesian macro-economics is named after one man, John Maynard Keynes (1883–1946). That is handy, but at the same time misleading; when Keynes published his celebrated book *The General Theory of Employment, Interest and Money* (1936),

---

*Incidentally, the word 'classical' can have many meanings. It is used here with reference to the theory that gives pride of place to the production function, the price mechanism and the substitution of means of production and which – and this is what is classical about it – has its roots in the historical beginnings of economic science. Some authors call this the neo-classical approach, and to them 'classical' means David Ricardo and his theory of low wage and ever-increasing rent.

the ideas contained in it were already to be found in books by many other authors. Keynes rejected Say's Law and showed how the total demand for goods and services could differ from a country's productive capacity. That had already happened before. In Sweden particularly, Say's Law had come to be doubted by many, under the influence of the work of K. Wicksell (c. 1900). The business cycle – that is the wave movement in production, prices and employment – had already attracted the attention of many, and such fluctuations are not easy to reconcile with the classical idea that the total demand for goods always matches the productive capacity. But it is true that Keynes succeeded in formulating the criticism of Say's Law in a way that impressed economists. It opened their eyes for them, and although many differed in opinion from Keynes, his book had tremendous influence.

Keynesian macro-economics concerns itself above all with the factors that determine demand. This is where it differs so much from classical theory: the latter pays more attention to production, i.e. to the supply side. In the classical way of thought total demand adjusts to the supply (we shall see later how exactly that happens), but in Keynes the opposite is the case: if there is inadequate demand, production falls. The level of expenditure is too low. This causes unemployment. It is no coincidence that Keynes's masterpiece saw the light of day at a time when a quarter of British workers were unable to find work. However, the level of expenditure can also be too high; that is called overspending, and also inflation. These departures from equilibrium form the Keynesian problem. They have to be explained in order to be combated. The first is the task of theoretical economics, the second of politics, which can be aided by economics. Keynesian economics has an obvious political continuation, in the sense that it helps us to fight deficient or excessive levels of expenditure.

Typical Keynesian thinking is that national income comes into the hands of the consumers, who spent it, and so the income returns to business. Capital investment also creates incomes, which are spent. The same is true for government outlays. There is something like a circular flow of incomes and spending: this circular flow has to be analysed and this analysis is the core of Keynesian economics.*

In the Keynesian reasoning production functions are also encountered, but they are usually very simple. Substitution – interchange of factors of production – is ruled out. Therefore, production is proportionate to the factor of production which is relatively most scarce. Except on a very narrow growth path, where the number of workers and the amount of machines are constantly an exact match, there is always labour or capital left over. In the short term it is often assumed that there is ample capital, so that an increase in demand can lead to an increase in production and in so doing can create employment. The level of employment is determined by the level of expenditure.

The third school is monetary macro-economics. It can claim a venerable past – the first monetary view was put forward in the sixteenth century by, among others, the Frenchman J. Bodin and the Italian B. Davanzati. These authors were anxious to know why prices were rising so much, and they ended up with an abundance of money as the answer. Since then many have concerned themselves with the money supply: whether this was perhaps excessive, or precisely too tight, and what effect it has on economic life. Conversely, some even go so far as to ascribe the major disturbances of economic life – such as unemployment and stagnation – to aberrations in the money supply. This is then the monetary school, which in our time is represented above all by the American Milton Friedman (Nobel prizewinner in 1976). The adherents are interested in the creation of money by the government and the banks (yes, indeed, banks can make money). They are also fascinated by the interest rate, the velocity of circulation of

* It would incidentally be quite wrong to describe Keynes as the inventor of the circular flow theory. The idea comes from the eighteenth-century French economist F. Quesnay, a kind of predecessor of Adam Smith, and it is also to be found in Marx's work. Moreover, the circular flow does not explicitly occur in *The General Theory*; it was brought forward by later interpreters of Keynes. *The General Theory* is, in fact, a difficult book, highly technical, badly put together, not free from contradictions – only later did it become clear what the author had meant. But then many ideas proved to be of surprising simplicity, and the book had already conquered the world of economists.

money (which is further explained in Chapter VII) and above all in the effect of all this on society.

It may be doubted whether there is in fact a complete monetary macro-economics. Usually the monetarists have a classical equilibrium system in mind, in which money forms a source of disturbance. But this source of disturbance is so fascinating that the monetary school often cannot think of anything else. That is the great difference of opinion with the Keynesians: they also see that there is such a thing as money, but they do not assign it such a predominant role. The Keynesian disturbance of the circular flow comes about because too little (or too much) is consumed or invested – the banks cannot help that. The dispute between Friedmanians and Keynesians occasionally flares up, and that is perhaps a sufficient reason in itself to speak of monetary macro-economics.

The three schools are opposed to each other, but one can also say that they supplement one another. A synthesis is possible and that is then the mainstream. Some representatives of the mainstream are of the opinion that this can best be called 'neo-classical' – in that case classical thought has absorbed the Keynesian revolution.* This is a defensible view, but I nevertheless consider it more educative to emphasize the differences in opinion. The reader is then faced with the necessity to form his or her own opinion. He or she remains responsible for his or her own image of society. Nobody can take away this responsibility. It would be fine if empirical macro-economics produced such clear insights that no one could escape them, but that is not so. One of the reasons why is discussed in the following section.

6 · QUANTITATIVE ECONOMICS

Economics speaks of quantities; since they can change, they are called variables. Employment, income, prices – these are all numbers. Economics is therefore always a quantitative affair.

Now quantitative relations between variables can be approached in different ways. One method is to take simple properties of man

---

*This is the view of P. A. Samuelson, in the standard textbook *Economics: An Introductory Analysis* (many editions between 1955 and 1978).

and society as the point of departure and from there, by logical reasoning, to try to arrive at knowledge of relations. This is the deductive method. For example, it is assumed that entrepreneurs aim at maximum profit. It follows from this that they will use an expensive means of production less than they will use a cheap one. If the price of a means of production, for instance labour, increases, then to achieve a given volume of production less labour will be used, and more capital. This type of reaction is stressed by classical theory.

A deductive reasoning of this kind operates with quantities. The price of labour – the wage – is a quantity, as is the extent of the demand for labour – employment. The reasoning tries to establish a relationship between wage and employment, and is therefore quantitative to a certain extent. But it tells us nothing about the extent to which wage increases lead to reduction of employment. Will the effect be great, or small?

Deductive reasoning contains a number of dangers. In the first place it is tempting to create the impression by an evocative argument that a given reaction will be quantitatively important. By utilization of purely literary artifices efforts are made to get more out of the method than it contains. But all the rhetoric in the world cannot explain whether employment will react sharply or not to wage increase. This is a question of empirical figures.

A second danger is that we give the relations a fine algebraic form and then pretend that we know reality with these relations. For instance, we write: L, the demand for labour, depends on the wage level W in accordance with the relation $L = L_o - \alpha W$. Here L_o is the part of L that does not depend on W (the intercept) and α is the regression coefficient. This demand function is a straight line. (Connoisseurs prefer a more complicated relation, such as $L = W \cdot \dfrac{1}{\lambda - 1}$, a result of classical theory. Here λ represents the share of labour in national income. The exponent $\dfrac{1}{\lambda - 1}$ shows by what percentage L falls if we raise the real wage W by 1 per cent. A quantity of this kind, which connects percentages together, is called an elasticity. If $\lambda = 0.8$, this means that the elasticity of the demand for labour is -5. It should be borne in mind that this is an arithmetical example, not an empirical truth.) Writing down such an equation is an excellent thing provided we always remember that the relation implies a hypothesis. The hypothesis states that L and a or λ remain constant in the course of time. A constant of this kind, which determines a relation, is called a parameter. However, the constancy has to be proved – that too is an empirical question. It may very well not be true, and then the equation has little point. The thing about Greek letters is that they deceive the observer into thinking that the quantity concerned is constant. Textbooks often create this impression, as do the graphs belonging to the equations.

The danger reaches a climax in model-building. This too is an excellent method, the crown on the work of deductive reasoning. Beautifully styled equations are set out side by side; the interaction of the variables is visible. There have to be as many equations as there are unknowns; then the system is solvable. The technique is indispensable when reactions operate against one another – the typical case in macro-economics.

Let us again take wage increase as an example. This summons up all kinds of contrary reactions, not only higher costs for the entrepreneur, but also higher money incomes for the workers and therefore an increased demand for some consumer goods; the latter reaction is stressed by Keynesian theory. Also higher prices, substitution of machines for human beings (and thus a greater demand for machines), lower profits (and thus a lower demand for machines) and lower exports. The effect on employment is the result of this. It is difficult to say how it will turn out, but one thing is certain – we must put the reactions side by side to be able to understand them. The model is essential for this.*

*The set-up of this book is therefore inspired by model-building. In Chapter II a classical model is presented, in Chapter III a Keynesian model – but both are still very incomplete. After Chapter IV, which is concerned with model-building itself, new elements are added one by one: foreign trade, government, money, growth. In Chapter XI the blocks are then combined, whilst the empirical side is also dealt with. Chapter XII is concerned with economic policy; there too we let ourselves be guided by model results.

Models serve to order our mind – but they can seduce us into overestimating our knowledge, because the relations that we have written down do not become firm and solid *just because we have written them down*. They are provisional hypotheses.

To convert these hypotheses into economic science they have to be empirically tested. That is the task of econometrics: a clever combination of deductive model-building and statistical investigation. The technique is varied nowadays, but correlation analysis remains the heart of econometrics, alongside more recent techniques like multivariate analysis and simulation. (Something more is said about these techniques in Chapter IV.) The aim of econometrics is to test the relationship suggested by deductive theory, and to estimate the parameters. Not until we have really estimated these parameters – that is to say when the Greek alphabet has been replaced by numbers that are found empirically – can we say that we have understood a relationship. (Filling in fabricated parameters, as is done in many textbooks, is not a proper substitute for the quantitative method. These 'arithmetical examples' are useful for exercising the mind – they are also to be found in this book – but can easily mislead.)

If we have all the strategic parameters at our disposal, we can also predict what will happen if a country is exposed to external shocks, such as an oil crisis, or to government measures. Without constant parameters no prediction is possible. In that case, come to think of it, the present day is also incomprehensible. Model-building can then create some order in our thoughts, but we still do not know what really matters.

Macro-econometrics came into being in the thirties, with Jan Tinbergen (The Hague),* Ragnar Frisch (Oslo) and others as pioneers. In 1969 they were awarded the first Nobel prize for economics for their work. Since then there has been a tremendous growth in skill. In some fields fairly reliable relationships have been found. But on critical points – viz. investments and profits – our knowledge is still deficient. As a result, the overall

---

*Cf. the monumental *Statistical Testing of Business Cycle Theories, A Method and its Application*, 1939. The research was commissioned by the League of Nations.

picture of the macro-relations too is still weak and the econometricians still have a lot of work to do. Whether they will ever arrive at big, reliable models, with well-estimated parameters that stay constant over many decades, remains to be seen.

CHAPTER II

Productive Capacity Determines National Income: The Classical Theory

1 · SAY'S LAW

In the last chapter incidental mention was already made of the fact that the 'classical' theory believed that the productive capacity of a country determines how much will be produced. An economy produces as much as it can. This is the maximum real national income. It is a highly strategic quantity, often referred to in this book as $Q^\star$. By introducing it we tacitly assume that this quantity is known.* Now classical theory is more or less heedless of the possibility of less being produced, since the classicists trusted that no great difficulties would occur in selling the goods produced. On the other hand they were not always alive to the possibility that a larger sale of goods might lead to a greater increase in productive capacity. Economic stagnation, retarded and also accelerated economic growth remained in the

---

*Unfortunately this is not so in practice. What can be measured – and with difficulty – is total production Q as the latter actually comes about. Capacity, on the other hand, cannot be directly established statistically. Above all if less is produced than is possible, for instance through a Keynesian depression, $Q^\star$ escapes direct measurement. Statisticians then measure unemployment, and regard this variable as an indicator of overcapacity, $Q-Q^\star$. This is only an approximate approach, because not all unemployment is caused by the depression. Labour may be of the wrong kind – and not match the demand – which is known as frictional unemployment. What is the capacity then? But even if sufficient demand is exerted by the consumers, it continues to be difficult to calculate what maximum production could be. Machines can keep on running longer than normal working hours; overtime can be worked. Sometimes bottlenecks occur in the one factory, or a whole branch of industry, while there is unused capacity elsewhere. Very specific problems appear when there is too little labour (for instance, skilled labour) and sufficient capital, or vice versa. The fact that we use $Q^\star$ as if it were a known quantity may allow us to forget these complications only temporarily. Many textbooks pass over the matter too lightly.

background; these are the very points that are elucidated by modern economics.

The confidence that the market makes it possible to sell all of the national product stems from Say's Law. As stated above, this amounts to the fact that a supplier only supplies goods because he demands other goods. Put in this way, this 'law' sounds rather mysterious. However, there is another way of putting it which is used more often nowadays, and which makes matters clearer. This description originates with the circulation of purchasing power. This idea is first found among the eighteenth-century physiocrats. They noted how the product of agriculture was urged along by the national economy. Owing to the fact that this view was rather distorted, the circulation theory was long in discredit. It began to enjoy a new vogue at about the same time as Keynesianism; in particular national bookkeeping contributed to this.

The simplest picture of the circular flow of goods and income is given below. The upper rectangle represents business. On the

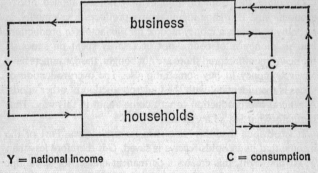

Y = national income   C = consumption

Fig. 1: The simplest form of the circulation

right-hand side the national product emerges; we shall assume for the moment that this consists entirely of consumer goods. These make their way to the households, which are represented by the lower rectangle. Arrow *C* represents this flow of goods.

Meanwhile the households have also supplied something to

business: the factors of production such as labour, savings, land. In return for these they receive every week, every month, or every year a money income. The sum of these incomes forms the national income, the central quantity in modern economics. This quantity is represented in the figure as an arrow Y; since it is a flow of money, it has been drawn as a broken line.

This therefore means that the households receive exactly the amount of money that they need to buy the national product.* The flow of money Y flows back from the households to business; the entrepreneurs receive in the form of revenue what they have spent on the factors of production, including the profit. National income and national expenditure are constantly transformed into one another. The line C represents consumptive expenditure. The modern version of Say's Law stresses this fact. If the households again and again spend the income they have received, the entrepreneurs have no difficulties with sales.

This is an important point. It shows how an increase in production creates the money income that can buy the extra production.

Of course this train of thought may not be applied microeconomically. If a shoe manufacturer produces a new model, in so doing he creates a money income for the factors of production, but his money is of course not necessarily spent on shoes. If the newly manufactured shoes are not bought, the consumers have received money to buy something else. The overproduction of shoes is then identical with the underproduction of other goods. A general overproduction cannot come about in this way. That is exactly what Say's Law means.

It is obvious that this 'law' has its weaknesses. Part of the income that households receive is saved. C is therefore less than Y. At first sight, this creates a permanent danger for sales. But fortunately part of production consists of the production of machines and buildings; these capital goods are sold from firm to firm. The investments have to be financed; this can be done by savings. If the production of capital goods I exactly equals

---

*The sophisticated reader is invited to forget for the moment that business income may be saved by firms, that machines are bought every now and then but are used continually, and similar dynamic complications.

savings S, the flow of purchasing power is unhampered. The classical view rests on the equality between I and S. Classical theory believes that this equilibrium will be taken care of. It is the capital market that provides the mechanism for this. Businessmen are always willing to invest more and more – from a macro viewpoint, sales are not a limiting factor. The bottleneck in the way of business expansion is S. The scarcity of savings is reflected by the rate of interest, i.e. the price that business managers have to pay for the use of capital. If savings go up, the availability of capital increases and more machinery will be installed. If entrepreneurs are slow to seize the opportunity, the rate of interest will go down and prod them into action. We see the invisible hand at work; Say's Law depends on it.

The mechanism can also be described as follows: productive capacity $Q^\star$ is given. Consumers decide to consume an amount C. They leave unused capacity $Q^\star - C$ to business for its investment I. Dynamic entrepreneurship plus the working of the capital market ensures that $I = Q^\star - C$. The latter equation is another way of stating Say's Law. The gap between productive capacity and consumption is always neatly filled by investment.

The flawless operation of the capital market and in particular the businessman's perpetual enthusiasm for investment are the two weak pillars of the classical system. Say's Law has been attacked, notably by Keynes, for being unrealistic, and rightly so. And yet the 'law' is not as meaningless as some assume. It forms a healthy counter-argument to the naïve view that a continuous increase in production must lead to a slump. For instance, many are afraid of the expansion of production in the underdeveloped countries. They fear that the world will presently be flooded with products. But they forget that this greater production automatically leads to a greater money income which, provided that it is spent in the right way, creates the market for the greater flow of goods. This does not mean to say that disturbances cannot occur, but these are anything but a necessary consequence of the expansion of productive capacity. Supply does in fact tend to create its own demand.

A related form of pessimism is somewhat more complicated. Some see a danger in the increasing productivity. If the same

factors of production keep on making more and more products –
for instance by automation – the flow of goods increases, but
incomes remain what they were. And therefore an increase in
production might lead to economic stagnation and unemployment.

But this pessimism, too, is based on a fallacy. For if the flow
of goods broadens, the price of these goods must drop. The
business firms, as a result of the increase in production, need
less of the factors of production to make one unit product.
When prices are lower the increased product can be purchased by
the same money income. But what happens if the prices do not go
down, despite the lower costs? In that case profits may increase,
so that Say's Law continues to be obeyed, unless a disturbance
in the spending of the money income has meanwhile occurred
because profits are less likely to be spent than wages. In that
case a drop in sales is probable, but this is not the result of the
increase in productivity, but of the disturbance in the distribution
of income, and the relatively high savings of those whose income
is derived from profit. Increased productivity can lead to specific
unemployment, which may be painful, but not to general unemployment – provided that the flow of income and expenditure
is undisturbed.

In later chapters we shall encounter a type of general unemployment which seems, at first sight, to be compatible with Say's
Law. Suppose that the equilibrium on the labour market is
jeopardized by excessively high wages. In that case labour will be
swiftly replaced by machinery. This replacement is a normal
aspect of traditional economic growth, but wage inflation may
induce business managers to engage in such a rapid introduction
of labour-saving machines and such a rapid scrapping of old
labour-intensive equipment that the result is unemployment. It
seems as if the invisible hand is paralysed by, say, the unions.
But on closer inspection unemployment will come about only if
the productivity of labour increases more quickly than production. The stagnation of production has to be explained – and
this is extremely difficult if we keep relying on Say's Law. In
other words, wage inflation can lead to unemployment only if,
at the same time, sales stagnate. And this stagnation is almost

always the result of a disturbed flow of income and expenditure.

Classical theory ignores the latter disturbances, unlike Keynesian theory; it disregards what the recipients of income do with their money. However, it has a sound view of the genesis of incomes. Let us follow this theory for a moment, and assume that all additional production also leads to an additional market. In that case the size of the national product is determined by productive capacity. What else should be said about this?

2 · THE PRODUCTIVITY OF LABOUR
DETERMINES PROSPERITY

A country's productive capacity is determined by a mass of factors differing greatly in nature. To make sense of them, they must be arranged in a certain way. This will be attempted below.

The starting-point is that according to Say's Law total production depends partly on the factors of production present – the quantity and the quality of labour; the stock of capital goods such as machinery, factories, roads, schools; the nature of the soil and the climate – and partly on the productivity of these factors of production. Productivity is defined as the ratio between the national product and the quantities of factors of production present. But this national product is extremely heterogeneous – it comprises shoes as well as newly built houses, road-building and the production of non-material goods, such as 'government services' (e.g. legal security and education). An attempt has to be made to solve this difficulty by reducing all products to a common denominator – money – and then making corrections afterwards for changes in the value of money. In this way an indication of the real income or the volume of production is obtained. In the second place the factors of production are also heterogeneous. The work of the office clerk, of the small shopkeeper, of the farmer, can if necessary be reduced via a sum of money to a common denominator with the productive services – also expressed in money – of capital and of land. But figures obtained in this way have little point.

Consequently another method is preferably followed. We do

not divide national production by the entire mass of production factors, but by the volume of only one factor, although this in itself is again fairly heterogeneous. Labour is often taken as this factor, but capital could also be taken. In the first case you find the productivity of labour, in the second case the productivity of capital. The productivity of labour is therefore defined as the national product divided by the amount of labour. It is a very rough and ready measure, but not unimportant.*

Strictly speaking, therefore, the concepts productivity of labour and productivity of capital are on a par. Now the strange fact occurs that they are of entirely different significance to the prosperity of a country. The productivity of labour has a decisive and immediate effect on welfare; the productivity of capital hardly has any direct effect. This may appear to be a strange paradox, but it is easily solved.

The prosperity of a country is determined to a considerable extent not by the total national product, but by the national product per head of the population. China has in total a greater product than Belgium, but there are relatively too many Chinese who want to share in this product; per head the average Belgian is at least twenty times better off materially than the average Chinese. Prosperity therefore depends on the national product divided by the number of mouths to be fed. The productivity of labour is identical with the national product divided by the number of pairs of hands. The ratio between the number of mouths and the number of pairs of hands is often more or less constant. It might even be thought that both numbers are identical. But that is not so: the working population is smaller than the consuming population. One can therefore at most assume that prosperity and the productivity of labour are in a fairly constant relation to one another. Not exactly constant, for if more women go out to work or if the school-leaving age or the pensionable age is changed, this relation also changes. It is determined by mainly sociological and institutional factors; at least, as long as Say's Law holds good and there is no unemployment. But if a slump occurs, and the ratio between the number of people who want to

* More subtle definitions making allowance for working hours will not be considered here.

work and the number actually employed changes, the ratio of labour productivity to prosperity is upset. Prosperity is then less than follows from the productivity of labour. The latter is the case examined by Keynes; he even believed that a higher productivity of labour would almost certainly lead to less welfare, because the risk of unemployment would be greater at higher levels of the national income.

But, given Say's Law, we see that it is the productivity of labour that determines prosperity to a considerable extent. This cannot be said of the productivity of capital. A country may have a rather high productivity of capital and still be very poor. It is possible that underdeveloped countries use the little capital they possess in such a way that it has a fairly high productivity per unit invested. But this does not mean to say that these countries are highly prosperous. The productivity of labour will be low, and in that case a high productivity of capital does not help much.*

A central element of the problem of prosperity is therefore labour productivity. The great international differences in prosperity – in the order of magnitude of one to twenty or more! – are correlated with this quantity. What determines the height of this productivity index? Before the factors are mentioned which are important in this respect, a warning may be uttered against a misunderstanding that ascribes fluctuations in the productivity of labour to fluctuations in the efforts or the skill of the worker. These personal properties are of course of influence, but their factual importance is overshadowed by more important factors. For we must remember that the definition of the concept 'labour productivity' means that the national product is divided by employment. If machines are added which make more product with less labour, the productivity of labour increases without the worker doing anything about it; in fact he will often not need to exert himself as much. Only in special cases – say a tennis player –

---

*This does not mean to say that the productivity of capital is unimportant. A high productivity of capital makes investment attractive, and the investments determine the stock of capital goods, which in turn helps to determine the productivity of labour. This point will be taken up in the chapter on economic growth.

is labour productivity directly correlated with the 'worker's' efforts and capacities. In outline, the elements that determine the productivity of labour can be understood in a simple way by using the concept of a 'production function', which has already been discussed in Chapter I. Let us call the amount of product Q, the amount of labour used L and the stock of capital goods K. The production function is $Q = F(L,K)$. We shall need this notation later for more complicated ends, but we are concerned here with the question of what determines the productivity of labour. For this purpose we define this strategic quantity as Q/L. Now if the production function is given – and is of a certain type, in which all variables may be divided by the same quantity* – we can write $Q/L = F(L/L, K/L)$. What this means is that the productivity of labour depends on a quantity that is equal to one (and which may therefore be omitted) and on the capital intensity K/L. In other words, the productivity of labour increases with the size of the amount of capital per worker, and with nothing else.

It should be borne in mind that this applies only at a given production function. If this changes, labour productivity can increase without an increase in K being involved. We call a change of this kind technical progress. The latter may consist entirely of new techniques, such as the introduction of electricity, or automation, but a more effective organization of the factory may be involved, so that the efficiency increases. The concept of production function serves among other things to separate the influence of the accumulation of capital conceptually from the influence of technical progress. In practice the two kinds of influence are often interwoven, and econometricians frequently have the greatest difficulty in keeping them quantitatively separate. For instance, R. Solow has suggested that in fact the whole of technical progress is embodied in new capital goods, but others have worked out that half of the increase in labour productivity is ascribable to the accumulation of capital and the other half to disembodied technical progress. We shall return to the many unsolved problems of technical progress in Chapter X.

* A function of this kind is called linear-homogeneous; this is explained later.

It is meanwhile certain that the growth in the stock of capital goods is important to the growth of labour productivity. This brings us to the ever-recurrent theme of investment, which will be considered in the following section.

3 · THE CAPACITY EFFECT AND THE INCOME EFFECT OF INVESTMENTS

In classical theory – for that is the subject of this chapter – the importance of investments to the national income was at all times recognized.* But only in the sense that investments increase productive capacity. The classicists did not make very much allowance for the fact that investments also have an entirely different result, viz. the creation of a money income. Nowadays it is said of them that they saw the capacity effect, but not the income effect.

The income effect means the following. If the entrepreneurs decide to build new factories or if the authorities construct a road, the factors of production are employed in doing this. They receive for this an income. With that income they can buy consumer goods – but these goods have not been produced. For the income has originated in the production of lathes and paving stones. If the recipients of the income wish to spend the whole of it on consumer goods, they will find that these are not available. To put it another way: there is too great a demand on the market for consumer goods. The income effect of the investments must therefore be compensated for by the decision to abstain from consumption: the recipients of the income must save. We shall have to consider this relation between saving and investing later, for it forms a keystone of Keynesian economics. But let us begin by explaining the classical view of it.

Since the classicists believed in Say's Law and always considered

*Investment here means the production of new capital goods. It must not be confused with the purchase of securities – investment in the other sense – and still less with not using income for consumption – saving, in other words. In Keynesian theory a sharp distinction must be made above all between investing in the sense of buying capital goods and investing in the sense of buying securities. It is a pity that English uses the same word for these two activities.

a sufficiently large market to be present, the machinery of production is in their theory always fully employed. There is no unused capacity. If an entrepreneur wishes to expand his production, he can do so only in one of two ways, either by increasing productivity or by withdrawing factors of production from other purposes to which they are being put. More shoes means less of something else. In macro-economic terms, more investment means less consumption.

An entrepreneur who wants to invest must have the necessary financial resources at hand. These are furnished to him by the savers: households and firms, and probably also by his own business. The households have received an income from production, but they do not spend this fully on consumer goods. They save, with the immediate aim of building up capital, but at the same time they help the entrepreneur. Without savings the latter cannot finance his business. (The bank can if necessary create credit, but this only helps the investor temporarily. In the long run he must consolidate from real savings.)

But not only do the saving households provide the financial resources by saving; they also make investment possible because, by their abstention from buying, they release the factors of production that can presently be employed in making capital goods. In the classical view saving is in a double respect the necessary preliminary to the real formation of capital. Savings and investments are in equilibrium with one another; the rate of interest attends to that. But saving is primary and investment secondary.

In this line of thought, which is almost diametrically opposed to the Keynesian one, the national money income remains constant. It is not influenced by investing. True, investing has an income effect – the classicists would not have denied that – but investing has been preceded by a drop in consumption. This of course also has an income effect, and these two neutralize one another. In the classical interpretation the production of capital goods replaces the production of consumer goods. Total production and total income remain the same. Consequently, in the classical reasoning there is little point in indicating an income effect of investments. It is a foregone conclusion that this effect will be compensated.

The full loading of plant and full employment, which form the economic milieu to which classical theory relates, have a further effect on investments. Productive capacity can be increased only if the consumers are prepared to abstain from purchases for consumption. If they do not abstain, and there is nevertheless a great urge to invest, a tense situation occurs. The investors and the consumers are as it were fighting for the scarce factors of production. This fight has been very vividly described by F. A. von Hayek.* We may therefore call this accentuated scarcity of the factors of production the Hayek situation. In such a case there is really inflation. Sometimes the investors win, and then large projects are embarked upon, but there are too few consumer goods. Sometimes it is the consumers who win: in that case an over-investment crisis threatens, not because there is no market, but because the factors of production are taken out of the hands of the investors. In both cases an acute shortage of capital threatens, a special variant which is the reflection of the scarcity of factors of production. It manifests itself in two characteristic ways: in the first place the rate of interest goes up, and secondly we see that large projects are abandoned uncompleted. After this special type of depression we see no empty factories, no unemployed workers – we see half-finished factories.

In this argument, which by no means need be unrealistic in all circumstances, saving is almost identical with economic progress, and consuming hampers the latter. Saving increases productive capacity, and consuming checks this increase. This order of things was radically changed by orthodox Keynesian theory. Of course, here too investment leads to a greater productive capacity, but it is problematic whether saving always leads to increased investment. I shall be discussing this in the next chapter.

4 · PLAYING WITH THE PRODUCTION FUNCTION

The heart of classical macro-economics is the production function: $Q = F(L, K)$. Fascinating things can be done with it. In section 2 of this chapter we have seen that, given L, K and the function itself, we can easily deduce labour productivity; we just

* *Prices and Production*, 1931.

divide all three variables by L. Then we have one of the basic relationships that determine real income per head. Call the number of people in a country N (whilst L is the working population). In that case L/N is the participation index: in Britain slightly less than 50 per cent. We can write the real income per head as $Q/N = L/N \cdot Q/L = 50\% F(K/L)$. This simple and instructive formula is true only if there is no mass unemployment. It states that real income per head depends on the participation index, the production function and the amount of capital per worker.

Matters become even more interesting once we know how high the marginal productivity of each production factor is. The marginal productivity of labour is the increase in Q that proceeds from increasing L by one unit, with a constant K. In the same way the marginal productivity of capital is the increase in Q that proceeds from increasing K by one unit, with a constant L. (Some readers will recognize here the partial derivatives of the function.) These quantities play a strategic role in the distribution of national income – classical theory takes the view that the wage rate is determined by the marginal productivity of labour and the interest rate by the marginal productivity of capital. We shall, of course, return to this (in Chapter IX), but it explains why the classical view is so interested in these derivatives of the production function.* The marginal productivities differ from the average productivities; they are always lower. This is because of the 'law of diminishing marginal productivity'. Though more capital per man yields more product, it does not do so proportionately. The marginal productivity of capital falls, and is therefore lower than the average productivity. This rule was formulated by David Ricardo at the beginning of the previous century, and still forms part of the arsenal of classical thought.

A production function worthy of the name should be specified in such a way that it incorporates diminishing returns (marginal

*We can also include variables other than just capital and labour. The latter production factor, for instance, can be divided into three kinds, depending on the level of education: graduates, people with a secondary education, people with a primary education. This is done by J. Tinbergen, *Income Distribution*, 1975, who endeavours in this way to track down the quantitative development of relative incomes.

productivity). An assiduous search has been made for such functions. Economists have found several, which at the same time satisfy requirements that can be made with a view to reality, for instance regarding income distribution among the factors of production. There prove to be several basic forms. The best-known is the so-called Cobb-Douglas function, which takes its name from two American research workers, C. W. Cobb and P. H. Douglas. In 1928 they produced the following empirical approach: $Q = L^\alpha K^{1-\alpha}$. Until around 1956 this was extremely popular among econometricians, since it has the property that the share of labour in national income is equal to a and the share of capital is equal to $1-a$. (The reader who really wants to understand this must differentiate the function. The marginal productivity of labour, i.e., the wage, is equal to $aL^{\alpha-1}K^{1-\alpha}$. The total wage bill is equal to L times the wage, i.e., $aL^\alpha K^{1-\alpha}$. This divided by Q yields a.)

With this, function distribution is fixed. We know the share of labour if we only know the production function. Capital intensity K/L can increase, but the share of labour nevertheless remains constant. That is because labour and capital can replace one another flexibly. A 1 per cent shift in K/L leads to a shift in price between K and L (that is to say a shift in the wage-interest ratio) which is also exactly equal to 1 per cent. Or, to put it somewhat differently, the elasticity of substitution between labour and capital is equal to one. This idea of substitution is highly characteristic of classical thinking; here too it proves to govern income distribution.

Unfortunately, reality is more complicated than the Cobb-Douglas function. Around 1956 other econometricians, including R. M. Solow, came to the conclusion that a different specification is probably better. They suggested: $Q = (L^\alpha + K^\beta)^{1/\alpha}$. With this function, substitution may proceed less flexibly than under the Cobb-Douglas function. An increase in K/L then leads to a growing share of labour – exactly what the statistics showed – which is why Solow-type production functions have come to occupy a leading place in classical thinking from 1956. There are many variants – as yet it is difficult to say which is the best of them. Considerably more empirical research will be required before something can be said for certain about this. We shall return to the matter in Chapter IX.

The production function, we have seen, is used in the explanation of the height of labour productivity, and in understanding income distribution; in the third place this mental instrument is useful if we wish to gain insight into economic growth. If Q increases, this can be ascribed to a bigger L or a bigger K. By using marginal productivity theory we can derive beautiful growth equations, as we shall see in Chapter X. But growth may also be due to a shift in the production function itself. This shift is called technical progress. It is defined as that part of the growth of production that cannot be ascribed to more labour and more capital. It is a kind of residual quantity – something that gives us a good deal of trouble in macro-economics. All kinds of things come under it: not only new technical processes (electricity instead of steam) but also better schooling of people, more effective management, handier ways of keeping records. As we have already seen, it is a difficult task to separate technical progress from the growth of the stock of capital goods, but in principle the concept of the production function makes such a separation possible.

Technical progress is an underdeveloped area in economics. This was made painfully evident at the end of the fifties, when M. Abramowitz and others discovered that the historical growth of real income was attributable much less to labour and capital than to a shift in the production function. We shall return to this in Chapter X, which is concerned with economic growth. For the moment what matters is that we note how useful the production function is for thinking. It orders our thoughts, and it is the most important function occurring in a classical set of equations.

Anyone who dislikes classical macro-economics would do well to attack the production function. This has been done by, among others, Mrs Joan Robinson and her school, which is sometimes named after Cambridge (England). She regards the use of this relation as a swindle and a harmful swindle at that (these are her own words). According to this school, lumping together all capital in one quantity K is impermissible. It is considered particularly wrong to calculate K by capitalizing the flow of incomes (interest) and then deriving the flow of incomes from marginal productivity. This is circular reasoning. I agree with this latter criticism, although my conclusion is that K must not be calculated by capitalization but by using the cost price of the machines. This is what econometricians do. The production function as an instrument of thought is defended by, among others, P. A. Samuelson and R. M. Solow, both from Cambridge (United States), and the discussion is known as the Cambridge-Cambridge controversy.

5 · THE STRENGTH AND WEAKNESS OF CLASSICAL THOUGHT

Classical macro-economics has something attractive, not to say fascinating, about it. It is a system. This will become clearer when we consider growth theory (Chapter X), where striking propositions will reveal themselves. The classical theory gives us a consistent view of reality, but it can easily degenerate into a kind of faith. It is tempting to come under the sway of the glorious equilibrium and brilliant harmony that classical theory constantly displays. Economic facts all fall into place; they are grasped from one central idea, namely that there is fundamental equilibrium between all economic quantities, and that this equilibrium is attained by the price signals. There is a control mechanism at work, invisible but highly effective, which translates the consumers' wishes into productive decisions. All the relevant information on scarcity is crammed into prices, and if we only put our trust in these price signals the invisible hand will attend to the rest. Whether we are concerned with the equilibrium of circular flow, or optimum allocation, or distribution of production between today and tomorrow (the 'length of the production detour'), or income distribution, or, as we shall see later, economic growth – classical theory always perceives a meaningful order. Moreover, the classical tenets, above all if they are formulated with the aid of differential calculus, are of unmistakable elegance, and that too gives some people the idea that the world makes sense. Anyone who has busied himself with this form of logic intensively and for a long time is liable to see economic reality as a very fine and marvellous thing which, via the revelations of the classical model, endeavours to make known a higher meaning. If, then, something nevertheless goes wrong in economic reality – unemployment, inflation, injustice – that must be the fault of human intervention in the control mechanism. In other words, the fault of governments, who hamper trade or levy taxes, or of pressure groups of employers and workers who rudely disturb the natural equilibrium. Thus classical macro-economics leads not only to a belief in the perfect nature of a completely free society, but also to a political recommendation: the government must refrain from interfering as much as possible, and employers' associations and workers' unions should preferably not exist at all. The ideological side of classical thought evidently contains a permanent temptation.

No wonder, then, that other observers of economic life have conceived a sometimes violent aversion towards classical macro-economics. They suspect classicism of an exaggerated regard for the existing order, of trying to explain things away and drawing a veil over conflicts, and of manipulation.* This criticism comes of course in the first place from the Marxists, who perceive the class struggle everywhere; but their criticism would carry more weight if they had not themselves made exactly the same ideological error, namely the intermingling of faith and science and the subordination of facts to what the ideology prescribes.

A second critical trend is the old classical view, originating from David Ricardo. The latter described at the beginning of the nineteenth century a situation in which an agricultural country is inhibited in its development because too large a piece of national income accrues to feudal landowners. Overpopulation keeps wages down and pushes rents up. Industrial profit is deficient. There is considerable luxury consumption: castles, lackeys. Stagnation, poverty, unemployment and conflicts characterize

---

*For instance, Mrs Robinson, whose dislike of the production function has already been mentioned, is of the opinion that the existing income distribution is defended. But that is a misunderstanding. Explaining the distribution is one thing, justifying it is another. J. Tinbergen analyses income inequality with the aid of a kind of Cobb-Douglas function, but finds income differentials definitely too great (*Income Distribution*, 1975).

this society. The modern followers of Ricardo recognize this situation in the capitalistic developing countries; they consider Ricardian theory more realistic for these countries than the neo-classical growth theory, with its smooth equilibria and its omni-present harmony.

The third trend to criticize classical macro-economics is Keynesian theory, which does not believe in Say's Law and from that standpoint arrives at entirely different views – see the following chapter for these.

My opinion on classical micro-economics is as follows. It is a way of thought constantly drawing attention to a number of fundamental phenomena, namely that goods, services and factors of production are scarce, and therefore demand a price in social intercourse. Such a price is not just anything; price determination basically makes sense. The latter comes into its own above all when substitution is possible. Substitution between products and substitution between capital and labour are of particular importance. (Later we shall see that substitution can also occur between domestic and foreign goods, and that the classical equilibrium on the balance of payments is based on that.) The price mechanism does not lead to perfect control of economic life – far from that, for cumulative disturbances of equilibrium can occur that are known as the wage-price spiral, and Say's Law also proves mainly an illusion. But the fundamental forces that classical theory spotlights are at work – under the surface, sometimes gently, sometimes strongly. How strongly they function is precisely what must be examined now. Scarcity penetrates allocation and income distribution. Capital accumulation causes production to rise and likewise the real wage, and if the elasticity of substitution between labour and capital is less than one, the share of capital in national income is accordingly reduced. These are interesting hypotheses that can be verified, for that is an additional advantage of classical macro-economics: it leads to empirical research work. That relates in particular to income distribution and growth.

We must therefore make use of the classical insights without allowing ourselves to be carried away by them. In difficult times too, when unemployment grows and people ask themselves what the government can do about it, the classical system has the meritorious property of opening our eyes to certain disturbances in the control mechanism of private-enterprise production. We must give these classical ideas the benefit of the doubt. We shall return to this contribution of classical theory to insight into the events of the seventies in Chapter XI.

CHAPTER III

Total Expenditure Determines National Income: Keynes's Theory

1 · THE BREAKING OF SAY'S LAW

Both Keynes and the classicists proceed from the idea that the national product, upon its creation, gives rise to the creation of a money income that can exactly buy this product. It *can* buy the goods. But in answering the question whether it *will* do so, the old and the new theories part company.

To grasp what is going on here, and to appreciate the heart of modern macro-economics, the reader must closely follow the coming argument. A number of symbols will be used in it, but I promise that this will not end in 'mathematics'. About all that is going to happen is addition and subtraction. It is, however, necessary to bear the following figure in mind. It is a somewhat more extensive variant of the circulation diagram on page 41.

The national product appears from business at the top right of the diagram. Its size is Q. This flow of goods (represented by a solid line) starts out but then divides into two parts. The larger part, consisting of consumer goods, makes for the households. This is C. A smaller part returns to business; it is that part of the production that serves to increase the stock of capital goods. This is I (investment).

These two flows of goods must be paid for. From the households to business a flow of money runs that is represented by a broken line, likewise of a size C. The flow of goods and the flow of money are quantitatively equal; they have to be, because both flows meet on the market for consumer goods.* To make a distinction between the flows – of course they are entirely different in nature – we speak of C (*goods*) and C (*expenditure*).

The same holds good for the investments. There too a flow of

* Supplying on credit can only effect a small time-lag in payment which is immaterial here.

money and a flow of goods keep each other in equilibrium. This splitting-off of Q is shown in the top right-hand corner as a small circulation. The broken line is I (*expenditure*).

Whilst Q leaves business, a flow of money Y, the national income, goes from business to the households. $Q = Y$, that is to say quantitatively, for in essence these are again two entirely different things; a flow of potatoes, milling machines, or trucks

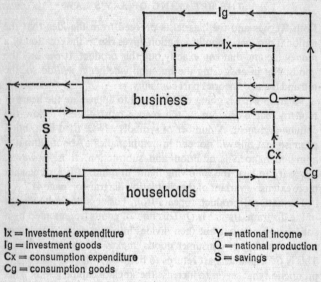

Ix = Investment expenditure	Y = national income
Ig = Investment goods	Q = national production
Cx = consumption expenditure	S = savings
Cg = consumption goods	

Fig. 2: Income and expenditure

is something quite different from a flow of money. The latter is drawn as a broken line.

Now this Y ends up with the households. In this simple circular flow they can only adopt one of two courses with it (later a larger number of possibilities will be put forward). They can consume the income or they can abstain from consumption. The latter is called saving. The flow of money for consumption is again called C, the total sum of savings S. C makes for the business firms, and S remains behind with the households. True, this money also goes to business, but it does not enter there in the form of a return but in that of a loan. Loans do not constitute incomes. They do not appear on the profit and loss account. Consequently, it makes a considerable difference to the entrepreneurs as to whether they get Y back again in the form of S or of C.

The total receipts of the entrepreneurs are therefore $C+I$. The latter is the amount that they receive from their fellow-entrepreneurs who have bought machines and other capital goods. Since these have to be produced by business, the entrepreneurs spend Y and receive in return $C+I$. The households receive Y and spend C. S is retained and later invested. This is the picture of the circulation on which Keynesians and classicists agree. The question now is, how can a Keynesian breach of Say's Law occur?

We saw that $Q = Y$. We also know that $Q = C+I$. (This is the division of the product among two kinds of goods.) But Y, which is equal to Q, is divided by the consumers among C and S. (This is the apportionment of the income among consumption expenditure and savings.) That is to say, $C+I = C+S$. Or $I = S$.

At first sight there does not seem to be anything sensational about this. Even the classicists knew that savings are equal to investments. But there is a great difference. In the classical view money was first saved and later invested. Investment was impossible before the savers had performed their task. But Keynes arrives at his celebrated $I = S$ without this reasoning. The mechanism that lies behind this equality looks entirely different in Keynes's theory.*

It looks as follows. Suppose that at a given moment the households wish to save a greater part of their income than formerly.

---

*We found $I = S$ by simple subtraction; in that case there are no mechanisms, only definitions. This way of proving that $I = S$ holds good if the income received by business ($C+I$) equals the income received by the households ($C+S$); in other words, under static conditions. If income grows or shrinks it is necessary to take time-lags into account; I and S are no longer equal by definition. In that case there is a mechanism at work that makes them equal. This point is only raised here for insiders. It led to an enormous discussion in the first years after the appearance of the *General Theory*, but has almost disappeared by now.

That is to say, C (*expenditure*) decreases. The receipts of the business firms, $C+I$, therefore also decrease. This is the first consequence. But at that moment, $C+I$ threatens to become smaller than Y. In that case there is a loss, or at least a reduction of profit. Since the profits are included in the national money income Y, at the same moment Y becomes smaller. This can happen in itself without production contracting. But the possibility of the latter happening is also great. In that case unemployment becomes probable. The money income decreases further and as a result the households receive less money. The result of their increased thrift is thus a smaller income! This compels them to cut down on their consumptive expenditure. In this way the receipts of the firms are again less than they already were, and once again a loss or a reduction in profit threatens. The dwindling money income cannot but lead to smaller savings – for saving is a luxury which cannot survive a drop in income. The process of contraction thus continues until the receipts of business firms are again equal to their expenditure. Or, to put it differently, until $C+I$ equals $C+S$. That is to say, until S has again become equal to I.

Here lies the starting point of Keynesian theory. If the savers proceed to save more, total expenditure decreases. As a result national income decreases – for that arises from total expenditure. If national income is lower, less is saved. In this way the equality of I and S, which for a moment threatened to vanish, is restored. The equilibrium between these two quantities is established by the variation of income, production, and employment. The rate of interest, which in the classical view provided the equilibrium, does not occur in this story.

Of course the classicists would have an answer to this. They would point out that an increase in savings does not lead to a contraction of expenditure but to greater investment, so that the total of the business firms' receipts $C+I$ remains unaffected. The Keynesians counter this with the following argument. In many cases the entrepreneurs will not react to the increased thrift with larger investments. Why should they? Investing means creating a greater productive capacity. There is no future in this if the households have just decided to cut down on their consumption. On the contrary, we may be thankful that investments remain at the same level. It is also conceivable that they will decline – and then the circular flow is completely disturbed, for in that case the total expenditure of business declines still further through the reduced sales of the engineering industry (see below, the savings paradox). As a matter of fact, in the Keynesian line of thought the greater thrift of the households does not lead to greater savings balances. These disappear again for the very reason that income declines. Consequently there are no surplus savings that can be invested. They have disappeared with the drop in national income.

At this stage it is too early to decide who is right. The essential thing is that the Keynesians have detached the decision about the size of I from the supply of savings. It is true that savings are equal to investment, but that is because national income controls the size of the savings. Y adjusts itself. National income and therefore national production are not given quantities determined by productive capacity; they fluctuate, and they do so in such a way that savings become exactly equal to investments. The latter are primary: savings proceed from investments via the size of the national income. As a result of this the national income may occasionally work out far too small. We then see unused productive capacity and unemployment. This is exactly the opposite of the classicists' world.

This relation can also be approached from another angle. Suppose that at a given moment a wave of optimism floods business. Although consumption is constant the entrepreneurs consider that it would be a good and profitable idea to increase productive capacity. They order from their colleagues in the engineering industry a number of lathes, shoemaking machines, agricultural implements, and other forms of equipment.* The sale of capital goods increases, as does production of them. Assume that there is still unemployed labour in those branches of industry. As a result these men find work. They receive an income that they did not have at first. The profits in the capital goods industry also

---

*The classicists would ask: how do the entrepreneurs get the financial resources to finance this? But note: in the Keynesian theory these resources appear as a consequence of investment, provided that the slightest start can be made, e.g. by bank credit.

increase. In other words, national income increases. This comes as a pleasant surprise to the households. They therefore proceed to consume more. Now something strange happens: the expectations of the investing entrepreneurs, which at first were perhaps based on nothing better than a certain unfounded optimism, are fulfilled. Through their orders the investors have created the income that leads to the consumptive expenditure which will proceed to justify their increased productive capacity. Everyone is happy about this course of events. So are the producers of shoes, propelling pencils, and chewing gum, for they see their sales increasing. Perhaps they in turn also invest more, so that income and consumption further increase. We clearly see here the cumulative process known under the name of multiplier effect.

Here too the question arises: will this process continue until the national economy finally explodes in an orgy of consumptive and investment expenditure? No. Because the increased income will lead not only to additional consumption, but also to additional savings. S accumulates, in such a manner that the increase in I is compensated in the long run. The additional investments have led via the increased national income to additional savings. And also exactly enough savings have been formed to help finance the investments. At this point the incomes of the firms, $C+I$, are equal to the expenditure $C+S$. Total expenditure is in equilibrium with national income. But the latter has increased, as has production, as has employment. Through the expansion of the circulation some unused productive capacity has again come into operation.

Anyone who comprehends this process no longer believes in Say's Law. He will no longer unquestioningly accept that there will always be a market for the total production. True, in the first instance the income required for this is created; but if this income is not consumptively spent to a sufficient extent, the flow of money and production will begin to contract. Overproduction will threaten.* The entrepreneurs rectify this by cutting down on

---

*I should like to point out at this stage that there is also a trend in modern economics that considers Say's Law to be broken in another way. It notes the withdrawal of money from circulation, which happens by the increasing of cash holdings ('hoarding'). This way of thinking is not neces-

production – but in that case the factors of production are no longer fully employed. There is no question of the entrepreneurs fighting in all circumstances for the factors of production. They may do, but not necessarily so. It is therefore not productive capacity that determines the real national income; total expenditure forms the determinant. Productive capacity is only a ceiling. Usually, the more orthodox Keynesians say, economic life is far below that ceiling. Idle machines and unemployment are normal phenomena if we do nothing about them. Some followers of Keynes consider economic stagnation to be the constant threat to the national economy.

It is highly problematic whether the older Keynesians, and also Keynes himself, are right about this. Their pessimism on this point has been abandoned by a later generation of Keynesians. But this does not detract from the fact that the relation of the macro-economic quantities as given above is accepted in broad outline by the neo-Keynesians. They follow the circulation idea and, with certain variants, regard national income as the quantity that establishes equilibrium in the system. This is characteristic of all neo-Keynesians: Y is not a given quantity emanating from productive capacity. National income is determined by a combination of investment and consumption, which we shall call total expenditure.

2 · THE PROPENSITY TO SAVE AND THE MULTIPLIER

We have now seen a number of the main features of Keynes's theory, and we must next study his train of thought somewhat more closely. This can be done by examining two quantities which played a large though still somewhat concealed part in the above, viz. the propensity to save and the multiplier.

What is the propensity to save? It is that part of national income that is saved. We shall call this quantity s. The propensity to save is a percentage. It may for instance be 10, or 15. More than 25 is

---

sarily at variance with that which has been followed here, but it does often lead to a somewhat different view of things. I shall come back to this.

improbable. Side by side with the propensity to save is the propensity to consume; this is designated by c and is equal to $1-s$. These concepts do not really appear in classical theory, for in the latter national income is a datum. That is to say, an increase in the propensity to save *pari passu* means an increase in savings. Both quantities run exactly parallel, and there is little point in introducing the propensity to save alongside savings S as a separate concept. Nor does the propensity to consume have a special place in classical reasoning.

In the modern approach, on the other hand, the distinction between s and S in particular is very important. For we saw in the preceding section that S equals I. According to orthodox Keynesianism (we shall be giving a more moderate view later), the size of savings is considered to be determined by the size of investments. Strangely enough, therefore, the savers have no say in the volume of savings! They are at the mercy of the fluctuations in national income. This looks at first sight like an absurd idea. For we have also drawn the conclusion that total expenditure is of vital importance to national income. And this expenditure is partly determined by the households. They decide what part of their income will flow on in the form of consumptive expenditure and what part will remain behind in the form of savings. This free and independent decision on the division of income is a privilege of the recipient of that income in a democratic society.

And in fact the recipient of income does decide for himself how he will divide his income among clothes, food, gramophone records, and savings. He is free in his choice He or she independently determines his or her own propensity to save. But in so doing he has not yet determined how much he will save! For the volume of his savings is the product of his propensity to save and his income. Saving is to a certain extent a luxury – as is the buying of records – a luxury that depends on income. Viewed macro-economically, income turns out to depend precisely on . . . the propensity to save! This is the heart of Keynesian theory, which we should now like to explain again, this time by means of the new concepts.

The savers determine the propensity to save and the entrepreneurs determine the volume of investment. Whatever the propensity to save proves to be, savings must, according to the circulation theory, equal investments. The quantity that creates this equality is, as we have seen, national income. It adjusts itself in such a way that $I = S$. Now, how large is that national income in that state of equilibrium? Exactly so large that the product of the propensity to save (determined freely and independently by the savers) and of national income equals the investments. In 'mathematical' terms: Y becomes so large that I equals $s.Y$. Here I and s are given, so that Y is determined: $Y = \dfrac{I}{s}$. National income is the quotient of investments and the propensity to save. If the investments in a country amount to five thousand million pounds, and the propensity to save has been fixed by the income-earners at 1/7, national income will proceed to be thirty-five thousand million pounds. This is the heart of Keynesian theory in a nutshell.*

From this relation it becomes clear what effect the recipients of income exert on the circulation. They fix the percentage that they wish to save. But by so doing they at the same time, in unconscious combination with the investors, fix national income. Since national income has a decisive effect on the volume of savings, afterwards exactly those savings come about that match the investments. The propensity to save has determined not so much the volume of savings as the national income. The effect of the decision to save is therefore enormous in the Keynesian system; but it is quite a different effect from what the savers themselves think. They do not know what they are doing. Perhaps through exaggerated thrift they are opening the door to a depression which perforce breaks them of the saving habit. Keynesian theory gives people control of their own fate – but they do not know it.

*The reader must grasp this proposition, but not learn it by heart. For it applies only to the simple circulation that we have in mind at present. In reality things are more complicated; we shall be concerned with this later. In fact the multiplier is much smaller. And it is not simply 'given'; the multiplier may depend on the national income and on other factors. This sounds very unpleasant to those who are looking for a Great Constant.

MODERN ECONOMICS

This obscure relation between the various aspects can be understood in another way. We can check what the position is with regard to the multiplier effect, which was touched upon in the preceding section. In this effect we encounter exactly the same quantities.

Let us assume that the entrepreneurs extend their productive capacity at a given moment. They give an 'investment impulse', to use the Keynesian jargon. This impulse is the income effect of the new investments. The circular flow swells on the left-hand side. The households get the extra income; part of it they use for consumption (a fraction c) and part for savings (a fraction s; $c+s = 1$). The part spent on consumption returns to business; it is an increase in revenue. If we call the investment impulse ΔI, then the households that receive this additional income spend a sum equal to $c\Delta I$. This again returns to business in the form of extra revenues. Consequently $c\Delta I$ is spent again on the factors of production, and as a result assumes the form of a second increment of income. Part of this, determined by the propensity to consume, is spent again on consumer goods. In the second round of the multiplier, therefore, a sum $c^2\Delta I$ makes its way to the business enterprises. In the third round this is $c^3\Delta I$. The multiplier process continues to work in this way. Ultimately national income has increased by a sum which is equal to all these extra impulses together. This total increase amounts in the first place to ΔI (primary effect) and then to $c\Delta I+c^2\Delta I+c^3\Delta I$, etc. Perhaps at first sight it might seem as if this infinitely long series displays an infinitely great sum, and that the multiplier process keeps on stirring up expenditure, an idea that occasionally passes through the minds of some enthusiastic laymen when they philosophize about the effect of (for instance) public works. But in actual fact the process of passing on and receiving income gradually peters out. For c is less than 1, so that c^2, c^3, etc., become steadily less. After the first impulse smaller and smaller ones follow. The impulses approach zero, and the increase in national income has a finite value. But nevertheless the increase in Y is greater than the original investment impulse. The ratio between the two is called the multiplier. It is defined as $\dfrac{\Delta Y}{\Delta I}$, and represents the proportion by which an additional investment causes national income to swell via income effects.

Now how large is this multiplier?

To understand this we must bear in mind that the multiplier effect ceases to operate if in the course of the increase in income a new equilibrium is found. This is the case as soon as the consumers have been able to save so much that S has become equal to I. The increase in investments, ΔI, has then 'leaked away' in its entirety in the form of savings. $\Delta I = \Delta S$. In this situation the entrepreneurs again receive as much from their customers as they put into circulation as incomes. The circulation is again in equilibrium. By bearing this in mind we can determine the size of the multiplier. For we know that ΔS must be equal to $s\Delta Y$. Consequently, in the final situation ΔI equals $s\Delta Y$. It follows from this that the multiplier, which we have defined as $\dfrac{\Delta Y}{\Delta I}$, must equal $\dfrac{1}{s}$. Or, to put it in another way, must equal $\dfrac{1}{1-c}$. The multiplier equals the reciprocal of the propensity to save.*

The doctrine of the multiplier can once more be described as the heart of Keynesianism. Perhaps the reader has gradually come to the conclusion that this theory contains a little too many hearts. But that is not so. Everything that has been said in this and the last section is a constant repetition of one and the same thing. The same economic event, viz. the income-creating effect of consumption and investment, has been approached from various angles. The story changes, the terms are different, but the essence remains the same. The question is always: how big is national income? And the answer is always: so big that savings equal investments, or, to put it differently, so big that the multiplier has provided sufficient savings, or, in yet other terms, so big that total revenues are sufficient to cover the total expenditure of

---

*In actual fact this propensity to save must be related to the part of income added or marginal income. We must not have the average propensity to save $\dfrac{S}{Y}$ but the marginal propensity to save $\dfrac{\Delta S}{\Delta Y}$. In the following pages the letter s is to be understood as this marginal quantity.

business, or finally, so big that the circular flows of money and goods are in equilibrium. This is the Keynesian mechanism.

It is definitely important. However, its quantitative importance can easily be exaggerated. I should like to warn the reader against a misunderstanding which is encountered among some adepts of the modern theory. They have grasped that the multiplier equals $\frac{1}{s}$; and they also know that the marginal propensity to save s may lie somewhere between 10 and 20 per cent. This leads them to estimate that the multiplier is about 7. That is to say that building a factory that costs a million pounds would cause the potential sales of business to increase by no less than seven million. This idea leads to a sort of Baron Munchausen economics: a national economy could pull itself up out of a depression by its own bootstraps. This view of things is misleading, for two reasons.

The first reason is that we have introduced here a simple form of circulation in which purchasing power leaks away in only one direction: savings. But in reality there are two other leaks, viz. taxes and imports from abroad. We shall come back to these. They lead to the multiplier being much smaller than would appear at first sight.

The second reason is theoretically rather complicated. It is connected with the fact that the multiplier operates in time. The new revenues which are the result of the income effects are not present forthwith. The Keynesian process of income accretion and additional consumption takes time. If only a single investment impulse occurs, income will not be lastingly raised to a higher level. 'Pump-priming' is therefore a misleading expression. If national income is to expand permanently, the investment level must be permanently raised. Incidentally, this can quite easily be the case if the additional consumption which occurs in the course of the multiplier process encourages the entrepreneurs to maintain or even increase the new investment level.

The fact that the multiplier operates in time also has the result that S does not immediately become equal to I. There is a time-lag. In the interim the entrepreneur will have to do his financing with other means than current savings. This gap can be filled by bank credit, to which we shall return in Chapter VII.

In the *General Theory* the stress tends to fall on the constant equality of *I* and *S*. There has been a good deal of discussion about this. Now more stress is laid on the time-lag. This can be done by what is called period analysis (D. H. Robertson and the Stockholm School), which follows the movement of *Y*, *C*, and *S* in time. Tables can be drawn up showing all this. I prefer to leave these exercises to those who fancy such things.

3 · IS KEYNESIANISM DEPRESSION ECONOMICS?

The development of modern economics, and in particular that of the political conclusions that can be drawn from it, has been harmed by the fact that many have characterized Keynes's theory as a special depression theory, a theory of idle machinery and unemployment. It would be dangerous, it is reasoned, to apply this theory to other situations, for instance inflationary ones, for it was not constructed for these.

This criticism is understandable. Keynes himself gave rise to it to some extent, and some of his followers in particular have promoted this belief. They were impressed by a theoretical system that was able to explain a low income. Classical theory believed that national income would always be maintained at such a high level by Say's Law that productive capacity would be fully utilized. The *General Theory* had shown that a lower national income was also possible. And more than that; national income could freeze at a low level, without any chance of recovery. Say's Law had been put out of operation, and the hope that a surplus of savings would lead to a revival of investments via a lower rate of interest had vanished. In the Depression, according to the Keynesian view, there *were* no surplus savings at all; as a result of the drop in national income these had disappeared, shrunk, been lost, just as national income had shrunk to a considerable extent. The circulation was just ticking over; there were no sales because there was no income, and there was no income because there were no sales. Moreover, this vicious circle was no abstraction, no pessimistic view of the future, but the reality of the 1930s. Small wonder that the Keynesians believed that their theory not only explained the Depression, but also predicted it for many years to come. Econo-

71

mists thought that they had discovered the forces that brought about a permanent slump.

Keynes himself developed a special theory on these forces in the *General Theory*. He was of the opinion that the propensity to save which, if it is too high, summons up depression and unemployment, would display a steadily rising trend. He based this belief on the fact that a higher income leads to a greater propensity to save. Rich people save a greater percentage of their income than poor people. The same holds good for rich countries. Rising prosperity and a growing national income form a threat to themselves. Our prosperity spells our downfall: poverty in the midst of plenty. To put it in technical terms: the marginal propensity to save increases with income. A further expression that ties up with what was said above about the fundamental determinations of prosperity: the higher the productivity of labour, the higher unemployment will be. The fruits of progress are spoilt by the monetary disturbances in the circulation.

This special relation between income and propensity to save is, however, doubtful when taken as a general law. Keynes had arrived at it by deduction, and in this respect he reasoned like an old-fashioned economist of the abstract school. He believed that pure logic, if at least it started from wide observation of reality, could lead to quantitative conclusions. This is a mistake, fostered by the special situation in the 1930s. The Keynesian system is a strictly logical structure. But it cannot express an opinion on the value of concrete quantities. These have to be filled in later. We need quantitative economics for this – a scientific technique about which Keynes was all too sceptical, to the detriment of his system, for now he incorporated an element – too great a propensity to save – which in later years proved hardly tenable.

For it is by no means the case that the propensity to save must be greater in the event of a larger income than in the event of a smaller one. The invalidity of this proposition is already apparent f om a comparison of the incomes of different people. Some income-earners in the middle classes find it more difficult to save than those members of the income classes immediately below the middle classes. And macro-economically, too, we can sometimes observe things that are at variance with Keynes's view.

The year 1956 gave a characteristic example of the converse in the Netherlands as did the year 1959 in the United Kingdom. In each year the national income of the country concerned increased enormously, but this did not make people any more thrifty; on the contrary. There were reasons for this which are irrelevant here, but which in any case were more complicated than the over-simplification that a higher percentage of savings results from a higher income. This oversimplification has contributed towards Keynesianism being wrongfully labelled the theory of 'depression economics'.

There was a further reason. One of Keynes's most influential followers, the American Alvin Hansen, developed an alarming theory about the permanent depression. He foresaw not only too great a propensity to save, but also a constant abatement of investments. Population growth would come to a stop, which was supposed to discourage capital outlay. True, technology would not stand still, but it would lead to increasingly compact and thus more limited investments. (Hansen thought that an instance of this lay in the switch from railways to airfields, which have a smaller income effect.) The entrepreneurs would become increasingly disheartened. Hansen's view was depression economics with a vengeance. This was, however, not due to the logic of the Keynesian system, but to the special premises that Hansen had incorporated in his theory. An insufficient distinction has been made between these two things – the logic and the figures. The opponents of this stagnation theory, as it is called, have used Hansen's pessimistic theory as an argument against modern macro-economics. Events were on their side to the extent that the post-war period in the Western world displayed the exact opposite of stagnation. However, their criticism of Keynes is misplaced, for Keynesian logic and the depression theory are two different things.

Despite the fact that Keynes personally had little faith in capitalism's ability to maintain a decent level of employment, his theory can be very well applied to a situation in which the factors of production are all in operation. That is also the reason why the *General Theory of Employment, Interest, and Money* is rightly called General. Keynes reproached the classicists with having dealt only with the special case of non-inflationary full employment. But there exists also the Hayek situation.

In the unemployment situation many economic activities have to be judged differently. The latter applies particularly to saving. The classicists saw saving as a fine and useful activity. It promotes the acquisition of property, and it increases productive capacity and with this future prosperity. Individual benefit and society's benefit coincide – one of the most comforting aspects of the classical system. But then Keynes comes along to tell us that saving is harmful. It reduces sales, slows economic life down to a jog-trot, and leads to unemployment, whilst moreover savings do not even increase as a result of it. Saving becomes suspect.

But this applies only if there are productive forces which are unused. If there should be a real scarcity of factors of production – which Keynes considers not very probable, at least in peacetime – the classical view holds good. In that case investment is possible only if the recipients of income are prepared to sacrifice part of consumption. *A fortiori* this is true in an inflationary situation. We can also put it in this way: in the Hayek situation consumption and capital formation are competing for the factors of production. In the depression consumption supports investment; they are not rivals, but help one another in that one supplies the sales for the other.

The *General Theory* therefore confronts us with two worlds: one in which unemployment prevails and machinery is used only in part, and another in which full loading of machinery and full employment predominate. In the first world national income is smaller than the productivity of labour allows; in the second the productivity of labour forms the factor determining prosperity. The Keynesian theory can grasp both worlds; but at first it believed that the former world would be the more probable one. Now this view of probability is dubious. For in fact the deductive theory cannot by itself teach us whether a certain national economy will yield a large or a small national income. The Keynesian system of thought merely arranges the variables that lead to a given result. Some of these variables have an expansive effect on the circulation: these are investments and consumption. Other variables – the propensity to save – have a contractive effect. The way in which they keep each other in equilibrium can be shown in the form of a general theory, but this equilibrium can be quantified only if we know the figures. We have here an example of what has been said in Chapter I about the shortcomings of the deductive theory and of the necessity of quantitative economics. This is all the more cogent because the economic system that we have described above is extremely simple in its set-up. It has been stripped of imports and exports, of taxes and of government expenditure. No allowance has been made for the fact that investments are not given but, as regards size, might sometimes react on consumption. To use the language of the next chapter, an extremely simple model has been used. If we introduce more variables – and this is necessary if we really want to give neo-Keynesian theory – the force field of opposed expansive and contractive factors becomes more complex. At the same time the need for quantification becomes greater. Only when we know the concrete figures can we say whether an economy is growing or shrinking, whether it is threatening to become bogged down in depressive stagnation or to soar up an inflationary spiral.

However, quantification presupposes a conveniently arranged theory. This is something that we do not yet have. The Keynesianism discussed in this chapter is still too elementary. Things will improve somewhat in the next chapter.

4 · THE ESSENCE OF KEYNESIAN THEORY

Since 1936 a whole library has been published on what Keynes really meant. No wonder that there are differences of opinion about this. All we know for certain is that Keynes was a man who often changed his mind, wrote carelessly, and read some books while leaving unread others that sometimes were more relevant.* We have a well-defined idea of what the essence of Keynesian

---

*An example is the work of Michal Kalecki, a Polish predecessor and contemporary of Keynes. When Kalecki tried to establish contact with Keynes in the thirties, he had little success. Keynes was not in fact prepared to assume that anything that was worthwhile could emerge from such foreign parts.

theory is – this idea has already been put into words in th
preceding sections, but I should like to say again what the essen
tial features are. Then I shall discuss some views held by others.

In my opinion investment is the crucial variable. In th
classicists there is a mechanism at work that gives I a ver
special value. If we call the productive capacity $Q^\star$ and con
sumption C, then once the consumers have established how muc
they wish to consume some unutilized productive capacity is lef
This is equal to $Q^\star - C$. The classical theory demonstrates a
equilibrium mechanism in which I becomes equal to this quantit
$Q^\star - C$. The room in the productive capacity is therefore exactl
filled. Now the essence of Keynesian theory is that this equili
brium mechanism is absent, so that $I \neq Q^\star - C$. If I turns out t
be greater, expenditure will be too high; in the other case expendi
ture will be too low. There is no guarantee that the investment
exactly fit the space left by the consumers. There is as a result n
guarantee that $Y = Y^\star$.

Everything therefore revolves around the factors determinin
I. In the classicists these are ultimately savings, and the mechan
ism is that of the capital market. In Keynes too $S = I$, but her
the independent quantity is I, and S adjusts to it. The invest
ments depend on all kinds of other things, but not so much on th
available savings. They are for instance determined by expecta
tions of the future, by the psychological mood among entre
preneurs, or by the incitement of new inventions. Financing i
arranged in one way or another, by bank loans perhaps, but sav
ings do follow on investments via the multiplier mechanism, s
that a shortage on the capital market is usually a temporary one
I can assume every possible value differing from $Q^\star - C$, an
that gives the disturbance of sales and the movement of nationa
income.

We can go a step further. So far we have viewed I in detach
ment from everything – an exogenous quantity. But we can als
assume that I depends on Y. That makes a Keynesian disequili
brium more likely. If savers save more, consumption declines an
sales therefore fall as well; if I reacts to this, not only does C fal
but also I. In the classical view, C and I move in opposite direc
tions, so that together they lead to $Q^\star$. In Keynes C and I possibl

move in parallel, and then anything can happen. Investment may even depend on the *change* in sales – in that case the national income becomes utterly unstable because everything revolves around investments. In the following chapter we shall consider further the factors that determine I, including the possibility that I depends on ΔY (the so-called accelerator).

Incidentally, we shall see later that in Keynes's government expenditure G plays a similar role to investments. There too an autonomous chunk of spending occurs that can give rise to underspending and overspending. Full cover of G by tax proceeds T does not offer any guarantee of spending equilibrium – that is the heart of Haavelmo's theorem, which we shall discuss separately because it throws such a clear light on the Keynesian view. Exports too are autonomous spending. Even the autonomous part of consumption has the same effect; C_o is on a par with I_o.

I feel that my interpretation is the simplest one: in a Keynesian world some components of expenditure are insensitive to the feedback mechanisms. As a result they enter circular flow like hard lumps. They cut across the equilibrium mechanism. But there are other interpretations of Keynesian theory, and I shall briefly refer to a few of them.

One alternative method of characterizing the essence of the Keynesian view considers the reason why the capital market mechanism does not work. For instance, one can say that in Keynes the rate of interest has no effect, either on S or on I. But this is a disputable interpretation of what Keynes wrote. In the *General Theory* investments most certainly depend on the interest rate, only the latter is not determined on the capital market. Keynes derives equilibrium interest from the liquidity preference and the available quantity of money – a special tenet that has meanwhile been superseded by other views (namely that interest is determined by the supply and demand of credit, whereby the demand comprises both I and the demand for money for cash-holding purposes, and the supply comprises both S and the newly created liquidities). We had better forget the notion of the insensitivity of I to interest.

It is somewhat better to define Keynesian theory as the analysis of the liquidity trap. What this means will not be properly

explained until Chapter VII; only a concise definition will b
given here. The savings that come about because savers try t
make S bigger than I enter the capital sphere without flowing o
to the income sphere. They linger there for a while, but meanwhi
the lack of consumption depresses national income, with th
result that the extra savings disappear again. The contraction c
Y is explained by this liquidity trap. I do not regard this story a
incorrect, but I do doubt to some extent whether it is characte
istic; depressions need not be accompanied by such an abundanc
of money in the capital sphere, but my objection is that this stor
belongs to the monetary way of thought. It is not typicall
Keynesian.

Another interpretation of what Keynes meant involves futur
expectations. The influence of interest on entrepreneurial decision
is as it were swamped by future expectations regarding sales an
profit. The Keynesian innovation has occasionally been describe
in this way: at last future expectations were done justice to i
macro-economics. I find this comment relevant, but I neverthe
less regard this as an insufficient characteristic of Keynesia
theory, since nowhere is there any mention of $Q^\star$ and of the wa
in which actual spending may differ from it. A number of moder
interpreters of Keynes in particular take this much too far. The
see the difference between Keynes and the classics mainly in thi
expectations issue – wrongly so.

Yet another fallacious explanation emphasizes the suppose
fact that in Keynes all prices are rigid, above all wages. Only i
this way could a deviation from the classical expenditure equili
brium come about. Anyone who reasons in this way is indee
trapped in the classical pattern of thought, because it is not at a
true that in Keynes prices and wages are fixed; on the contrary
the *General Theory* contains a whole chapter on what happens
money wages change. Prices and wages are not rigid, but Keyne
considers them unimportant. The macro-supply of and the macro
demand for just about everything is inelastic. Employment doe
not react to movements of the wage level – this view is typicall
Keynesian, and we shall encounter it again in Chapter IX. Tota
production does not react to the price level. It is not so strang
that Keynes arrived at this idea, because the study of circular flo

prepares us for it. If all prices rise, incomes rise. If all wages rise, costs of production rise, but also revenue. Changes in these variables produce opposite effects, and therefore perhaps more or less disappear if we consider strategic relationships. There is a clear point here calling for quantitative examination.

It is indeed my opinion that Keynes found prices and wages rather uninteresting. And yet I would prefer not to make this the central point here; we must not characterize a theory by means of a negative property. Moreover, the fact that Keynes leaves the price mechanism out of things can be rectified. A complete theory must for instance make allowance for the wage-price spiral and its effects. Such a theory then retains a Keynesian framework but is less limited.

Finally, there is a view of Keynes that says that everything revolves around the multiplier. This is the Keynesian Great Constant from economic life. It is an argument used by both supporters and opponents. The supporters see in the multiplier a quantity that is more reliable than the velocity of circulation of money – in this they are at variance with the monetary school (which is discussed in Chapter VII). They are also of the opinion that the multiplier lends itself well to quantitative research. The hypothesis which has then to be tested is that the autonomous impulses are proportionate to the movement of Y. I am not an enthusiastic proponent of this reasoning – the Keynesian multiplier is constant in the textbooks, but not necessarily constant in reality. Empirical research sometimes tends to display variations in time, which is not surprising – we shall encounter the factors determining the multiplier again further on in this book, and the multiplier will then prove that the factors include variables, such as the burden of taxation. I do not consider it incorrect to speak in the first instance of the multiplier as a fairly stable quantity, provided that we don't build a whole theory on it.

If, however, we do build a whole theory on it, strange ideas emerge. These are intelligently exploited by the opponents of Keynes to show what a silly mess the *General Theory* is. Henry Hazlitt, who called Keynesian theory one of the biggest intellectual scandals of our time, advanced the following criticism.* Define

* *The Failure of the 'New Economics', 1959.*

the ratio between the national income of the United States an
the income of Henry Hazlitt as a fixed quantity, the HH mult
plier (this has a value of about one hundred million). Suppo
that the national income of the United States is too low; there
deflation and unemployment. But there is no cause for alarn
because there is an inexpensive way of remedying deflation: th
Treasury gives Henry Hazlitt a few thousand dollars and the H
multiplier attends to the rest. Total income increases by thousand
of millions of dollars.

This criticism makes a good point and clearly shows where th
danger lies of assuming constant relationships. Of course, Hazli
makes the whole matter look ridiculous. And yet I should like t
derive from his criticism the lesson that the fixed multiplier ma
not be blown up into the central tenet of Keynesian theory. A
advanced version of this theory operates with a multiplier whic
in turn depends on many variables. The real constants are at
greater depth. Where precisely? That is *the* big problem of en
pirical science (More about this in Chapter IV.)

Finally, I am against defining Keynesian theory in a purel
political respect. And yet it is often specified as that theory whic
is aimed at full employment, or the prevention of inflationary an
deflationary gaps, and thus gives a number of recipes for budge
ary and monetary policy.

Sometimes Keynesian policy is even further narrowed dow
to a public works policy, overlooking the fact that other goverr
ment expenditures can likewise be used as instruments, and tha
the same applies to taxes. Still other people say that Keyne
really wanted to promote a low interest rate. I am dead again
such political definitions, because it is not a good thing to confu
analysis and policy recommendations. The *General Theory* cor
tains both; the book endeavours to replace the classical theory b
a 'general' one, but at the same time to make a contribution t
the combating of unemployment. There is no objection to th
latter, but Keynesian *theory* is a theory of the interplay of cor
sumption and investments, not a recipe for statesmen. Ho
macro-economic theory and macro-economic policy can be kep
apart, while the theory is nevertheless helpful to econom
steersmanship, can be found in Chapter XII.

5 · THE STRENGTH AND WEAKNESS OF KEYNESIAN THEORY

So far we have emphasized the heart of Keynesian theory: the movement of national income. This attends to the identity of saving and investing, and to the disparity between income equilibrium and expenditure equilibrium. Circular flow receives maximum attention. We shall later see that this method of reasoning can be extended in different ways. We can regard investments as a variable (and ask ourselves what determining factors lie behind them), and we can make allowance for government expenditure and taxes. We shall also involve international trade. The simple Keynesian theory can therefore be generalized, but it continues to be a way of thought that constantly draws attention to the demand side and leaves those other elements of economic life in the shade. I would like to include some of them here: it is no coincidence that they are the things in which classical theory has always been greatly interested.

In the first place, in the most simple Keynesian reasoning, productive capacity is given. Investments create money income; the fact that they also increase productive capacity is overlooked, at least in the simpler versions of Keynesian theory. This is of course an irksome restriction if we proceed to consider the development of production in time. For this reason allowance is quite definitely made for a capacity effect in the somewhat more extensive variants of Keynesian theory. But this starts from the simple idea that investments lead in proportion to additional productive capacity. If the stock of capital goods increases by x per cent, production also increases by x per cent. Another way of saying this is that the capital coefficient is constant. Two followers of Keynes – E. D. Domar and R. F. Harrod – have built on this constant capital coefficient a growth theory that has become rather popular and that will be explained in Chapter X. We shall see there that this constant has highly destructive effects on the stability of the national income. What we are concerned with now is this: as long as the Keynesians maintain the assumption of a given productive capacity, they are engaged in explaining short-term phenomena whereby the movement of expenditure dominates everything. If they abandon the assumption of a given productive capacity and concern themselves with economic growth, they adhere to another limiting assumption, namely that the relationship between production and the stock of capital goods is constant.

Why do they do so? Not out of silliness, but to gain a clear view of the world. In this way the full light falls on the role of spending, and above all on that part of it which we call investments. The latter have an income effect on national income and also a capacity effect; these two can be made equal to one another, and then a typical Keynesian equilibrium emerges. This equilibrium income determines how much labour will be used. In Keynesian thought, employment adjusts to production. In the following chapter there is a graph which illustrates this. Spending is the great driving force, determining everything via fixed coefficients. Employment is a passive variable.

This is a limitation of Keynesian theory that can also be described as the mirror image of classical macro-economics. *There* everything revolves around substitution. Labour and capital can replace one another, and in the organization of production the entrepreneurs will pay attention to the relative prices of labour and capital. Say's Law attends to total sales. In Keynesian thought exactly the opposite occurs: the movement of sales is the big variable, but the relationship between the amounts of labour and capital within productive capacity is a fixed one. The price relationships between labour and capital can do what they like, but the entrepreneur pays no attention to them. He is impervious to this kind of price signal, and pays attention only to sales. Adam Smith's 'invisible hand' is absent from the Keynesian model.*

This set-up of Keynesian theory has far-reaching consequences that we shall encounter again and again. Where international trade is concerned we shall see that the classical price mechanism (the rate of exchange) is largely eliminated by the Keynesian view. When we are discussing wages we shall see that in a Keynes-

*A remarkable consequence of the Keynesian predilection for fixed relationships between the amounts of product, labour and capital is that the Keynesians in actual fact have no distribution theory.

ian world these can rise beyond all proportion without affecting employment, a view whose realism has greatly to be doubted and which led in the seventies to great mistrust of Keynesian theory. When we discuss growth, we shall see that in the Keynesian interpretation this depends in particular on investments, and that the amount of labour used is adjusted to these investments in a fixed ratio; this too is at variance with recent experiences.

And this is not all. The Keynesian view does not ignore the substitution effects in which classical theory is so greatly interested; it also deals with the financing problems of the firm with striking lightheartedness. It has been remarked here and there in the above that it does not matter so much whether investments are financed from savings or from bank credits. But bank credit means the creation of money, as we shall presently see, to the surprise of some readers. Now the monetary school finds that the very point around which everything revolves, and firmly dissociates itself from the Keynesians, here. This controversy will definitely appear again in this book. The Keynesian neglect of financing further means that the theory may not be applied to countries with an acute shortage of savings and an underdeveloped banking system. For then I is restrained by S, and no multiplier process is started to produce S. Keynesian theory is therefore of limited significance for developing countries.

All this shows that Keynesian theory entails a drastic reduction of reality and may never be elevated to a kind of faith. It analyses the interplay of incomes and spending and explains how inflationary and deflationary gaps occur. There are situations to which it cannot be successfully applied, but as long as inflation and deflation are with us, we shall need Keynesian theory.

CHAPTER IV

How do we Build a Model?

1·FORMAL AND EMPIRICAL MODELS

The word 'model' means different things to different people. Sociologists and political theorists in particular use it rather loosely; they speak of the Yugoslav model (firms are run by the workers) or the French model of 'indicative planning' (the government draws up a plan for the expansion of the various sectors of the economy and tries to achieve these targets, among other things by directing additional bank credits to the sectors that have priority). Fortunately, most economists confine the term to systems of equations. Economic variables are brought together in such a way that their relationships come to the fore. The upshot of this exercise is to find the constant elements in the changing situation. National income, capital stock, exports and imports, the level of prices are perpetually on the move – but perhaps there are constant relationships between these magnitudes. These constants are called parameters. The mathematical form of the economic relationships and the numerical values of the parameters, taken together, is what we call the economic structure. The business of economic science, as I see it, is looking for this structure.*

---

*The following example may illustrate the nature of a parameter. Take the equation $z = ax+by$. When we first examine this, we see five variables. But most people will feel that a and b should be given a definite numerical value, say 3 and 5. In this second stage of the reasoning, the equation becomes $z = 3x+5y$. Now a and b are turned into parameters, and we have three variables left. (The strange thing is that almost all observers will choose a and b, not x and y, to be fixed! Greek letters are even more tempting.) These constants determine the relationship between x, y and z. If x and y (the independent variables) change, they influence z (the dependent variable); the influence (or 'regression') is given by the parameters (or regression coefficients). The paramount problem is of course: how do we proceed to fix these parameters? One way is to invent a number at random – this is

Models can be classified in various ways. The most important distinction is that between formal and empirical (or econometric) models. Formal models contain a theory, cast in algebraic or graphical form. They are relatively easy to draw up, and constitute a first step towards empirical work, but unfortunately the second step, that of econometric analysis, is not always taken. Formal models flourish in the classroom and in the textbook. This is excellent, provided that teachers and students know what they are doing: formalizing their own thoughts in an understandable way. This is necessary, but also dangerous. By scribbling on a blackboard we suggest that certain relationships are strategic, while others (those that are left out) are not. We also suggest that certain relationships assume a definite form; this is called specification. The straight line is very popular, for obvious reasons. And we imply that certain quantities are constant. For instance, in simple Keynesian theory the marginal propensity to consume does not change when income changes. The latter suggestion is interesting but unproven. By writing such a quantity as a Greek letter we may strengthen the suggestion, but that is no proof either. Greek letters are helpful but seductive. They create beliefs and that is not economic science.

Genuine economic science consists in the building *and the testing* of economic models. Only when sufficient empirical work has been done can we pronounce on the structure of economic life; only then can we make predictions. When predictions fail, theories must be rejected. The structure that we assumed to exist proves to be non-existent.

Empirical models are much more complicated than most formal models. The models in this book are characterized by utter simplicity. They are meant as preliminary steps down a long road. The equations are unspecified, or the specifications are the most elementary ones that the human mind can devise. Only in Chapter XI will a few remarks be made on the work of the empiricists. These remarks will be disappointing to those who

what I did here. In economics coefficients are often chosen with an eye to reality. So we get 'numerical examples', a useful but dangerous method. The best way to determine parameters is by econometric research.

are strongly influenced by classroom exercises and who are led into the belief that economic life is characterized by a few well-defined relationships.

The battle between the great schools – neo-classical, Keynesian, monetarist – can be elucidated by model-building. But here too the danger exists that models become masters of the human mind instead of useful arrangements for discovering what we are actually thinking. The final aim should always be a synthesis – that is, a more or less comprehensive system of equations which lends itself to empirical verification or falsification. The schools should submit themselves to these tests.

In this chapter, we confine ourselves to the use of models for expository purposes. I want to show the difference between classical and Keynesian thinking, that is, I want to stress the importance of investment. The models are the most simple ones that can be devised. In later chapters new elements will be added to these skeletons.

2 · A CLASSICAL SKELETON

We start with Say's Law. Income recipients save, and their savings S react to the rate of interest R. Thus $S = S(R)$. Businessmen invest, and their investments react to the same rate of interest R. Thus $I = I(R)$. The capital market equates saving with investment. $S(R) = I(R)$. This suggests that any level of national income Y can be sustained; firms receive the same amount of money that they have spent on the factors of production (including profits). But this suggestion is not yet spelled out. We have three (unspecified) equations and three variables, a bloc describing the capital market.

We can compile a similar bloc for the labour market. The supply of labour $L^\star$ depends on the wage level W. Thus $L^\star = L^\star(W)$. The demand for labour L also depends on W. (Here marginal productivity lurks in the background.) Thus $L = L(W)$. The labour market equates supply with demand, so that $L^\star(W) = L(W)$. This means full employment and a given wage level.

The third bloc describes production. The supply of labour $L^\star$

is given; the stock of capital $K^\star$ is given; the production function is given. And so the level of production $Q^\star = (L^\star, K^\star)$ is obtained. Labour productivity H follows immediately; divide $Q^\star$ by $L^\star$ and we get $F(K^\star/L^\star)$. This expression tells us that labour productivity is determined by the amount of capital per worker and the production function. With the aid of one additional quantity, the quotient of the labour supply $L^\star$ and total population N (this quotient is called the participation ratio – in Britain it is slightly under 50 per cent), we find real income per head. It is $Q/N = F(K^\star/L^\star)L^\star/N$.

The model is almost trivial. It contains two blocs (capital market, labour market) of three equations and one bloc (production) of one equation (production). Seven variables are determined by it: Q, L, S, I, R, W and Q/N. One quantity, $K^\star$, and one quotient, $L^\star/N$, are given. But, trivial or not, production, investment, income distribution among labour and capital and real income per head are all determinate quantities. The only variable missing is Y, the national money income. This is often added as an afterthought, by multiplying Q by the price level P. (Chapter VIII will explain how P is determined. Classical theory favours the type of reasoning that derives the price level from the quantity of money – the quantity theory.) But classical theory is basically about real quantities.

The interesting point in this classical model is the smooth equilibrium and the neat determinateness of everything. There is full employment. This condition may be disturbed in three ways. Somebody (trade unions or labour-type governments) may push the wage level up above its equilibrium level. Somebody (an oppressive, restrictive government) may prevent businessmen from investing all available savings. Or there may be frictional unemployment; in times of rapid micro-economic change this type of unemployment may be quite substantial, and some observers would add that it will be increased if unemployment benefits are not much lower than wages. These three types of unemployment can be understood within a classical framework. The ideological point is that they are always caused by external factors or by slow adaptation. The model as such does not produce a surplus of labour. That is, the human mind refuses to see unemployment as something that is generated by the economic system.

3 · A KEYNESIAN SKELETON

The equations that we need are, in words, the following. There are three of them.

No. 1. *National income equals the sum of consumption expenditure and investment.* (This is an outcome of the proposition that $Y = Q$; see section 1 of the previous chapter.)

No. 2. *Consumption depends on national income.* In the previous chapter we have designated the relation between consumption and income as the (average) propensity to consume. Let us take the simplest case, that in which the relation between the growth of the income and the extra consumption resulting from it is constant; this relation is the marginal propensity to consume. Part of income is 'autonomous', that is, it does not depend on current income. In that case the average propensity to consume drops as income rises. This is the case discussed by Keynes. It is still insufficiently realistic, but can do excellent service as a first approach.

No. 3. *Investments are given.* This means that they do not depend on the other variables in the model, especially total expenditure. This is a fairly improbable assumption, one that we shall have to change later. We shall have to consider further the question of which factors determine investments. This will be done in the next section.

This simple set-up gives us our model. There are three equations, of differing nature. The first is a simple sum; it represents an equality, without quantities being involved other than the variables that we want to find out: $Y = C + I$. The second is a 'regression equation'; it can take the form $C = C_o + cY$. The coefficient c represents the extent to which Y is influenced by C; in general such a quantity is called a regression coefficient. In this case the regression coefficient is called the marginal propensity to consume. The third equation ($I = I_0$) is hardly a real equation; it is merely a piece of notation to say that we do not bother to analyse the variable I.

These three equations determine the three quantities we want to know. National income is equal to $\frac{1}{1-c}(C_o + I_o)$. Here c is supposed to be constant; $C_o + I_o$ represents the autonomous part of total expenditure. C is, of course, known when Y is known. It is a simple affair.

A pleasant feature of this model is that it can be represented in the form of a graph that gives a clear summary of Keynes's theory. The graph shown in Fig. 3, or at least the top part of it, is therefore held in great esteem by the neo-Keynesians.

On the horizontal axis national income Y has been plotted. This is a money flow; its size is what we want to find. On the top part of the vertical axis we have the sum of consumption and investment. This sum $C+I$ represents the total production of, and expenditure on, goods and services. In Keynes's theory $C+I$ and Y are equal, as emerges from the first equation. This first equation will be represented in the figure by a line which passes through the origin at an angle of $45°$ to the axes. For every point of this line $Y = C+I$. The point of equilibrium will therefore have to lie on this line in any case.

Next the line $C = C_o + cY$ is drawn: the consumption function. This is a straight line that intersects the $45°$ line. At the point of intersection consumption equals Y; at this point, therefore, the whole income is consumed; nothing is saved (and nothing is invested). The national economy is 'stationary' here. It moves constantly in the same channels; productive capacity does not expand. Left of the point of intersection capital is eaten into: savings are negative. Right of the point of intersection the national economy begins to save. The savings are represented by the difference between the $45°$ line and the consumption line.

To arrive at the total expenditure, the sum invested I must be added to the consumption function. The curve is shifted in an upward direction over a distance I. In this way we find the total expenditure function $C+I$. This gives the total expenditure in relation to the national income.

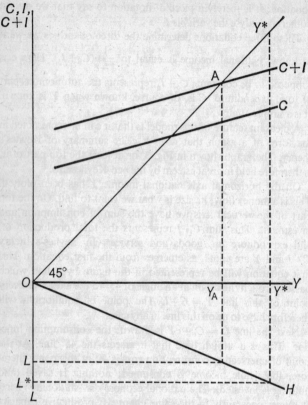

Fig. 3: The simple model

The point of intersection *A* of this total expenditure function and the 45° line is the Keynesian point of equilibrium. There the entrepreneurs get back exactly the sum that they spend on the factors of production, including their profit. There is no reason for swelling or shrinking of the flow of money and goods. The national income has been determined. It is represented in the graph by OY_A. No other point can exist (permanently), for it implies a discrepancy between receipts and expenditure of business.

There is consequently only one size of national income possible: that size at which this income generates exactly as much expenditure as its own size. A national income that evokes less expenditure than its own size shrinks. A national income that evokes more expenditure than its own size expands. The circulation is at rest only at A. This is the essence of Keynesian theory.

The size of the income OY_A is not related to the community's productive capacity. It may work out smaller than would be possible with the available working population and the level of labour productivity. This is represented in the graph by extending the vertical axis downwards. On this is plotted L, employment. The relation between L and Y is a straight line in the fourth quadrant, given by H. The gradient of this line is determined by the productivity of labour, which we have defined as national product (national income) divided by the quantity of labour used: $\dfrac{Y}{L}$. Accordingly as labour productivity lies higher, the straight H becomes increasingly horizontal.

This H line helps us to determine whether total expenditure on goods and services does or does not yield a satisfactory national income. We produce the perpendicular AY_A downwards, and go to the left from the point of intersection with the labour productivity line. There we find a point L. This is the employment that results from the model. But perhaps this is too small, in the sense that unemployment ensues. Let L^* represent full employment, the point at which the whole working population is employed (apart from frictional unemployment, seasonal unemployment, and the like). By returning to the Y axis via the H line, we find the national income that would be needed for the state of full employment. It is the most desirable result that our model could show. In the state of affairs that we have depicted, employment is too small. Unemployment is LL^*. National income is also too small: LL^* has never come about. Why not? Because the total expenditure was too small. It was only AY_A.

The determination of unemployment can be linked to the three-equation model by one additional equation. The demand for labour L equals Y/H, in which H, labour productivity, is given. (In classical theory H was determined by the model itself!) We found that $Y = \dfrac{1}{1-c}(C_o + I_o)$. Unemployment $L\star - L = L\star - \dfrac{1}{H} \cdot \dfrac{1}{1-c}(C_o + I_o)$. This is the Keynesian approach to unemployment. It suggests that employment is determined by autonomous spending on consumption and investment, the marginal propensity to consume (this being a parameter) and labour productivity, which is given (but growing with time).

This skeleton is less trivial than the classical one. It points to a possible fundamental disequilibrium in the labour market. L may be smaller than $L\star$ because actual income Y is smaller than capacity income $Y\star$. The difference between $Y\star$ and Y is called the deflationary gap. But note that Y may also turn out to be higher than $Y\star$. In this case there is full employment, but another disequilibrium pops up: tension in the labour market and rising prices. Because $Y = QP$ and Q has reached its ceiling $Q\star$ (given by $L\star$ and H), P must go up. This is the inflationary gap; more is spent on C and I than productive capacity allows. The Keynesian train of thought leads us to believe that price inflation is caused by overspending. The monetary factor (inflation being caused by too much money) is pushed into the background. This point will be taken up in Chapter VIII.

The differences between the classical and the Keynesian views are brought clearly to the fore by comparing the two models. In the classical model S determines I; in the Keynesian model S does not even appear: I is determined by something we do not yet know ($I = I_o$). This is probably the most crucial difference between the two models (we shall deal with the determinants of investment in the next section). But it is also remarkable that the classical model contains two prices (W and R) as equilibrating forces, whilst in the Keynesian model these magnitudes are absent. (Small wonder, will be the neo-classicist's comment, that the Keynesian's world is one of disturbance and disequilibrium!) Also, in the Keynesian model labour productivity is given; it determines the demand for labour. In the classical system labour productivity is explained by the amount of capital per worker – it does not determine employment. Finally, the classical system explains income distribution – the Keynesian system does not.

As I see it, the determination of investment is the most crucial difference between the two schools. Let us consider it in somewhat more detail.

4 · WHAT DETERMINES INVESTMENT?

Model-builders have various options in answering this question. They may follow the classical trail, and write that the amount of savings determines investment. Perhaps this is realistic in countries where business is thriving, people do not save and there is no banking system that can create finance. The actual situation in Western countries suggests that we adopt another view. Let us first turn to Keynes's own ideas, as expressed in *The General Theory*.

Keynes himself had a very concrete theory about the determinants of I. If the entrepreneurs are considering buying new machinery, they have in mind a certain additional profit that is to result from this. By capitalizing these profits of successive years the value of the new capital good to the enterprise is found. In this capitalization the rate of interest plays a big part; the higher the rate of interest at which you capitalize, the lower the value. Now it is always possible to point to a certain rate of interest that makes the value of the additional capital good equal to its cost. Keynes calls this rate of interest the marginal efficiency of capital, in my opinion a somewhat artificial term which often gives rise to confusion with related concepts. And Keynes's investment theory amounts to the fact that the entrepreneur will buy the capital good in question if its marginal efficiency is higher than the rate of interest at which he can borrow money.

But in Keynes's theory this rate of interest is not determined by the supply and demand of savings (after all, S and I are equal), but by people's liquidity preference and the quantity of money. Thus the quantity of money influences investments via the rate of interest. Keynes borrowed this strategic effect of the monetary factor from a Swedish economist, K. Wicksell (*c.* 1900). Many neo-Keynesians do not follow him in this. They consider total expenditure and its movements more important to *I* than the financial sphere.

The argument that the rate of interest determines the size of *I* is not illogical, but it seems hardly realistic. In fact the rate of interest probably plays a minor role: one of the reasons for this is self-financing out of profits, a matter for which insufficient allowance is made in orthodox Keynesian theory. It has been one of the first fruits of quantitative economics, and in particular of the investigation performed by Tinbergen,* that the rate of interest has proceeded to play a somewhat more modest part in economic thought. The influence of interest had been overestimated not only by Keynes but also by various classical and other authors.

The marginal efficiency of capital no longer plays an important role in economics. It is one of the aspects of the *General Theory* that has not been able to hold its own. But in one respect it has brought an old truth to our notice again. Investments are to a considerable extent determined by expectations for the future, and therefore by psychological factors. For this very reason the prevalent mood among entrepreneurs is of tremendous importance to economic equilibrium. If they take an optimistic view of things and buy more capital goods, there is a good chance that the income effects which this will evoke will prove them right. The expectations for the future tend to realize themselves via the flow of goods and money. This psychological influence may be a reason simply to accept investments in the model as given.

But this is a makeshift solution. Entrepreneurs do not act on whims; the determinants of investment lie not only in the psychological but also, and in particular, in the sober sphere of business. Expectations with regard to future sales are the entrepreneur's guide.

The effect of sales on capital outlay entails a complication. At first sight it does not seem implausible that a 10 per cent rise in sales must lead to a 10 per cent increase in productive capacity, and therefore also to a 10 per cent increase in investment. But this is not so; the increase in investment tends to be greater.

This remarkable thing can best be explained by starting from

* *Statistical Testing of Business Cycle Theories,* 1939.

the difference between investment for replacements and investment for expansion. In the normal course of business, machinery is constantly being written off and replaced. This leads to a level of gross investment that is needed to keep up the stock of capital goods. Part of the sales of the capital goods industry is based on this. Now to this part are added the investments for expansion. They can give the sales of machinery a strange look. Let me illustrate this by an example.

Let us suppose that a shoe factory makes 100,000 pairs of shoes a year. It has ten machines at work, each of which lasts ten years. Their age is spread uniformly over the years, so that every year one machine is replaced. The engineering firm that makes these machines therefore sells one a year. Now the sales of shoes increase by 10,000 pairs, or 10 per cent. To meet this additional demand one new machine is purchased. The sales of the engineering firm now rise from one to two shoemaking machines; an increase of no less than 100 per cent. The percentage by which the sales have increased has increased tenfold in passing from the shoes to the machines. This is known as the acceleration principle. Accurately formulated, it implies that investment is proportional not to sales but to the increase in sales:

$$I = a . \Delta(C+I).$$

This is the investment equation which we would have to include in our model if the acceleration principle effectively described reality.

However, the acceleration principle, though remarkable, is not quite realistic. The entrepreneurs do not react entirely in this spirit. Productive capacity is not as rigid as the acceleration principle assumes. In actual fact the increases in consumption do spread in intensified fashion to the investment activity, but this intensification is not as accentuated as the acceleration principle assumes. If there is overcapacity, the principle does not work at all. The acceleration principle is moderated by a certain flexibility. This may be expressed in an equation which implies that investments are determined by the difference between the stock of capital goods desired by the entrepreneurs and the actual stock. The former then depends in turn on the expected expansion of sales. The regression coefficients of this equation show how lively the acceleration will be; it may be great or small, according to circumstances. Such a relation is called the flexible accelerator.*

But another view of the investment equation is possible. This type of investment equation has a devastating effect on the stability of national income. Suppose that people save more than before, or that sales are reduced by factors from abroad. Consumption falls. Production decreases. Machines are not used to capacity. Businessmen are confronted with a negative difference between the desired and the actual stock of capital. This is very bad for investment. In the primitive Keynesian model investment follows its own course ($I = I_o$), but if we introduce an accelerator, flexible or otherwise, I falls sharply, taking consumption with it. Production and income get in a very vicious spiral.

Note that this spiral originates in an innocent-looking event. The growth of expenditure is slowing down. Initially, sales are still growing, but their increase is less than before. This triggers the downward movement. The more one thinks about it, the more convincing the idea seems that capitalism is utterly unstable. Observers of the British situation in the seventies will recognize a fateful interdependence. Perhaps they will be tempted to believe that they fully understand the sorry situation of employment and the mechanism that has led to this. But the accelerator does not tell the whole story.

There is another form of the investment function that is both obvious and disturbing. It says that investments depend on profits. On expected profits, but perhaps actual profits may be used as a proxy. Retained profits are a source of finance; in this sense we come close to classical thinking. Profits are also an incentive and a determinant of the psychological climate among businessmen; in this sense we come close to the Keynesian view. There is nothing mysterious about this. The trouble is, however, that once we include profits among the independent variables of the investment function we should explain them; and that is very

* R. M. Goodwin, 'Secular and Cyclical Aspects of the Multiplier and the Accelerator', *Income, Employment and Public Policy, Essays in Honor of Alvin Hansen*, 1948.

difficult. There are many elements in the economy that nfluence the level and the development of net profitability: increases in money wages, movements in tax rates, shifts in the competitive position of important sectors of production, shifts in the international division of labour. Profits are difficult to predict, the more so because they form a rather small difference between two big quantities: revenues and costs. Profits are volatile.

All this spells trouble for the model-builder. By introducing such a slippery element into the investment function, the whole set-up becomes slippery. Investment is a strategic element in the macro-economic interdependencies – it may stabilize or de-stabilize national income and employment. Now we can see that it is difficult to choose between various possible forms of the investment function, while at least one plausible variable – profits – tends to weaken the reliability of the whole model.

The easy way out is to hand the problem to the econometricians. We just tell these smart technicians that we have listed a number of possible variables that explain investment: savings, the interest rate, the change in sales, the amount of unused capacity, profits after tax; and they are requested kindly to report which of these variables performs best. Alas, the econometricians have not found a satisfactory solution either. Their correlations do not stand up, the parameters of the investment function tend to become pretty soft, in particular under quickly changing conditions like those of the seventies.*

In these circumstances there is another way out. The economist tries to make separate estimates of the volume of investments for the next year. This can be done by questioning business firms. Theoretically, the method boils down to dealing with investment as an autonomous variable – a somewhat improved way of saying that $I = I_o$. This solution is not elegant, but it works. Given the

---

*There is some comfort in the fact that part of gross investment is inspired by the wish to replace machinery that has been scrapped. These replacements are a rather stable element in the situation. They can be explained as a fixed percentage of the existing stock of capital – unless tempestuous wage inflation leads to accelerated scrapping. See Chapter XI for this point.

state of economic theory, perhaps it is the best we can do. However, the procedure makes it impossible to look ahead for more than one or two years.

5 · THE UNSETTLING ROLE OF TIME

So far we have been describing static equilibria – that is to say, variables have been related to one another that referred to the same point in time (such as L and K) or to the same period (such as Y, C and I). Adjustments to new situations occur quickly in these models. At first sight the rate of change is not so important. If a new impulse is generated, for instance by rising or falling investments, this has spent itself after a few periods. The new equilibrium described by the model is established after a while – does it matter much if this happened somewhat earlier or later?

Yes, it does indeed. Around 1930 various authors, including A. Hanau, discovered that delayed supply adjustments could lead to fluctuations – and that is not the same as a new equilibrium. This is called the Cobweb Theorem (because the picture of the lagged supply curve, the demand curve and the ensuing price movements look like a cobweb). The pig market in particular displayed violent fluctuations in the prices and the quantities sold, owing to the fact that pig-breeders reacted in natural, lagged fashion to price signals. Overproduction alternated with underproduction and prices went up and down with great regularity.

In macro-economics too time lags may lead to fluctuations. This was sharply described for the first time by Michal Kalecki, Keynes's Polish predecessor. Suppose that consumption depends on the national income in the preceding period plus a constant, say 4. So $C_t = 4 + cY_{t-1}$. Suppose further that investments are governed by an accelerator, i.e. $I = a(Y_{t-1} - Y_{t-2})$. Each variable is provided with a time index. A model of this kind is called a dynamic one. What I have written down here is again characterized by extreme simplicity: a consumption function and an investment function. An income equation of the usual type completes the whole: $Y_t = C_t + I_t$. We can fill in C and I in the latter equation and then get $Y_t = (c+a)Y_{t-1} - aY_{t-2} + 4$. National income depends on its own value in two earlier periods. An equation of this kind is called auto-regressive. So far it looks as if we have introduced only a minor complication into the Keynesian model.

But the results are surprising. The reader can establish that for himself by working out a few numerical examples. For this purpose we have to give Y_1 and Y_2 'starting values'. Let's put them at 100 and 110. Next parameters c and a have to be fixed. A lot depends on this. If we choose $c = 0.6$ and $a = 0.5$, national income develops as follows: 100 – 110 – 111 – 107 – 102 – 99 – 98 – 98 – 99 – 100 – 100. After that the national income is at rest and everything remains the same. We see a fluctuation heading for equilibrium; nothing to get excited about. But if we had set the parameters as $c = 0.6$ and $a = 1$ (so that the whole increase in income is invested) a wave is generated that becomes increasingly violent. Y assumes the following values: 100 – 110 – 116 – 116 – 110 – 100 – 90 – 84 – 84 – 100 – 116 – 126 – 126 and then wilder and wilder. The model proves to be rather sensitive to the choice of the parameters. If we were to put c at 0.8 and a at 1 again, Y would already be trebled after nine periods!

What do we learn from this? In the first place, something that is known to everyone who studies cybernetic systems: time lags can summon up nasty disturbances. In this sense the above exercise is rather trivial. The second conclusion is that our economic models do not only have to be well specified as regards the form of the equations – the time lags also have to find a place in them. This considerably aggravates the econometrician's task. And in the third place the intensive study of dynamic models can easily arouse the feeling that fluctuations in income and employment are entirely inevitable. The partisans of this school think that these waves are an inevitable part of a society in which people, firms and governments react to one another in delayed fashion. There is little that can be done about this, for a government which wants to combat the deviations easily makes them bigger. A nervous policy is just as much a destabilizer as a retarded control circuit. Stop-go is not a mere accident or the result of poor statesmanship; it is the natural consequence of tinkering with a delicate control mechanism. This type of fatalism is a sophisticated and glum version of the old theory of the invisible hand.

Dynamic models have been endemic to economics for some time now. Attempts have been made to explain shorter and longer waves by means of them. The seven-year movement – often called a *Juglar*, after its discoverer – and the thirty-year *Kondratieff* can be generated by a model, through a suitable choice of equations, parameters and time lags. This is called simulation, one of the great games of present economics. Whether these mechanisms also exist in reality is nevertheless anything but certain. It is not even certain that the Juglar and the Kondratieff exist in reality.

More recently dynamic models have been applied on a world scale in order to analyse the influence of population growth, pollution, bottlenecks in the area under agriculture and the supply of natural resources. This is the work of, among others, Jay Forrester and Dennis Meadows and it has become very well known through the report *The Limits to Growth* (1972) for the Club of Rome. These models contain many feedbacks and time lags, as a result of which overall world production performs wild fluctuations. The computer willingly produces long series of figures. This report has occasioned great alarm. In itself this is excellent, but the scientific importance of such simulations must not be overestimated. The equations have not been at all econometrically tested. Most of the variables, such as pollution on a world scale, have not been measured. The parameters have been filled in more or less at random. The computer runs must therefore be regarded not as predictions, but as possibilities. They are numerical examples, just like the above example of a violently fluctuating national income. It is certainly useful to explore such possibilities – among other things because in this way we can investigate the sensitivity of the results when the parameters change. This is also of importance to politics; the fight against undesirable developments sometimes amounts to changing parameters. But running a computer containing a simulation model is not quite the same as genuine empirical science.

I hope that I have shown that all respectable models are dynamic. This is a great delight to some model-builders. It makes simulation possible and even inevitable. Modern models are computerized and generate long runs. But at the same time these dynamics complicate the art of model-building enormously. The outcomes are sensitive, not only to changes in parameters, but also to changes in time lags. This is grist to the sceptic's mill. Sophistication and scepticism go hand in hand.

CHAPTER V

The Impact of International Trade

1 · THE CLASSICAL VIEW OF THE BALANCE OF PAYMENTS

In these times of international turmoil the balance of payments is the focus of much concerned attention, especially in Britain. But this attention is not new. From of old, economists have reflected on international trade. Classical theory saw the invisible hand at work – the price mechanism would attend not only to the equality of savings and investments but also to the equality of exports and imports. The Keynesian view arrived at a different conclusion: deficits on the balance of payments are quite possible, even over longer periods. So are surpluses – one country's deficit is another country's surplus. The debate seems to be perennial. It originated when the mercantilists, sixteenth- and seventeenth-century writers on practical matters, gave their recommendations to the governments of their time.

These mercantilists had a clear purpose in mind: they wanted to make the country in which they lived a strong one. The best way to strength was wealth – above all wealth in terms of gold, since with gold mercenaries could be mustered and fleets could be fitted out. How is gold to be obtained if the country has no gold mines? The answer is foreign trade. By selling other countries more goods than are imported from them a favourable balance with these countries is created; this was once upon a time covered by gold, and it still is today in a certain sense. The difference between imports and exports was called the balance of trade. It was later realized that the gold balance with which the mercantilists were concerned was also affected by other items not directly concerning trade: the proceeds of services, the interest on debts, and the like. All these items together, including the balance of trade, were subsequently given the name of balance of payments. This is therefore a list of transactions with other countries, over a given period (generally a year) which give rise to payments.* If the incoming payments are greater than the outgoing ones, the balance of payments is called favourable. In that case gold (or foreign currency) enters the country. In the opposite case – that is to say when the country, roughly speaking, buys more abroad than it exports – a drop in the gold stocks is the obvious consequence The mercantilists therefore aimed at a favourable balance of payments. One of the ways in which they did this was to check imports of finished products as far as possible by import bans and the like. The Navigation Laws of the middle of the sixteenth century were also an attempt in this direction.

The mercantilistic view was combated by later writers. From Adam Smith onwards economists went to a good deal of trouble to make it clear that a favourable balance of payments cannot be maintained in the long run. For, so ran the criticism of mercantilism, if the balance of payments is favourable, and therefore gold pours into the country, the medium of payment (in this case the gold coin) will become abundant. More money means higher prices. The country that receives gold becomes an expensive country. But an expensive country prices itself out of foreign markets. It will lose its foreign customers to other, cheaper countries. And so exports decline to a level at which imports of gold are no longer necessary; the price level then comes to rest, and imports and exports are equal to one another. This is the classical theory of the equilibrium of the balance of payments. Exports cannot lastingly exceed imports; the prices attend to the equilibrium. In this train of thought an adverse balance of payments leads to the export of gold and a drop in prices; exports increase; and the deficit on the balance of payments cannot therefore be maintained any more than the surplus on the balance of payments.

* If we speak below of the balance of payments, we mean the current payments, i.e. excluding movements of gold and capital. The equilibrium of the balance of payments is equilibrium on current account (imports and exports, service transactions, donations, returns on capital, transferred profits). 'Export' is therefore a short way of saying 'all current transactions that bring in foreign exchange'; it should not be understood in its narrow sense of export of goods.

The attentive reader will have encountered a typically classical idea in this. It is the price system that establishes equilibrium. We have also encountered this in the equilibrium between S and I, where the rate of interest – the price of capital – in the classical view attended to the equality, as in general the price of a good has the function of bringing supply and demand into line with one another. Small wonder, therefore, that the import and export argument fitted so well into classical theory. And small wonder, too, that the modern theory differs in its view of this as well.

Let us examine this classical equilibrium mechanism a little more closely. The first link in the reasoning is that gold enters the country because the balance of payments is favourable. (This is the mercantilistic aim.) The second link is the rise in the price level in the country receiving the gold. This link is rather weak, firstly because 'gold' is here put on a par with 'money', and this need not always be so. But there is more. As we shall see later, it is not necessary that a country in which the supply of money increases experiences a rise in its price level. It is also quite possible that the greater quantity of money stays inactive, so that the rise in prices does not happen. And it may also be that a greater demand for goods gives rise to a greater supply, so that prices remain the same for this reason. The latter can occur in particular if there are many unused instruments of production, if machines are standing idle and workers are unemployed. The import and export argument does not make much allowance for the latter situation; quite logically, for it is part of classical theory, and classical theory does not recognize unemployment, since it has firm confidence in Say's Law.

An increase in prices is therefore not a certain, though a possible, consequence of a favourable balance of payments. But let us assume that the rise in prices really does occur. The country in question then becomes an expensive country compared with others. However, the foreigner is not directly concerned with the internal price level of the supplying country. He is concerned with the number of units of his own currency that he has to pay. And this is governed not only by the price of the supplying country, but also by the ratio between the prices of the two currencies.

This is the rate of exchange. The rate of exchange is therefore of just as much importance in determining whether exports are attractive or not as the price in the supplying country's own currency. The competitive position of a country on foreign markets depends on its own price level in relation to the prices of other countries, and on the rate of exchange. It is worth taking the trouble to remember this truth; it will stand us in good stead when we extend the model to form a realistic reproduction of reality.

The rate of exchange is sometimes fixed, sometimes not. Under the gold standard the rate is automatically fixed, but that arrangement ceased to exist in 1931. Between 1945 and 1971 the rates of exchange were influenced by the Central Banks; they had agreed (Bretton Woods Agreement, 1944) to prevent fluctuations by a buying and selling policy and to make a non-recurrent adjustment from time to time only (devaluation occurs if one's own currency becomes cheaper, revaluation in the opposite case). After 1971 this system was abandoned. The rates of exchange were left to the currency market and began to float. Thinking along classical lines, the floating rate has a typical function in bringing equilibrium to the balance of payments. Whilst older classicists started from a fixed rate (they lived under a kind of gold standard) and a variable price level, modern classicists rely on both the price level and the floating rate, the latter being obviously the more flexible variable.

The neo-classical equilibrium theory of the balance of payments, then, says that the rate of exchange tends to make imports and exports equal. If exports happen to be larger, the foreigners must make net payments to the exporting country, as a result of which the currency of that country, measured in other units of currency, becomes more expensive. In this way the competitive position of that country is weakened, and exports will again decline. Moreover, through the change in the rate of exchange, the country's imports have become cheaper. Its inhabitants will proceed to buy more foreign goods. As a result of this, imports increase. In this way the favourable balance of payments disappears again. The rate of exchange has led to a new equilibrium, even without further intervention of the price levels in the countries concerned.

It is a tempting theory. What is wrong with it? We can find this out by examining the circulatory effects of the balance of payments.

2 · THE INCOME EFFECT OF EXPORTS

The reader will doubtless recall from Chapter II that one of the remarkable differences between classical and Keynesian theory lies in the fact that the first makes no allowance for the income effect of investments and the second does. Investment means production of capital goods, i.e. the application of production factors which in return for their assistance receive an income. Classical theory does not need to pay particular attention to this – after all, one of its fundamental premises is full loading and full employment, so that labour and capital put to work by the investments had first to be diverted from other uses in which they were also earning an income. But in modern economics, where allowance is made for idleness of factors of production, the position is different. There investing leads to an investment impulse in the circulation, which spreads further via the multiplier.

Now this difference in outlook is directly concerned with the balance of payments. For in this respect there is a clear analogy between investing and exporting. In both cases instruments of production are used to make a product that does not reach the consumer, at least not the domestic consumer. And yet this consumer, as a recipient of income, has received the money created in the course of the production process. The worker, the entrepreneur, the furnisher of capital in the export industry earns his income: export has an income effect. But the product that they jointly produce withdraws from the circulation. It crosses the frontier and disappears. Domestic purchasing power continues to search for goods that are not there.

The income effect of exports is inflationary; it causes money income to swell. Will this lead to a disturbance? No – for at the same time goods are imported from abroad. These have been produced, have had an income effect, and have led to an extra demand – but this process was enacted over the frontier. If the import goods enter the country they arrive there without bringing the corresponding income with them. It is a good thing that exports provided this income. In this way the circulation is complete again. Exports attend to the income effect, imports attend to the matching goods.

We must bear this process in mind if we want to understand the Keynesian equilibrium mechanism of the balance of payments. We see a similar process occurring to that in saving and investing. The investments provide income, but not goods ready for consumption; the inflationary effect of this is neutralized by saving. S equals I; the multiplier sees to this or, to put it another way, the movement of national income. The latter fluctuates in such a way that saving and investment are brought into balance with one another. Exactly the same happens with regard to imports and exports. These can also be kept in equilibrium by national income and its fluctuations.

To form a clear picture of how this works, we must imagine a community in which there is no saving and no investing: a stationary economy. We shall call the exports of goods and services X (from eXports), and imports M (from iMports). The problem is the following: is there a tendency towards equilibrium between X and M and, if so, where does this come from?

Let us suppose that the balance of payments is in equilibrium at first, and that exports increase at a given moment owing to the fact that a new product is being made for which there is a ready market abroad. We shall call the additional exports ΔX. This additional production has an income effect; the additional income impulse $\Delta Y = \Delta X$. This sum goes to the households. They do not save (or so we have assumed) and therefore they can do only one of two things: buy domestic consumer goods or buy foreign ones. The ratio in which they divide their income among the two categories forms an important quantity in our reasoning. We call this quantity the (marginal) propensity to import, defined as the ratio between extra imports and extra national income. In letters: $m = \dfrac{\Delta M}{\Delta Y}$. Of the additional income ΔX an amount $m\Delta X$ therefore goes to the import goods; the rest $(1-m)\Delta X$ is spent on the consumer goods produced by domestic business. The entrepreneurs therefore see their receipts increase by this amount. To meet the extra demand they must engage new factors of production who appropriate the amount of additional receipts, convert it into income, and return the sum $(1-m)^2 \Delta X$ to business. Do you see the multiplier effect? The original income impulse from the export firms spreads through the whole system. Again and again a portion is diverted to imports. The process stops when all the extra income has leaked away abroad. In that case ΔM equals ΔX; imports and exports have both grown equally. The balance of payments, which at first had become favourable through the increase in exports, has again been brought into equilibrium.

The characteristic thing about this recovery of equilibrium is that the rate of exchange has nothing to do with it. Nor has, in our reasoning, any change in prices manifested itself. The equilibrium-restoring factor is national income. This quantity increased to such an extent that it caused higher imports which were ultimately equal to the increase in exports. When this had happened, the firms got back from the consumers that sum which they had spent on the factors of production. The circulation then continued along the same path without swelling or shrinking. But, compared with the original situation, national income, employment, and the use of existing machinery have increased.

How much has national income grown through the increase in exports? An answer can be given to this question that is entirely analogous to the answer that we gave to the question: when has Y grown enough to make S equal to I? The reasoning can follow two paths. The total increment in income equals $(1-m)$ $\Delta X + (1-m)^2 \Delta X + (1-m)^3 \Delta X$, etc. In this way we find the sum of a descending geometric series. The reader who considers this too scholarly an approach can take another route. He can bear in mind that the increment in income ΔY must be such that it makes ΔM equal to ΔX. There is consequently equilibrium at $m \Delta Y = \Delta X$. From which it follows that $\Delta Y = \dfrac{\Delta X}{m}$. The growth in national income equals the increase in exports divided by the propensity to import. We can also put it this way: the primary income effect of exports must be multiplied by $\dfrac{1}{m}$ to find the total income effect. You will not be surprised to learn that this factor $\frac{1}{m}$ is the export multiplier. It is a quantity that is strictly analogous to the factor $\frac{1}{s}$ which we have encountered before, and which shows the amount by which national income increases as the result of an income impulse from increased investments.

This is the Keynesian equilibrium mechanism of the balance of payments. It is obviously something quite different from the classical view. Before further explaining this difference, let us have a look at a circular flow which is subjected not only to the influence of international trade but also to that of saving and investing. In other words, we are adding to the model that was set up in the preceding chapter in all too simple a form.

3 · THE MODEL BECOMES MORE COMPLETE

The results of the last section and those of the preceding chapter can now be combined. We are now starting on the assumption that three kinds of goods are produced by business: consumer goods, which make their way to the households; investment goods, which are sold by the one entrepreneur to the other, and export goods, which disappear over the frontier. This situation is shown in the following diagram. From total production a money income follows that equals $C+I+X$. This money income goes to the households (in so far as it does not remain in the enterprises as their own savings). These households can do three things with it: they can spend the income on home-produced consumer goods, they can spend it on consumer goods produced abroad, or they can save it and then invest it. It emerges from the circulation diagram that the income Y received is divided among C, M, and S.

The circulation is now in equilibrium if business receives as much in return from its customers as it has spent on income. In symbols: $C+I+X = C+S+M$. Or $I+X = S+M$. This equation replaces the oversimple $S = I$ from Chapters III and IV and the oversimple $X = M$ from the last section.

This equation again throws a new light on economic events.

We can see from it how the inflationary impulses from investments and exports have finally to be restrained by deflationary purchasing power absorptions S and M. Only when the sum of saving and importing has become large enough to offset the sum of investing and exporting is national income at rest.

This important mechanism can be illustrated by means of the multiplier process. Assume an increase in investment activity.

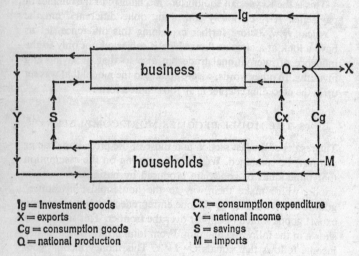

Ig = Investment goods	Cx = consumption expenditure
X = exports	Y = national income
Cg = consumption goods	S = savings
Q = national production	M = imports

Fig. 4: The circulation including foreign trade

The extra income that results from this finds its way to the households. In so far as they spend it on additional consumer goods new revenue is created. But part of the income will also leak away. This can happen both through imports and through saving. We therefore see that the extra investments can sometimes lead to extra imports of consumer goods. It cannot be said in advance how the extra money will be spent. Only the ultimate apportionment among imports and savings is certain: this is given by the propensity to save and the propensity to import. Saving and importing form the leak through which the original increment of income resulting from investments has flowed away. But not only the income effect of the investments must flow away through this leak; the income effect of exports must also be compensated in this way.

In view of this we can now draw up a somewhat more realistic formula for the multiplier. We had originally found a multiplication factor that was equal to $\frac{1}{s}$. This gives an exaggerated impression of the total increase in income. Upon closer examination the double leak proves to lead to the multiplier being equal to $\frac{1}{s+m}$.

For the reader who wants to see this proved: $S+M = I+X$. Since $S = sY$ and $M = mY$, we have $I+X = (s+m)Y$, or $Y = \frac{I+X}{s+m}$. An impulse, either in investments or in exports, ultimately propagates itself in income in accordance with the factor $\frac{1}{s+m}$. Or: the multiplier equals the reciprocal of the sum of the leaks.*

Besides a better view of the multiplier we now have a more realistic outlook on the relation between savings and investments. From the simple Keynesian theory you might gain the impression that a shortage of capital can *never* occur. Every investment begets its 'own' nest-egg – although, for the individual, this marrying-up process may not be relevant. It may be that the savings are formed in an entirely different part of the economic system, so that the original investor cannot make use of them for his financing, but even in that case the savings have come into being all the same. However, it now proves that this naïve Keynesian belief is based on an illusion. A discrepancy can quite easily occur between I and S. Not only *can* it form, it probably *will*. And we can also state the exact size of this discrepancy. For we know that $I+X = S+M$. It follows from this that $I-S = M-X$. The 'savings deficit' is made good by the deficit on the balance of payments.

*I have assumed here that the average and the marginal propensities are the same.

This somewhat surprising proposition does not only help us better to understand the relationship between saving and investing. It also gives us a new theory of the balance of payments. For we find that the balance of payments will be adverse according as more is invested and less saved. The two deficits on the balance of payments and on the capital market belong together like Narcissus and his reflection.

This Keynesian conclusion does not fit into the classical theory. A deficit on the balance of payments is in the classical view hardly within the bounds of possibility in the long run, and certainly not if there is a free rate of exchange. For the country will see its currency become cheap; the foreign customers will again be keen to buy the product of the country in question, and equilibrium of the balance of payments will again be established. But now we see that, whatever the rate of exchange, the balance of payments will permanently continue to display a deficit as long as a marked urge to invest is combined with a low propensity to save.

Anyone who considers the sixteenth- and seventeenth-century mercantilistic theory in this light has a greater appreciation of it than the classicists had. The mercantilists wanted to acquire gold by a favourable balance of payments; the classicists thought that this would not prove successful. Now it seems to us that it would. However, not via the policy of import barriers advocated by the old mercantilists, but by a deliberate regulation of the flow of goods and money. If a country wishes to collect gold, it must make sure that a slight deflation prevails. The savings surplus $S-I$ finds expression in the balance of payments as an export surplus. We could phrase this recommendation to mercantilistically-minded governments differently. We could say: restrict imports, but not by an obtrusive and difficult policy of tariffs or quotas. Do not do so via customs officials and government offices that divide a pre-set quantity of imports among the would-be buyers. Instead, do it via national income. Ensure that the flow of national income is hampered in such a way – we shall see in the next chapter what powerful means of doing this are available – that imports, which depend on Y, remain relatively small. Keeping down national income, in combination with the promotion of exports, proves to be an efficacious means of achieving a favourable balance of payments. But the gold thus obtained has its price. If great care is not taken it is bought with unemployment and idle machines, with too low a production for the home market and with too low a rate of economic growth. In short, with a depression.

However, it is not the sole advantage of the Keynesian theory of the balance of payments that neo-mercantilistic recommendations of dubious value can be derived from it. Its more useful side is that we learn from it why some countries in the post-war years were beset with a constant drain of foreign exchange. The reason for this lay particularly in too great imports, which themselves were caused by too large a national money income, which in its turn can be attributed for the greater part to the necessary expansion of productive capacity, which was inadequately compensated for in its income effects by savings. The ambitious investment programmes – vitally necessary for increasing productive capacity and the productivity of labour, and so increasing prosperity – did not match the insufficient thrift. Or, to put it differently, the sum of consumption and investments was too great. Exports did not go badly, but they were outdone by the imports resulting from the multiplier.*

This inflationary interaction can be understood by the theory outlined here. Consequently we cannot do without it if we are to see what happened in Europe after the war. But that is not the only positive side of modern macro-economics. It also gives us a realistic view of the importance of the rate of exchange. We shall now discuss this.

4 · THE RATE OF EXCHANGE DETHRONED?

It thus proves that the equilibrium of the balance of payments, and also its disequilibrium, can be explained without bringing

*There is, however, a complication. If a country tries to spend more than it can produce the relationship between extra imports and extra income may increase. The goods that cannot be produced are sucked into the economy from outside. In other words: the marginal propensity to import is not a constant; an inflationary gap causes this quantity to rise (and the multiplier to fall).

price relations, and also the rate of exchange as a special price relation, into matters. M is made equal to X, or the sum of M and S is made equal to the sum of I and X, through the movement of national income. The movement of prices seems to be completely detached from all this. Now does this mean that the rate of exchange is without the slightest importance for the balance of payments? This would be a premature conclusion. For in the above we have come across a relationship in which the rate of exchange does indeed appear. It is the relationship between exports and the factors which determine the size of these exports.

We may again state that exports depend on two factors. The first is the overall foreign demand. This is a quantity on which a country cannot exert much influence, although nowadays attempts are being made to control the international economic situation by joint consultation. If the size of the total foreign market is given, the question is: what share a country will have in these total sales? This depends on the competitive position which that country occupies in respect of other countries, which is composed of three elements: the quality of the product (in relation to what other countries have to offer), the price level of exports in relation to the prices asked by the other countries, and the rate of exchange. In this respect we can therefore say that the rate of exchange helps to determine exports. As exports cause income effects at home, creating direct and indirect employment, income and prosperity, the rate of exchange is an important quantity for the community. It has definitely not been dethroned by the circulation theory, but has been given another place in the system.

From the above we can draw a conclusion regarding the most desirable level of the rate of exchange. In the footsteps of classical theory a country should devalue if its balance of payments displays a deficit. But this is too rash. It is possible that such a country must deflate. This is something quite different. It must ensure that expenditure becomes smaller and that the circulation contracts. Devaluation must be applied if exports stagnate, if unemployment and slackening of effort become endemic in the export sector. It then becomes time to strengthen the competitive position and to give business a helping hand by devaluation. Now flagging exports are not the same as a deficit on the balance of payments. True, the first can lead to the second. But this is not necessarily so. For it may be that a decline in exports leads to a multiplier process through which the income is affected to such an extent that imports shrink. In that case the equilibrium of the balance of payments is not disturbed, but employment decreases. Consequently, it may never be derived from the existence of an equilibrium on the balance of payments that the rate of exchange is at the right level. Even then devaluation may be called for to arouse the national economy out of its lethargy.

Unfortunately, the positive effect of devaluation on exports and employment may quickly disappear. Devaluation increases the price level, in domestic currency, of imported goods. Importers will shift these increases to the consumer. If the wage level is tied to the consumer price index, money wages will rise. This leads to a weakening of the competitive position abroad. This mechanism becomes particularly vicious when a price–wage–price spiral is going on. Devaluation may add fuel to this process, and the spiral may wipe out the initial advantage of devaluation.

The above implies a strong argument against the free rate of exchange. Some neo-classicists tell us that it will promote equilibrium in the balance of payments. But if a country is suffering from an inflationary gap, and total spending is too high, its currency will fall and fall. Exports will be stimulated, but via the multiplier this will lead to even more spending and to a great deficit.

If a country suffers from an inflationary spiral – wages and prices chasing each other – the continuous depreciation of the currency will be even more dangerous. In both cases the float will make that inflation gallop even harder.

This is, of course, the tragic story of Britain in the seventies. Between 1970 and 1977 the pound sterling lost about half of its international value. But this floating depreciation did not visibly restore Britain's competitive strength, because the wage-price spiral was going on at the same time, nor did it re-establish equilibrium in the balance of payments of full employment. Italy supplies us with another sad example of inflation, depreciation and stagnation.

The prospect becomes even gloomier when the possibility of speculation is taken into account. A firm believer in classical equilibrium might even expect speculation to be a stabilizing force; when the price of a currency becomes exceedingly high, speculators pour their holdings of that currency on the market, and depress its price. But this beneficial mechanism only works in relatively quiet markets. When the swings in the rates become substantial, expectations of further increases and decreases begin to play an enormous role, and they act as powerful de-stabilizers. When, moreover, the massive amounts of currency are available for international capital movements, flitting from country to country, the float becomes a highly dangerous thing.

The experience of the early seventies has borne out the most pessimistic predictions. At first, the flexible rate of exchange took the mild form of a widening of the margins between which the rates are allowed to vary. But soon, under the pressure of speculation, the fixing of the rates by Central Banks was abandoned altogether. After 1971, when the link between the dollar and gold was severed, the international currency markets became chaotic. A colossal amount of floating money – owned by banks, international corporations, wealthy people generally – moved perpetually from Zurich to Rome and from Bonn to Tokyo, bringing the rate of the dollar to unprecedented depths, and dragging the international payments system from crisis to crisis. This has nothing to do with stabilizing any country's balance of payments. It is bad for trade, bad for morale, bad for inflation, and it is only good for a few rich people. It is a nuisance to the public and it endangers government policies in many ways. It is also a disturbing element in the European Economic Community; the floating rates threaten the delicate policy fabric of the Community.

Of course we should be aware of the fact that a fixed rate is not a cure-all against international instability. Rate fixing by Central Banks does not do away with the surplus of dollars floating around on the capital markets of the world. Moreover, it is no good to have rates of exchange fixed at the wrong level. The latter may occur when governments refuse to devalue for reasons of prestige. Obviously Britain has suffered a good deal from the idea that the pound is a sacred cow (the suffering started in 1928, but became sharper in the post-war decades), and the United States did themselves a good deal of harm by maintaining too high a rate for the dollar in the sixties. The great art of choosing a country's correct rate of exchange, and defending it once it has been chosen, remains one of the most troublesome issues in economic policy.

5 · INTERNATIONAL RELATIONSHIPS: ORDER OR CHAOS?

From the above something emerges that we already know, namely that the incomes in one country depend on the incomes in other countries. We have merely systematized this interdependence to some extent. Two strategic relations are concerned. In the first place the exports of one country depend on the income development abroad; in model-building the volume of world trade is therefore often included as an exogenous variable. In the second place import prices are important; a price increase of imported goods may end up in the wage-price spiral. In the seventies this has led to very violent inflationary phenomena – in the mid seventies import prices increased by about 50 per cent, resulting in a tremendous shock.

The international linkage of economic quantities means that a country has a considerable interest in a balanced development in other countries. This is immediately evident in a deflationary development. If demand is deficient in one country, its neighbours suffer as a result of stagnating exports. This can make its effect felt via the multiplier. In this way the trouble spreads until such time as everyone is affected by it. Here Keynesian theory emphasizes a disagreeable possibility which was not unknown in itself, but which assumes a somewhat grimmer appearance. If the correct policy is absent – that is to say, if the national governments inadequately pursue $Y = Y^\star$ – international trade will be subject to continuing instability.

This is therefore quite a different view from that of the classicists. They pointed to the order inherent in the international division of labour and to the natural equilibrium of the balance of payments. Governments could disturb this harmonious pattern only by hampering trade. The classical economists rightly indicated that welfare is harmed when countries protect themselves by import duties and quotas against imports from other countries. Not only the welfare of the supplying countries – their own as well. A protectionist country harms the international division of labour everywhere, and thus productivity. This classical reasoning is perfectly correct, and it is simply a pity that the obstinacy with which economists defended it was often exceeded by the energy with which the industrial and agricultural interests championed protection. But, in addition, modern circular flow theory shows that import duties and quantitative restrictions are not the only obstacles to international trade. At least as serious are the disturbances in the pattern of trade caused by reductions in purchasing power. These can dislocate trade and harm welfare even more severely than protectionism.

The threat that emanates from a delayed growth of national income is felt more strongly by some countries than others. A high X/Y ratio easily leads to an ideology in which free trade, international cooperation and a joint cyclical policy are regarded as urgent. This quotient, which is about equal to m, characterizes the economic openness of a country. For Britain the ratio is somewhat over one-third; for the Netherlands it is well over a half. Other countries have much lower ratios; for the United States it is below 5 per cent, and for this reason alone it is understandable that the American ideology of free trade is occasionally criss-crossed by protectionist measures.

The principal parties interested in international trade that is not threatened by disturbances of purchasing power are, however, the developing countries. Their gigantic problems, which this book will not further consider, become completely insoluble if their exports, vulnerable as they are, are harmed by a downswing of the world economic trend. The resultant losses of foreign exchange can easily exceed the foreign aid received by many times. Even if there should be absolutely no other reason for a

Keynesian policy than the needs of the developing countries, such a policy ought to have high priority.

The Keynesian view of international relationships thus entails that countries must follow an active policy in order to maintain equilibrium. That is a political recommendation. But at the same time this view means that there is a considerable chance of international disturbances. That is the factual or perhaps the scientific side of the matter. Experience between 1945 and the seventies has proved those right who made allowance for stubborn disturbances. The surpluses and deficits on the balance of payments have not been done away with, not even between the developed countries. The United Kingdom had to contend with persistent deficits that no devaluation and no Keynesian policy could eliminate. The United States also saw the appearance of balance of payments deficits, which undermined confidence in the dollar. The fixed rates of exchange, the cornerstone of the Bretton Woods Agreement (1944), were abandoned at the end of the sixties. In 1968 the Central Banks dropped the fixed price of gold on the London market. The dollar, which had seemed the stable element in world trade, was detached from gold in 1971. The Smithsonian Agreement (1971), by which the countries tried to save something of support of each other's currency so as to keep fluctuations in the rates of exchange within bounds, proved a failure. Floating rates became a general thing. Even the countries of Europe that jointly form the European Economic Community were unable to maintain fixed rates of exchange among themselves. True, in 1972 they concluded the 'snake' arrangement – a watered-down version of the Bretton Woods system, in which the rates of exchange are allowed to fluctuate within certain margins – but Britain did not take part and France soon opted out. In the mid seventies the snake covered only a few countries (including the German Federal Republic and the Netherlands). The floating rates of exchange are a nuisance within Europe, notably in agricultural policy. As early as the beginning of the seventies international economic order seemed to have become a lasting travesty.

In addition, 1973 brought the oil crisis with the subsequent large increase in oil prices. Since then the international economic situation has stagnated. In 1974 a recession broke out in all Western countries, followed in 1975 by a real, be it very short, depression – a fall in production.

Industrial production declined everywhere: in Japan by 11 per cent, in the United States by 9 per cent, in Britain by 5 per cent. At the same time unemployment grew: in Britain to 6 per cent, in the United States even to 8·5 per cent.

These dramatic events have upset confidence. If this were a political book on the future of the world economy, the principal questions would be as follows: will the various countries get out of their difficulties again? Will full employment be restored in the United States, the EEC and Japan? Will the monetary system be remodelled? Will the oil dollars flow on to the developing countries? And in fact the question of the future will concern us in the final chapter. However, this book is not concerned primarily with political prophecy, but with macro-economics as a science. In that case the questions are somewhat different. They are as follows: can we understand why international economic relationships are so unstable? Do we have an explanation for the recession after 1974? To put it more sharply: does science have a model with sufficiently hard parameters that explains what happened?

To start with the last question: there are world models that generate 'global' variables by simulation, but these serve a different purpose from linking together flows of trade. As we saw in the preceding chapter, they have been set up with a view to the problems brought to our attention in particular by the Club of Rome. The interlocking of national economies as described at the beginning of this section is analysed by so-called link models. The point of departure here is various existing models of national economies that are linked together.* As these sets of national equations are modelled predominantly on Keynesian lines, they emphasize income and spending flows. From this there follows a remarkable stability, not in income and spending, but in international relationships. Import and export ratios of the various countries prove to be rather constant with time. In that sense we

---

*Cf. the pioneering work under the direction of R. J. Ball (ed.), *The International Linkage of National Economic Models*, 1973.

are concerned with fairly firm relationships – certainly not with an unstructured chaos. However, it must be borne in mind that this structure does not rule out movements in income and trade figures; the balance of payments of various countries may not even show violent movements. But the turbulence is at least understandable.

While classical theory considers the order in international trade and Keynesian theory perceives fluctuations in growth but regards these as closely interrelated, there is a much more alarming view. That is the monetary one. The basic cause of international instability is sought in money, and more particularly in the defects of the international monetary system. International financial transactions are of such a nature that substantial sums of money can be moved from one country to another. This is partly a matter of speculation – from of old, a destabilizing factor – but in part they are also relatively normal movements of capital which are merely somewhat shifted. These capital flows react to differences in interest rates, but also and above all to future expectations. The latter can change quickly, and as a result capital moves in uneasy waves through the world and the picture becomes more erratic.

In this monetarist way of thinking an important part is played by the fact that the oil-exporting countries have proceeded to lay their hands on an enormous part of international liquidities since 1974. The surplus on the current account of the balance of payments of these countries in 1974 for instance was $60,000 million, and by the end of 1975 they had over a quarter of world reserves at their disposal. This may increase still further in the coming years. These countries have only a slight domestic spending capacity. Part of this money is invested on the European capital markets, but there it does not flow on sufficiently to the income sphere to be really spent on consumer or investment goods. Worldwide income flows are thus disturbed by hoarding. This leads to world depression. This view of the events of the seventies is defended by F. Cairncross and H. McRae in their book *The Second Great Crash* (1976). They claim that the second great depression (the first started in 1929) has already begun and will continue on its disastrous way through the world. Only by a deliberately produced increase in spending in the developing countries can the evil be averted, but that calls for international help on a tremendous scale, and it will not be forthcoming.

For the time being this sombre prophecy does not seem to be borne out by the facts: world trade has not declined since 1973 – in 1974 the increase in volume was 4 per cent, in 1975 there was in fact a fall (by 2 per cent), in 1976 the increase was again 12 per cent and for 1977 it was 4 per cent. Such figures do not suggest a fatal and deeply eroding depression, but indicate delayed growth. However, these few figures are of course not enough to refute the monetarist view of world events. Nor do they say much about the development of world trade that we may expect in the somewhat longer term. It is my personal belief that the monetarist view, though not very illuminating with respect to national events (at least in 'normal' times), must certainly be considered when it comes to international problems.

Evidently we encounter a problem here which is not only un-solved but also greatly exceeds the bounds of this book. And yet it was necessary to consider it. The models used by macro-economics easily create the impression that we understand every-thing – at world level that is certainly not the case at all (and hardly so on the domestic front); the international situation remains an unpredictable and uncontrollable source of disturb-ance for domestic economic events.

CHAPTER VI

The Role of the Budget

1 · GOVERNMENT EXPENDITURE, TAXES, AND NATIONAL INCOME

We started with a particularly simple flow of incomes and expenditure, in which only consumer goods were produced. After this, investment, i.e. the production of capital goods, was brought on the scene, and we found that with this complications arose which finally led to Keynesian theory. This was then applied to a third kind of goods: export goods. We are now coming to a fourth category which again is admirably suited to a Keynesian analysis. This category is formed by the 'products' of the government.

The word products is between inverted commas. The question whether the government does or does not produce anything has long been the subject of controversy and doubt. The nineteenth-century classicists – and this opinion was held in particular by J.-B. Say – denied that government activity was productive. As the government unmistakably employs factors of production – especially labour – such a view leads to the conclusion that this is a pure waste, which must be restricted as much as possible. Even now the idea is often encountered that the government is really unproductive.

The idea is of course untenable. The government has a number of absolutely essential functions. To fulfil these it must employ productive forces. These have a certain productivity, and they produce something. The only question is what this 'something' is exactly. It is a peculiar and moreover heterogeneous product. Some parts of it are just as tangible as the products of business – the coal of the British National Coal Board (but this is not a proper example, for the mines can also be operated by private entrepreneurs). Part of the government's productive output is not tangible, but nevertheless is visible: services of roads, parks, national theatres. But the most characteristic are the extremely tenuous but nevertheless very real products such as legal security, well-regulated traffic, the right supply of money, a balance of payments in equilibrium and full employment, social security and social welfare, and the like. If all is well, these ethereal things are promoted or produced by the government. They form a 'product'. We do not need to philosophize further on this, except

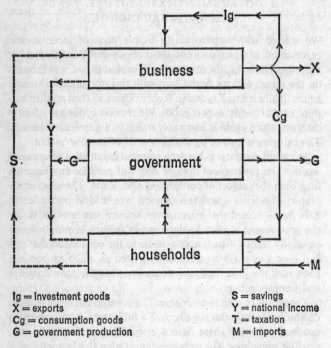

Ig = Investment goods   S = savings
X = exports   Y = national income
Cg = consumption goods   T = taxation
G = government production   M = imports

Fig. 5: The circulation including foreign trade and the government economy

in one single respect. Much of government output is character-ized by the property that it cannot be sold on the market to con-sumers. For only a minor part of the product can payment be demanded in the form of fees from those most directly concerned. This does not apply to the greater part; the product is not marketable. It is also called 'collective'. Payment has to be regulated in another way: via the levying of taxes.

The reader must bear these well-known matters in mind for a moment, for they are most relevant to Keynesian theory. While C flows to the households and meets half-way a flow of money heading for business, the government product, which we shall call G, goes differently. G leaves the government, which we therefore regard as a production economy (but which we draw separately in the figure, because it is so special) at the top right, but then does not make for the market for consumer goods. This flow of output is scattered far and wide; it is distributed for the general good, *urbi et orbi*, for the households and for business. But meanwhile a money income has been created, equal in size to G, which ends up in the hands of the factors of production. They cannot spend it on the government product, for that is not for sale. They therefore have too much money. If they were to spend it on consumer goods, there would be inflation.

This situation is the twin of the one which we have encountered with reference to exports. There too we have the making of a product that disappears. The recipients of income who have helped to create it cannot spend their income on the export goods, and they cannot fully spend it on consumer goods produced at home – for $C+X$ is of course larger than C. Too much spending seems unavoidable. But then imports come to the rescue and check this inflation. Something similar happens with the relation between saving and investing. There too we have a product that does not come on the market for consumer goods and an income that therefore cannot be spent on consumer goods. And there too we have a compensatory, deflationary flow of money: S. This striking analogy is the starting point of the modern theory of public finance.

The deflationary flow of money that must compensate for G is the taxation T.* T is drawn off by the tax authorities from the flow of income Y. It does not make much difference to circulation analysis where exactly this happens (though it most cer-

---

*The Exchequer has forms of income other than real taxes: fees, fines, profits from state concerns. The first two categories are included in T; the state concerns are usually put under the business sector. For they produce a marketable product that is paid for over the counter.

tainly does to other problems – such as the position of the taxpayers!). Various places are conceivable. In the figure only one has been drawn: the income goes from business to the households, from where part of it is led to the Exchequer; this is the flow of money T.

Now the reasoning which we learned earlier can again be applied to these quantities. As long as the inflationary components I, X, and G – which create incomes but no consumer goods for the home market – cause national income to swell more than the deflationary components S, M, and T – which use up these incomes without affecting home demand – hold it down, the entrepreneurs will continue to receive more from the households and the investors than they spend. This surplus is again translated into income, and this increases the flow of money. National income is in equilibrium only when $I+X+G = S+M+T$. It becomes manifest that saving, importing, and paying taxes have the same effect on the circulation, however different they may be in their importance to the national economy or to individuals.

And a second proposition comes to the fore. The size of national income depends not only on saving and investing, but also on the other components. An extra impulse in investments creates not only savings, but also imports; and now we find that taxes may also result from it. The same applies to government expenditure. If this increases, one of four things happens: savings increase as a result, or imports, or consumption, or taxes. In practice all four happen, until such time as national income has once more found its equilibrium value. The circulation is then again at rest. The proportions in which the income effect is divided among the four uses to which income is put are given by the ratio between the propensity to save, the propensity to import, and the 'propensity to tax' or tax rate.

The latter is a new element; it is usually called 'tax burden'. There is an analogy with the propensity to save s and the propensity to import m. It is defined as $\dfrac{T}{Y}$. The marginal tax burden t

$= \dfrac{\Delta T}{\Delta Y}$ shows how much taxes increase for a given change in Y.

These fractions are fixed by the recipients of income, but in a manner quite different from the way in which the propensities s and m are fixed. They do this as citizens; via the electoral system, Parliament, and the Cabinet they ensure that t is expressed in fiscal laws. A noteworthy feature of this is that these laws do not provide for a given tax revenue T. Whilst in general the appropriation acts state how large government expenditure G may be, there is no such system regarding taxes. These come about via the effect of the multiplier. The law fixes the tax rates and T then follows from Y. Incidentally, the marginal tax burden is higher than the average; this comes from the progression. So t is not a constant but depends on Y.

Now that we have finally got the government inside the circulation, we can state the real value of the multiplier. Everything that has been said about it so far has been a preliminary exercise, which may have a misleading effect because it suggests to the reader much too high an estimate of the multiplier. In fact the following reasoning is the only complete one: if national income is in equilibrium, $I+X+G = S+M+T$. An income impulse given either by exports, or by government expenditure, or by investments, therefore leads to an increment of national income that is $\dfrac{1}{s+m+t}$ times as large. This is the multiplier. It is much smaller than the reader who has stopped at $\dfrac{1}{s}$ might think.

There are many remarkable views on taxes, some correct, others less so. One of these, which in my opinion is correct, should be mentioned here, because it is rarely heard: taxes do not form a burden for the community, and therefore the term tax burden is misleading. This sounds incredible. Everyone who has to pay tax sees as a result his spendable income decrease, and does this then not hold good for the whole?

The answer is no. This is best illustrated by assuming that one day taxes are suddenly abolished while G is maintained. In that case spendable incomes would increase, but if full employment had already been achieved, no extra real income would result. Tremendous over-expenditure would occur, which would drive up prices, to the detriment of those whose incomes would not rise so quickly. The burden would be shifted from the taxpayers to the victims of the increased prices. For in fact it is not taxes that cause a sacrifice to be made, but the use of the factors of production by the government; as a result of this the product is sacrificed that otherwise could have been made with that work and that capital. Against that cost we have the government product. Taxes do not form an extra burden, but are only an instrument for dividing the cost among the members of the community in a fairer manner than the increase in prices would otherwise have done, and at the same time they serve to keep the circulation of money within bounds. The fact that taxes do not form a sacrifice – unless they become so high that they harm the real income, which happens in a depression – is one of the curiosities and apparent paradoxes which characterize macro-economics. Taxes demonstrate once more that macro-economics and micro-economics must not be confused with one another.

2 · BUDGETARY EQUILIBRIUM

By budget we mean below the confrontation of T and G. We are therefore ignoring for a moment the fact that the appropriation acts contain only predictions of T and authorizations regarding G, whilst in the circulation this 'paper' side of the matter does not count as much as the actual development of the flow of money. We say that the budget is in equilibrium when $T = G$. This differs from the usage followed by some to the extent that tax revenue (in the broad sense, i.e. including other current government income) must equal *total* government expenditure; often the budget is said to be in equilibrium if T equals the 'current' part of G. According to some, government investments ought to or might be paid for out of loans, not out of taxes. Behind this there lies a profound difference of opinion about the way in which the government ought to finance its activities, a difference of opinion that will not be discussed until later. Let us say for the time being that we speak of budgetary equilibrium when there is no borrowing at all, but all expenditure is covered by current government income T. The national debt in that case is constant.

The position of this budgetary equilibrium in the Keynesian theory is a strange one. An illustration of this is to be found in a model which again is very simple in set-up; true, there is government expenditure and income, but we ignore foreign trade and also saving and investing. Production consists of consumer goods and government services. The recipient of income can do only two things with his income: consume or pay taxes. (A strange situation, but no stranger than a situation as discussed in our simple model: there, money was saved, but no taxes were paid. And taxes are even more difficult to think away than savings. But let us try it all the same and place ourselves in that strange world in which C and G form the national product.)

If it is decided in this simple model to increase government expenditure (for instance, new civil servants are engaged to alleviate the difficult existence of those civil servants already employed), whilst the fiscal laws remain unchanged, the uninitiated would predict a deficit on the budget. For G becomes larger than T. But the reader of these pages, who is gradually being transformed into a Keynesian, knows better. He sees how new income is created (the new civil servants, who have just left school and so have not been withdrawn from the production of consumer goods, receive a salary); he sees how this income is used to purchase consumer goods which were not demanded before; he sees the receipts of business increase, and with them national income; in short, he predicts a multiplier process. This will end when the new flow of income is compensated by the increment of tax revenue. We consequently see that the Treasury will attain a new equilibrium, although government expenditure has increased while the tax burden has remained constant. Only the Keynesian is not surprised by this. He knew that ΔG would lead to ΔT, just as (in the simple situation in which all that happens is consumption, saving and investing) ΔI leads to ΔS. This relation is already of practical importance in that it weakens a certain view of budgetary equilibrium. The idea has occasionally been put forward that equilibrium between government income and expenditure cannot have an inflationary effect. But that is not so, any more than it is true to say that $S = I$ provides a guarantee against inflation. For it is quite possible that the higher tax revenue has come about only by the grace of a swelling of income; a swelling of income which has perhaps brought national income to the right of the point at which $Y = Y^\star$. That is, part of T is due to an inflationary swelling of income. Likewise a balanced budget is no guarantee against too large or too small national expenditure.

Let us now return to the more realistic representation of the circulation of money, in which business and the government together produce consumer goods, export goods, investment goods, and government services. Will there also be an automatic tendency towards a balanced budget in this? The answer is in the negative: for we know only that the sum of taxes, imports, and savings will equal the sum of government expenditure, exports, and investments. But the system does not establish any particular equalities between S and I (capital market), M and X (balance of payments), and T and G (budget). These equalities can be disturbed one by one, while the total system is nevertheless in equilibrium. And more than that: the disturbance of the one equilibrium leads to a disturbance of equilibrium elsewhere. Applied to that part of the system with which we are concerned in this chapter, this means that the budget will get out of balance if $S+M$ does not equal $I+X$. If there is a lot of saving and a lot of importing, the tax revenue drops. If there is a lot of investing and a lot of exporting, it rises, without anything necessarily having happened to the tax burden.

We can also turn this way of thinking round. What does a balanced budget mean? It means that the sum of savings and imports is equal to the sum of investments and exports. Is it desirable for the budget to be in equilibrium? We do not know; at least it is not evident from this relation. For why should an equilibrium between these two sums be so desirable? If budgetary equilibrium is an aim worth striving after, it is certainly not due to this relation! From the point of view of economic balance, the equality of government income and government expenditure is of no particular importance.

In classical theory, which still governs many minds, this is quite different. There the balanced budget is a golden rule, which may be departed from only in so far as productive investments are financed by long-term loans (or, in exceptional cases, in so far as surpluses are created by means of which the national debt is redeemed). This, too, is understandable. For the national economy that the classicists had in mind is characterized by full use of the productive forces. Moreover, in that economy there is equilibrium of the balance of payments; the rate of exchange attends to that. And there is equilibrium between saving and investing; the rate of interest attends to that. In these circumstances government expenditure must also be covered by government income. If tax revenue is less than government expenditure, inflation rears its ugly head (unless the government drains off so much capital from private investments that the latter decrease). The particular equilibria between X and M on the one hand and S and I on the other hand render necessary such a government policy that T equals G.

The Keynesian theory does not believe in all these particular relations. For in fact they need not be realized. The total of taxes, savings, and imports is brought into equilibrium with the total of the inflationary components by the multiplier. This overall equilibrium does not imply a balanced budget.

And yet Keynesian theory, like the classical one, lays down rules for the budget. It is these rules that form the essence of Keynesian policy. In their more orthodox form they are known by the name of Functional Finance: a term which some politicians, late adherents of the classical school, unknowing adepts of the theory of particular equilibria, identify with (at choice): pernicious modernism, irresponsible extravagance, too much power in the hands of the authorities, the fanaticism of intellectuals with their heads in the clouds, the imposition of an excessive burden on later generations by a national debt run wild, inflation, opening the door to a depression, chaos, communism, and dictatorship. Let us have a look at this.

3 · FUNCTIONAL FINANCE

The essence of the new rules for public finance can best be understood if for a moment we ignore international trade, which in any case did not play an important part in the original Keynesianism.

The overall demand for goods and services is then made up of consumption expenditure, investment, and government expenditure, $C+I+G$. The production resulting from this must be such that it exactly occupies the available productive capacity, no more and no less. The equilibrium must satisfy the requirement that the point A (Fig. 3, p. 90) is reached: the True Equilibrium, also characterized by the absence of inflation and deflation. The national money income is then at its best level. This point does not come into being of its own accord; it is not a 'natural' equilibrium. The government has to create it. There are two instruments available for doing so: government expenditure and the tax burden. These quantities must be so manipulated that the national economy displays an optimum total expenditure. This manipulating of public finance is called Functional Finance. This expression comes from one of Keynes's most fervent followers, A. P. Lerner,* who has repeatedly advocated this policy.

There are thus two instruments: t and G. Since it is confusing to discuss both of them at the same time, we shall assume for a moment that the tax burden is given, and that the circulation is therefore regulated by varying government expenditure. This was also the idea that most occupied Keynes himself; the extent of government expenditure could be varied by performing or postponing public works. An old idea – it already occurs in the nineteenth century – but one that has acquired a theoretical foundation through the new macro-economics.

The extent of government expenditure needed for full employment can be established without difficulty by means of our simple model. The equilibrium in the model is determined by $C+I$ (see p. 88). If this sum of private expenditure and investment after deduction of tax is too small to yield full employment, G must fill the gap. But not all of the gap; there is also a multiplier. G should be made equal to the deficit in expenditure divided by the multiplier.

On the other side, the total tax revenue is equal to the average tax burden times Y and it is improbable that this amount equals G; this would be so only by chance. The budget will therefore not

*In his article 'Functional Finance and the Federal Debt', *Social Research*, 1943.

be balanced. In the case that we have in mind there is a deficit on the budget. If Members of Parliament should criticize the Chancellor of the Exchequer for this, he can refer to the rules of Functional Finance. However, he must be prepared for a question which will also have entered the reader's thoughts: what about the increase in the national debt that results from this budgetary deficit? Is this increase an innocent one, or even desirable? Or does it threaten the national economy in some way or the other? We shall try to answer these questions in the next section, just as ministers sometimes ask for notice of a question.

Meanwhile, we can consider the case in which $C+I+G$ does not yield a deflationary situation but an inflationary one. The government can get rid of this by decreasing G or by increasing t. The latter will reduce private expenditure $C+I$. As a consequence T may become greater than G: a budgetary surplus turns up. This is, however, not the goal of the deflationary operation. It is a by-product of the stabilization of Y at a level $Y = Y^\star$.

Up to now t and G have been examined separately. But the new rules for public finance have the most point if they are applied to the income side and the expenditure side together. For instance, a depression can be eliminated by a combination of tax cuts, which cause $C+I$ to increase, and increased expenditure. The aim, the right size of $C+I+G$, can then be more easily achieved than by manipulating t and G separately.

This is Functional Finance in outline. No budgetary equilibrium, but a deliberate manipulation of t and G which compensates for the surplus or deficit of the expenditure of households and business. The government no longer aims at a balanced budget, but at a balanced national economy. Public finance becomes the greater regulator of activity.

But is this possible just like that? Does an unbalanced budget not mean that there is danger of inflation? This question is too complicated to be fully answered at this stage. For complications can arise from the national debt and the stock of money, subjects with which we have not yet dealt. But we can even now refute the popular misconception that a deficit on the budget must *per se* lead to inflation. As long as the equilibrium lies to the left of A (Fig. 3, p. 90) and too little is being spent, a certain degree of reflation is desirable. This is precisely the aim of Functional Finance: reflation, increased expenditure, increased production, the re-employment of productive forces. Activity must be so encouraged that it arrives precisely at the point A. If it goes any further, there is inflation, and Functional Finance must again come to the assistance to combat this evil. Precision work is therefore demanded of the government, and we may shortly ask ourselves whether governments are capable of doing this. But in this more theoretical stage of the reasoning there is no harm in this. The aim of Functional Finance is to prevent inflation, not to invoke it.

The new rules also give us a new look at the function of taxes. It is obvious to assume that these serve to fill the Exchequer, and to make it possible for the Chancellor of the Exchequer to put at the disposal of his colleagues in office the funds required for government expenditure. But this view is too unsophisticated for the Keynesians. Taxes serve to keep total expenditure within bounds. The government can always get hold of money – by borrowing and if necessary making some. But it has to take care that the nation's expenditure stays at the right level, that $C+I+G$ stays within the limits set by the factors of production.

This new view has something refreshing about it. It seems simplicity itself. But we shall see that a number of complications have been omitted from it. We shall now consider the first of these. It is the question of the national debt which the government owes its subjects.

4 · THE NATIONAL DEBT

The reproach that Functional Finance causes the national debt to increase immoderately can be parried by pointing out that the budget will not always display a deficit to fulfil its regulatory function. There are times when total expenditure threatens to display a deficit, so that a budgetary deficit must keep the circulation going; but then there are other times in which a budgetary surplus is required to protect the national economy against inflation. In the cyclical fluctuations the public debt varies, but it in no way needs to be constantly increasing. The permanent increase of the debt does not fit into the doctrine of Functional Finance as such, but rather into the stagnation theory, that is to say the view that expenditure in the private sector will constantly be too small for productive capacity. But the stagnation theory has been abandoned; the experience of the post-war years has shown that inflation can be at least as obstinate as deflation.

From the fluctuation of deficits and surpluses on the budget some economists, influenced rather by Keynes, have deduced that the budget does not need so much to be in equilibrium over a period of one year (the normal duration of a budget) as over a whole business cycle. Budgetary equilibrium thus remains the norm, but the period changes. The budget period must really comprise a whole business cycle. In this way an attempt has been made to reconcile Keynesian budget policy with the classical one. Just as happens with such well-meaning compromises, the theory of the anticyclical budget has brought little enlightenment and has confused minds to a not inconsiderable extent. The train of thought seems to be connected with the concept of regularly returning waves in economic life, waves which in length and amplitude display a uniform and thus predictable rhythm. This is the favourite idea of the old-fashioned cyclical theory. In actual fact economic life does fluctuate, but the waves are not nearly so regular and above all not nearly so predictable that a government could base a budget policy on them. Anyone who has been concerned with the practice of an anticyclical policy will shake his head at so theoretical a set-up. And if in addition the idea of a budget covering several years is attached, whereby expenditure must be specified for a number of years ahead, it requires little imagination to hear the bitter laughter of the civil servants and the politicians, who already have trouble enough with the one-year budget. This is quite apart from the difficulty that nobody can estimate where exactly a country is in the business cycle at the moment when this system is introduced.

The proponents of the long-term anticyclical budget have therefore done modern views of financial policy a disservice. They have distracted attention from the fact that Functional Finance directs the Chancellor of the Exchequer to act every year as he thinks fit, to accept fluctuations in the public debt as long as they do not exceed all bounds, and not to worry about the periodicity of what is believed to be a business cycle.

But when does the national debt exceed all bounds?

A very widespread view on this is the following. The national debt imposes on posterity the burden of interest and redemption. It may therefore be contracted only if posterity inherits not only the increased debt, but also the government investments which can cover the extra expenditure with their profit-earning ability. It is often said that a generation that does not follow this principle robs its children of their future. And in this respect a further distinction can be made between the very strict view that money should be borrowed only if the investments concerned can show a profit from the point of view of business economics – such as an electricity works, a railway line, a swimming bath – and the somewhat more flexible idea that it suffices if the general productivity of the country has increased through the investments – e.g. roads and bridges. Feelings have often run high in debates between the strict and the flexible. At this moment they interest us less; for both groups of debaters are wrong.

The first mistake they make is to think that the national debt as such represents a burden on posterity. An internal debt means that the government must pay interest and redemption to some of its subjects after other subjects have furnished these sums. Money is transferred from the pockets of the one to the pockets of the other. As the state's taxpayers and credits form part of the same national economy and of the same generation, the national economy as a whole does not become any poorer or any richer from the transfer. It may not therefore be said that an increase in the national debt burdens posterity. This cuts away the ground from under the moralistic view of the balanced budget. This view regards the public debt too much on the analogy of a private debt. It confuses macro-economics with micro-economics.*

---

* However, in classical theory the idea that the creation of a government debt puts a burden on future generations may be defended as follows: I depends on S. If the government borrows parts of present savings, present investment will suffer and therefore future labour productivity and welfare will suffer also. This is only acceptable if government investments are increased. In other words: in classical theory government should borrow only

The misunderstanding regarding the 'burden' is a particularly obstinate one. Many regard the refutation of it as a sophism. Perhaps the following will help. Our heirs will have to live under a burdened government; that is unpleasant for them. But at the same time they inherit the government bonds. This compensates for their distress. In a certain sense the one cancels the other out. Anyone wishing to debate with supporters of the naïve burden theory can use this argument. He can say – jokingly – that the present generation could greatly favour posterity by considerably increasing the public debt. For our children are enriched by securities which provide an income without their having to work for it. But I fear that the opposite party will go home with the feeling that they have been done.

There is a second reason for criticizing the prejudiced view that the government debt will *per se* burden later generations. Even if this debt should cause difficulties in the future – this can very easily be the case, though for other reasons than the naïve burden theory assumes – then it should be borne in mind that a deficit on the government account yields benefits which need not consist in the profit-earning ability of the capital goods purchased by the government. For the theory of Functional Finance teaches us that the extra government spending keeps the circulation going. This means that consumption is higher than it would have been. But it also means that private investments are higher; for, as we have seen, these depend on consumption, and even to a somewhat greater extent (acceleration). Owing to the budgetary deficit not only is national income saved from a decline, but also the expansion of productive capacity can continue. Without a deficit on the budget later generations might perhaps get a smaller stock of capital goods; the productivity of labour and prosperity would be harmed by this. In return for the greater national debt we have not only the inheritance of a bundle of government securities but at the same time something that is much more important: a

---

for investment purposes. This moral prescription collapses if we drop the view that I depends on S. It should also be noted that in this classical view the burden on our children is not caused by the *existence* of a public debt but by its *creation*, an important distinction that is often lost sight of.

larger national income in the future. Quite apart from the specific projects which the government financed with the loans! These have nothing to do with the matter; in principle they cannot even be pointed to any longer. There is no connection between the budgetary deficit and certain detailed items of expenditure; there is only the macro-economic connection between the deficit on the budget and the too small total expenditure $C+I$, which we want to remedy.

Perhaps the compliant reader has now gradually come to the conclusion that the size of the internal national debt is completely immaterial. After all, he reasons, it merely entails a transfer of money from one pocket to another, which does not make the national economy any richer or any poorer. But once again, things are not as simple as that.

For this transfer has certain consequences. The taxpayer forks out more money to provide his fellow-citizens with interest and redemption, and his reaction to this may perhaps be less enterprise. Too great a transfer of income and capital also causes a decrease in the propensity to save, and thus makes the national economy less proof against a future threatening inflation. Sometimes the new government bonds are difficult to place, and the government must have recourse to short-term debts, which may also entail a tendency towards future inflation. And finally a big national debt is just the thing to create in the minds of its holders the illusion that they are richer than they actually are. The national debt may not make the community poorer, but it certainly does not make it richer. And if the state's creditors are given a false feeling of wealth, there is a chance that the propensity to save will suffer, again with inflationary consequences. (The latter is sometimes called the Lerner effect of the public debt.)

It is therefore evident from this short summary of the drawbacks of too large a national debt that the latter's size is not entirely immaterial. However, it is something quite different if this debt is regarded as a burden because it seems to weigh heavily from a micro-economic point of view, which it does not, or because it can create monetary problems in the future, which it may. The first is a misunderstanding, the second a real difficulty, although the extent of this difficulty must not be exaggerated. All the same, a Chancellor of the Exchequer may not forget this side of the matter. For this reason alone Functional Finance is a less simple matter than is occasionally suggested. There are still other reasons for this; they will be discussed later (Chapter XII).

5 · A CLEAR-CUT HYPER-KEYNESIAN MODEL

One of the propositions defended in this book is that we can clarify our minds by writing down formal models. The Keynesian view of the budget is a case in point. I suggest that we formalize the ideas set forth in the preceding section and that we build a little income-expenditure model which includes a government sector. This exercise will not only create order in our ideas but will also produce a new and rather unexpected result, known as the Haavelmo effect.

We saw that national income can be written as $Y = C + I + G$. We can leave international trade out of the picture. Consumption is supposed to depend on income after tax, in the following manner: $C = C_o + c(Y - T)$. That is, we assume that the marginal propensity to consume out of disposable income is a constant, which is a not unreasonable assumption. Let us also assume that I and G are both given: $I = I_o$ and $G = G_o$. Moreover, we start from the special case (which will be made less special later) that all taxes are levied as lump sums; they are unaffected by national income. Thus $T = T_o$. A simple world.

Yes, but a world in which peculiar things happen. Watch what happens if we increase government expenditure by an amount ΔG whilst at the same time increasing taxes by an equal amount ΔT. Additional expenditure is covered right from the start (and not after the multiplier has done its inflationary work) by additional taxation – a tax policy that would appeal to an observer with classicist leanings. Now we would expect national income not to be affected by this operation. For ΔG is added to it, ΔT is subtracted from it and because the two are equal nothing happens to Y. Or, in other words, because the budgetary deficit does not change there is no impact on national expenditure.

But our little model leads us to a different result. National income is $Y = \dfrac{1}{1-c}(C_o + T_o + G_o - cT_o)$. That means that the multiplier of G is $\dfrac{1}{1-c}$. The multiplier of T is only $\dfrac{-c}{1-c}$. The sum of the two multipliers equals one. This has the surprising consequence that the simultaneous increase in G and T by an equal amount $\Delta G = \Delta T$ leads to an expansion of national income by the same amount. $\Delta Y = \Delta G = \Delta T$. (If the reader does not follow this or does not believe it, he or she may go back to the original equation and increase both G and T by an arbitrary constant – the result will be that Y increases by the same constant.)

The proposition that an increase in government expenditure, covered by an immediate increase in taxation, makes national income go up by an equal amount is called Haavelmo's theorem.[*] I have written it down in its strong form, that is, I have assumed that all taxation was of the lump sum type. If we start from the more realistic position that at least part of T depends on Y, we might write $T = T_o + tY$. In that case the multiplier of G equals $\dfrac{1}{1-c+ct}$ and the multiplier of T_o equals $\dfrac{-c}{1-c+ct}$. The sum of these two multipliers is smaller than one. However, it is greater than zero, and zero is the intuitive conclusion from classical theory. A balanced budget multiplier between 0 and 1 might be called the weak form of Haavelmo's theorem.

By way of numerical illustration, if the marginal propensity to consume equals 0·8 and the marginal tax rate 0·5, the multiplier of government expenditure equals 1·7 and the multiplier of autonomous taxation – 1·3. These are small numbers – but the point is that they are different. The multiplier of an increase in the level of the budget equals 0·4. (In an open economy, where imports constitute another leak in the income flow, the multipliers are even smaller.)

Before we try to find out what this little exercise means in theory

[*]T. Haavelmo, 'Multiplier Effects of a Balanced Budget', *Econometrica*, 1945.

140

and in practice, let us concentrate on the way in which the Haavelmo effect crept in. What did we introduce into our model that led to this strange outcome? Perhaps the reader should look for himself or herself. If this quest proves unsuccessful, the following may help. Obviously G and T are treated in an asymmetrical manner. G is, by definition, part of national income. But in the first Keynesian equation T is not subtracted from Y. Taxation enters into the second equation – the consumption function – and this happens in such a way that T is not fully subtracted from C. If consumption were reduced by the full amount of the tax, the Haavelmo effect would disappear. In fact, this is the ancient classical or Ricardian consumption function – it says that taxation is a burden on consumption and on nothing else. However, in our model we assumed that T reduces C by an amount cT; the rest of T, $(1-c)T$, is a burden on saving. One deflationary component overlaps another, and this leads to an inflationary result. This overlapping was smuggled in at the moment we said: 'it is not unreasonable to assume that people consume according to $C_o + c(Y-T)$, that is, they keep the marginal propensity to consume out of disposable income constant'. The exercise is instructive, if only for learning what unexpected consequences reasonable assumptions may have.

The theoretical importance of Haavelmo's theorem is that it shows us the workings of the Keynesian model. A naïve and mistaken version of Keynesian theory tells us that this theory is all about budgetary deficits. Slumps should be fought with deficits and inflation with surpluses. A more sophisticated version of Keynesian theory points to the fact that the deficit $G-T$ does not appear in the Keynesian model. It is a result, not a cause; the policy instruments are G and t, the tax burden. $G-T$ is not an instrument. Moreover, this quantity does not appear in any equation as an independent variable. This is quite different in monetary theory – there the budgetary deficit is one of the crucial causal factors in the whole system, because $G-T$ may lead to the creation of new money on behalf of the government. The idea that the deficit is important is not a Keynesian but a monetary conception. The Haavelmo model stresses the asymmetrical effect of G and T. It rests on the assumption that taxes are partly paid out of current savings. These savings do not affect investment. It draws the full consequences of the small three-equation system outlined in Chapter IV. This model may therefore be regarded as a hyper-Keynesian one. Monetarists do not like Haavelmo's theorem, they call it trivial or artificial, or just bunk.

Now what is the practical importance of the Haavelmo effect, if any? It seems to me that it may shed some light on two possible configurations. The first relates to the depression. Governments may try to get rid of a deflationary gap by increasing public spending without increasing the budgetary deficit. A constant deficit may prove to be politically expedient if parliament (or the government itself) is critical of the level of public debt.

The second situation is more to the point. It relates to a steadily increasing level of government expenditure – a phenomenon that has been with us for many decades. Around 1900 the public sector in most Western countries stood at less than 10 per cent of national income; the figure is now well over one-third (and if we include social security, over a half). Governments have found it extremely difficult to increase taxation accordingly. But suppose that they continuously succeeded in covering the new levels of G with new amounts of T – even up to the point where budgetary deficits could have been avoided. Then Haavelmo's theorem tells us that even in that seemingly reassuring case we might expect a good deal of inflation. Neutral finance implies not a balanced increase in G but an overbalanced one.* Because this overbalancing has not happened in practice, Haavelmo's theorem contributes to our insight into a long-run tendency towards inflation. Britain's deficits on the balance of payments may, perhaps, be understood in this light.

But the clear-cut model not only shows us that national income may well expand under the influence of a growing budget – it also draws our attention to the theory's own limitations and weaknesses. These are the things that are taken as given. The most conspicuous sore spot is $I = I_0$. Government expenditure and taxation are supposed to have no impact on private investment – an easy assumption but not a convincing one. If we drop it, the

---

*The amount of overbalancing can be deduced from the model. If the effect of ΔG on Y is to be zero, ΔT should equal $1/c\Delta G$.

model loses much of its pleasant determinateness, and Haavelmo's theorem may be reversed. This is the subject of the next section.

6 · THE FULL IMPACT OF THE BUDGET: THE UNKNOWNS

Up to now we have been talking about budgetary effects that fit into the Keynesian approach, that is, income effects. But there are others. Firstly, public spending summons up various capacity effects. Roads and bridges increase production capacity. This influence of G on Q can be measured in principle, although that is not easy. With education it becomes even more difficult. Legal security also increases Q, and here measurability becomes an absolutely unattainable ideal. Sometimes new laws make production more cumbersome – high costs of implementing social security are an example of a negative impact of this kind on private productivity. In econometric practice all these capacity effects are taken together labelled as technical progress and this portion of the growth rate of $Q^\star$ is given. In part this growth is the work of the engineers, in part it comes through better education and in part it results from better organization and planning (let us at least hope the latter). The precise influence of G is not categorized and thus remains obscure.

Secondly, taxes summon up a number of capacity effects too. These relate among other things to the labour supply – an old bone of contention among economists. Will higher taxes on wages lessen or increase the supply? Will the productive effort expand or contract? Formal micro-models neatly show that both reactions are possible, but what happens in fact is uncertain. Quantitative research has yielded little more than that a higher marginal tax rate leads to earlier retirement in the case of some free professions. For most people, working hours are fixed and the question is only to what extent they will accept overtime. The tax burden has a negative effect on this, but to what extent? Reliable quantitative answers are not available. The same applies to the effect of taxation on schooling. There is an opinion that high marginal tax rates (plus low pay differentials) cause the incentive for additional schooling to decrease considerably;

but another view indicates that in the choice of the type of school the non-financial incentives are more important than the financial ones. Here too science has not yielded any solid results on which macro-economics can base itself.

A strategic capacity effect of taxes runs via investments. There is no doubt that a higher rate of taxation on profits harms investments. In the simplest case this impact is quantified by including the after-tax profits in the investment equation as an explanatory variable and assuming that its influence will be linear. True, in doing so we have introduced the whole uncertainty of profits, but at least we have a linear relationship. In this way we get a clear model. But it is suspected that the influence of tax rates (including social security premiums) on investments is more complicated – that strong effects occur as soon as certain threshold values are exceeded. Curvilinearity is a popular theme in the political economy of taxation. Businessmen say, even in good times, that a slight tax increase will have disastrous effects; some authors (Colin Clark, C. Northcote Parkinson) have described the critical ceilings with verve. Twenty-five per cent is crippling, 30 per cent is fatal. Meanwhile the burden has become much greater. So far macro-economics has been unable to provide quantitative certainty about this curvilinear effect of taxes on investments. It gets no further than conjecture.

And there is something else. New taxes are borne in part by consumers, and in part by firms. Little is known about this proportion. We do know who pays the taxes to the tax collector; the statistics show this. However, between the levying and the paying of taxes lies passing-on. Even an increase in a profits tax may lead to a price increase.* The shifting of various types of tax lends itself excellently to formal model-building; in such a model elasticities of supply and demand (written in Greek

---

*The well-known micro-models of the equilibrium of the firm (marginal costs are equal to marginal income) lead to the conclusion that a profits tax cannot be passed on – the price at which profit is maximum remains the same. But in practice firms refuse to accept a lower return – 'normal profit' is partly restored. To what extent this restoration of profit occurs is greatly disputed. It has occasionally been calculated that passing-on

letters) play a big part. Almost nothing is known about these elasticities from the macro-economic point of view. Sometimes firms succeed in shifting tax increases in their entirety to the consumers – sometimes this process is a difficult one. The degree of passing-on, in times when taxes gradually creep up, makes a tremendous long-run difference for after-tax profits. Here we encounter a strategic unknown: the development of profit. (It will thwart us on other occasions too, in particular when we are discussing the wage-price spiral.)

In the light of the above, considerable doubt must be cast on Haavelmo's clear theorem. As I is a negative function of T (or of t), the influence of T on S (on which the theorem is based) can easily be eclipsed. In that case a negative effect of a balanced budget occurs. Dutch econometricians, working with a model that contains a strong negative influence of taxation on the stock of capital, have sometimes calculated that this is minus two. That means that for every civil servant who is appointed, three people become unemployed in the private sector! This result has been sharply contested. It seems to me exaggerated, and at most valid in times of a strong profit squeeze. But, once again, we don't really know. We are working with unknown parameters.

In the interdependence of public sector and total economy one last causal factor also operates: that of the budgetary deficit. In the classical view this is borne above all by investments, because the government skims off savings that would otherwise have gone to the private sector. In the Keynesian view $G-T$ is pretty immaterial; it is a loose end in the model. Functional finance more or less disregards it. But things are quite different in the monetarist view. The budgetary deficit is partly covered by the creation of money. This gives monetary inflation, as a result of which prices rise and various side-effects occur. Investments are perhaps stimulated by this creation of money instead of being restrained, which means that the uncertainties increase. This monetary side of macro-economics is dealt with in the following chapter. It will

---

exceeds 100 per cent! This strange result was found by M. Krzyzaniak and R. A. Musgrave, *The Shifting of the Corporation Tax*, 1963. Their research was sharply attacked. All kinds of other figures appeared, and perhaps 50 per cent is not such a daft estimate. But we don't really know.

prove there that it is difficult to choose between the monetarist and the Keynesian view on purely scientific grounds. My preference is Keynesian, but others think differently about it.

The conclusion from this last section is unpleasant. A number of strategic influences of the budget can be mapped by economics, but our quantitative knowledge of the reactions is limited. The capacity effects in particular are difficult to estimate, and the investment equation, which is slippery enough as it is, becomes even more tenuous through the fiscal influence. As the effects of increased expenditure and higher taxes operate against one another, the net result is uncertain, also as regards direction. That is already disappointing from a scientific viewpoint – it is no less annoying for economic policy. The failure of full-employment policy in the sixties may partly be traced back to this kind of uncertainty.

Does the above mean the 'end of Keynesian theory'? No. The Keynesian relationships between budget and income flows remain important ones. However, they can be criss-crossed and eclipsed by other effects of a more classical nature, which moreover are less accessible to quantitative analysis. Keynesian theory can be blamed for making light of our ignorance, but not for being wrong itself.

CHAPTER VII

The World of Money

1 · WHAT IS THE THEORY OF MONEY?

I should imagine that there are few economics subjects which the layman finds as mysterious as monetary theory. Money in itself is a rather mysterious affair – we are daily concerned with it, and it plays an important part in our lives, but most of us have only a faint notion of where it comes from, how the monetary system is regulated, what forces act on it. People suspect that bankers have something to do with it, but banks are obscure institutions and it is not easy to get an idea of what goes to make up a banker's daily round. And if, on top of this, theories are developed about these mysteries, some are inclined to surmise an extreme of scholarship far beyond their comprehension. And yet this awe is exaggerated: the essentials of money theory can be grasped without any great effort, although in this field, even more than in other fields of economics, imagination should be tempered with common sense if strange views are to be avoided. Illustrative of this is the fact that many reformers of society who have more nerve than special knowledge set their sights at monetary matters. They want to abolish money as being the source of all economic ills, or they want to saddle us with monetary systems the efficiency of which may, to put it mildly, be doubted. These reformers often suffer from a lively imagination and a lack of critical sense. If they had been a little more hard-headed they would have realized that their plans do not hold water and that in any case money is much less the real *bête noire* of society than they think.

This chapter is an attempt at hard-headedness. It will try to give the problems arising out of money a more modest place than is often done by economists. This will annoy a number of experts. I may warn the reader that this chapter is based on highly subjective opinions which the author happens to hold.

Let us first look at the subjects money theory deals with. If I see matters aright, there are five.

The first problem relates to the 'nature' of money. Formerly quite a lot was written on this more or less philosophical subject, above all by German economists, but the subject is hardly topical nowadays. Of course we have to know what money is; right, then, it is a good – any good whatsoever, irrespective of its physical nature or further properties – which is generally accepted by people in exchange for other goods. You can pay your tailor with coins from the Mint or with banknotes (from the Bank of England); but if you give him a hundred-franc note from France he will look askance and perhaps prefer not to make use of your offer of payment in this form. Consequently, the French franc is not money in Britain; it is not generally accepted. Nor can you pay your tailor with a claim which you have on someone else, unless this 'someone else' happens to be a bank. This is a most important point; claims on banks are accepted as money, at least among businessmen, and therefore *are* money. It is sometimes asserted (in examinations, for instance) that these special claims are not genuine money, but that view is not to be recommended. Every businessman knows that his bank balance is money, good money, ordinary money (unless it is a savings account – you cannot pay people with that; the savings account is 'near-money').

We do not need to say much more here about the 'nature of money'. To track down this deeper essence, you can go into the historical development of money (beginning with shells and oxen, passing via the Italian goldsmiths and the Maria Theresa thaler to the situation today), but this exercise has little point for our purposes.

Of greater importance is that part of money theory that concerns itself with the functions of money. Money is above all a medium of exchange, i.e. it has the function of facilitating the exchange of goods. If there were no money, the producers of goods would have to search for a partner who needed their product at that very moment – quite a business for the butcher and the baker, let alone for the car manufacturer. In other words, the medium of exchange saves work. But money is also a measure of value. The pound is used in the same way as the gallon and the kilowatt, viz. as a fixed unit in which other quantities are expressed. The value of a house is measured in pounds. The unit of account and medium of exchange usually coincide, but in difficult times they differ; exchange is then performed by means of almost valueless monetary units (e.g. marks), but accounting is done in gold or in dollars, or in cigarettes. This difference is a sure sign of deep monetary disorder and of social disruption.

Money is not only a unit of account and a medium of exchange; it also represents one of the many forms in which a rich man can keep his wealth. It is a 'store of value'. This aspect of the matter will concern us more deeply – for we shall see that this is one of the areas where there is a difference of opinion between the monetary school and the Keynesians.

A third subject with which money theory usually concerns itself – and most thoroughly – is the 'monetary system'. In the nineteenth century and the first decades of the twentieth century the discussion centred above all on the relation between money and precious metals. Money was originally metallic currency – gold and silver coins. Later the goldsmiths issued I.O.U.s which could be exchanged for gold, and later still bankers adopted this custom. In this way there came into being the banknote, a piece of paper issued by a large national bank which on demand could be exchanged for gold. This state of affairs, in which all kinds of money in a country, and in particular the banknotes, can be exchanged at the central bank for gold at a fixed price, is called the Gold Standard. The nineteenth century was the heyday of this arrangement. There were also situations in which silver, or even gold and silver side by side, occurred as a basis for the supply of money. A great deal was written about the pros and cons of these standards, and the problem became particularly pressing when the Gold Standard was suspended during the First World War, reinstituted after the war, and then abolished in the 1930s under the pressure of the Depression. The acceptability of paper money is no longer a special problem today; banknotes are accepted, not because they are convertible into gold, but because people know and trust that others will willingly accept them in payment. They are money because everyone regards them as money.

And the same is also the case with the claims on banks. They are money because you can pay others with them. These claims – they are called deposits – can be exchanged at the bank for coins and banknotes, but you don't need to do this before you can use the deposit for making a payment. I should like to give somewhat closer consideration to this point, because it relates to the creation of money.

Most people think that money is made by the state, and that is partly true, too. And through the central banks – in Britain the Bank of England, in the U.S.A. the Federal Reserve System – banknotes are issued. But what many do not know is that about half of the supply of money is manufactured by other than the state and the Central Banks. This half is the money on deposit or bank money: the claims on the private banks. Such a claim comes into being through the transactions between the bank and its client; the government remains outside it.

The claim on the bank – the deposit, that is to say – can be created in two ways. The first way is by the client taking coins or banknotes to his banker. He thus acquires a claim which he can use to pay others with. In fact the community's supply of money does not change as a result of this. It might be thought that it has changed, because a sum of cash has been transferred from the client to the banker (the quantity of cash is constant), whilst moreover the claim on the bank has been newly created, and thus has been added to the existing quantity of money. True, this view of the transaction is not illogical, but the economists consider another view more suitable. It is their custom not to regard the coins and banknotes which are being kept in the bankers' safes as part of the stock of money. This is just an economist's habit. And therefore the depositing of money in a bank is a substitution of money; cash has disappeared out of circulation and has been replaced by an equal amount of bank money. The total quantity of money has remained the same.

But now note the other way in which a claim on a bank can come into being. A banker can give a businessman credit. The bank then 'opens an account' in the books and gives the business-man the right to 'draw' on this account without his first having put money into it (right of overdraft). In other words, a claim is born out of nothing, and this claim is money, for the businessman can pay his creditors with it. As long as this deposit is outstanding, the community's quantity of money is increased. But this means that the banker and his client, in unison, have managed to make money that did not previously exist. The bank is therefore not only a storehouse and a clearing house for money; it is a money factory.

This truth is not generally known. Even some bankers believe that they only lend the money that they have received from others. They ignore their own creation of money. The economists became aware of this creation of money about a hundred years ago (one of the first to see this possibility was a Scotsman, H. D. Macleod), and it goes without saying that since then the banks have attracted their attention greatly. In manuals and textbooks many pages are devoted to this creation of money, with particular reference to the extent to which the banks, against their liabilities, must have a certain amount of cash in the till. This 'cash ratio' has to exist because some businessmen approach the bank for payment of their claims in banknotes or currency notes.

Many special publications on the operations and the signifi-cance of banks have seen the light of day, which is only to be expected, since banking has a long and extensive history. The organization of banking differs in various countries and times. So do the place and the function of the Central Banks – generally the only banks that issue banknotes. There is a rich field for study here. But for a rough idea of how a national economy works it is not necessary to go into these institutional matters.

The problem of monetary systems embraces considerably more than has been briefly outlined here. The international side of monetary arrangements is also of theoretical and practical im-portance. Under the gold standard the rates of exchange (i.e. the prices of the various national monetary units expressed in terms of each other) are fixed by the gold contents of the different currencies; it will be clear that this must be so, for every currency is connected to gold via convertibility and, given a free trade in gold, the price of gold is about the same throughout the world. If the gold standard is abolished, the rates of exchange cease to be fixed; they can then move freely and are determined by supply and demand. If governments do not wish to have fluctuations in the price relationship of the various currencies, they can try to manipulate the rate by buying and selling foreign exchange. They can sign conventions with each other, fixing the rate. The Central Banks of the countries concerned are then obliged to buy and sell each other's currency at a fixed rate. This was the situation under the Bretton Woods Agreement (1944), which also set up the International Monetary Fund, a kind of watchdog for a monetary system with stable rates of exchange and more or less stable balances of payment.

Unfortunately, the balance of payments of many countries proved to be stable in the wrong sense: they showed an almost permanent gap. Britain was of course the best-known example, along with the developing nations, but the United States also had a deficit in the sixties and the seventies. This led to the abandonment of rate fixing (see Chapter V, section 4) and to the more or less managed float. After the dramatic increase in oil prices the international monetary scene became more and more chaotic: countries like Japan and Italy were confronted by almost unmanageable gaps in their balance of payments and sought to remedy this by contracting their internal flow of purchasing power. This type of policy may lead to 'stagflation' (a recession combined with sharp price increases) or even 'slumpflation' (decreasing production with sharp price increases); and the evil may prove to be contagious. The IMF simply cannot cope with such a chaotic international situation. It is obvious that the internal equilibrium of many countries is threatened by the present international monetary chaos, but these tremendous problems cannot be dealt with in this small book, which concentrates only on national issues.

Let us return to these. We have listed three: the nature of money, its functions, and the monetary system. Our inventory comprises two other subjects: the value of money and the effect that money has on economic events. The last two are of great importance for our purposes.

The value of money is an old problem, which attracts attention again and again, and about which new views are constantly being formed. The next chapter deals with it.

We shall first try to form an idea about the effect of money on the circulation of income and expenditure. To put it another way: to what extent must we include in our model special relations showing the effect of money on the economic process? We shall see that differences of opinion may arise over this matter, in that some neo-Keynesians are not prepared to ascribe an important role to the money factor, whilst others regard this precisely as one of the great weaknesses of the Keynesian system. It is to this problem that the rest of this chapter is devoted.

2 · MONETARISM

The most pronounced form of monetary macro-economics is referred to as monetarism. To some people, including myself, this is an ugly expression. Monetarism may entail a kind of narrowing of the mind. Some people think about nothing but sex; the hyper-monetarist thinks about nothing but the quantity of money. Precisely because I am not a monetarist, I shall try in this section to give pride of place to the scientific intentions of this school of thought.

Very generally speaking, monetarism asserts that money is *very* important in society. This general formula can give rise to misunderstandings: it could be taken to mean that the monetary school has a certain theory about the behaviour of individuals, for instance, that they allow themselves to be very greatly guided in their daily lives by financial motives and that people are mad about money and prepared to do the strangest things to get their hands on it. Now monetarism does not say that. Nor is it of the opinion that society is highly commercialized, that monetary *quid pro quos* form a first-class regulation of human relationships, or that the government must create as many financial incentives as possible to have people participate in economic transactions. Monetarism does not praise the market. It so happens that Milton Friedman, who is the leader of the monetarists, does favour the market but that is bound up with a number of Friedman's conservative political ideas. These ideas cannot be directly derived from the scientific approach to the economic relationships, and it is with the latter that monetary macro-economics is concerned.

Monetarism says that the major variables of macro-economics, and in particular national income, investments and the price level, are mainly determined by the quantity of money. Of course, in addition, real quantities are involved – there is not a single monetarist who will deny that productive capacity is important, or that the existing stock of capital goods affects production. But, given these strategic variables, which are analysed by classical theory, the monetary school believes that fluctuations in economic activity, and above all general price movements, are caused by the money supply. Changes in the money supply manifest themselves in the individual households and business firms in that they can proceed to buy more, and because they can do that most of them will.

An increased quantity of money has in addition indirect consequences, namely via the interest rate. That operates as follows: if somebody has more money on his hands and he does not want to consume more or make further capital investments, he buys securities. If this happens on a large scale, it will increase the price of those securities, which amounts to reducing the interest rate level. A bond bearing a fixed rate of interest that becomes more expensive yields a lower interest measured as a percentage. This drop in interest forms an incentive for entrepreneurs to invest, and that has a positive effect on national income. The circulation of money penetrates every nook and cranny of economic life, and influences decisions everywhere. As a result, all macroeconomic variables are strategically dependent on the circulation of money. If we know how the latter quantity will develop, we also know how national income will behave.

This short sketch of monetarism shows that it is a genuine scientific theory in the sense of Karl Popper. It is a hypothesis that can be tested. In its simplest variant this hypothesis assumes the form of an equation for Y, which makes this quantity proportionate to the money supply M. Thus $Y = k.M$. This is the monetary income equation. The quantity k is the income velocity of money.* This quantity could at first sight very well be a variable that assumes different values depending on the phase of the economic development. But that is not the view of monetarism. In the extreme monetary view k is a constant. In other words, the quantity Y/M can occasionally differ slightly from its equilibrium value, but that does not last long.

If k, the ratio between national income and stock of money, is a genuine hard parameter, this means that every increase in the stock of money M leads to an increase in Y by an amount $\Delta Y = k . \Delta M$. It may not happen immediately, but after some time the value of k desired by households and business is restored. We can therefore give k a new name: the monetary multiplier (a name that comes in handy when we presently compare monetary theory with Keynesian theory). This is the essence of monetarism, that the creation of money governs the movement of the national money income.

To get a complete view of the monetary world we must have an idea of this creation of money. That can be done by assuming that M is an autonomous quantity, which is established by the 'monetary authorities': $M = M_o$. But, as I have already remarked, the introduction of such autonomous quantities is often a poor solution. In this case it is evident that in reality not only monetary authorities exist – that is to say a Chancellor of the Exchequer and a Central Bank, who initiate a fixed supply of money – there are also commercial banks that produce money just as a manufacturer of lubricating oil does with his special product. Such entrepreneurs keep an eye on their clients' needs. The money supply thus reacts to the demand for money. Evidently this demand depends on national income.

This gives us an opportunity to balance the monetary model. We introduce a money supply function, $M = \emptyset(Y)$, which

---

*The symbol k is used elsewhere in this book for the rate of growth of the stock of capital goods. The symbol M is used elsewhere for imports. To avoid confusion, the discussion of monetarism is quite detached from the rest of the book. The income velocity is to be distinguished from the velocity of circulation of money, which is usually called V, and which is discussed in the following chapter.

represents the way in which the monetary authorities and the banks adjust to the need for money. The form of the equation could very well be determined by the fact that it becomes more difficult for the banks to give more credit as the money already out on loan has a greater volume. In that case the supply function is a curve, as shown in Fig. 6. Part of M remains autonomous – that is the part of the money supply that came about through financial operations outside the needs of the public. An instance of this is money that comes from abroad through a surplus on the balance of payments. In this figure we plot Y on the horizontal axis. That is not a very obvious procedure, because Y is precisely the quantity that we want to know about, but we do so in order to tie in with Fig. 3, illustrating Keynesian theory. On the vertical axis stands M. The monetary income equation is a straight line through the origin. The money supply function is a curve flattening towards the right. The point of intersection of the two determines the national income which in fact comes about. It lies where Y assumes a value: $Y = k \cdot \emptyset(Y)$. This point of intersection is called the monetary equilibrium.

In this reasoning national income can change in various ways. One very striking way is that the money supply function shifts upwards. This is an autonomous injection of money that may occur from the government sector (the government finances a budgetary deficit with newly created money) or from abroad (a surplus on the balance of payments: foreign currency is converted into domestic money, which finds its way through business, households, the capital market). The impulse is multiplied by the monetary multiplier k, and national income finds a new equilibrium.

The monetary model can analyse other situations as well, such as the effect of monetary policy. The Central Bank intervenes and imposes a credit restriction on the banks. The money creation function rotates, with the result that the point of intersection moves to the left.

I think that the two-equation model is the most simple and consistent representation of monetary macro-economics, just as the three-equation model from Chapter IV is the simplest and most consistent representation of Keynesian macro-economics.

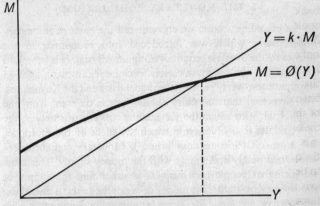

Fig. 6: A monetary model

But we must bear in mind that we have depicted only a framework. One can easily be a supporter of the monetary school and still not believe in a fixed value of the income velocity of circulation of money (a belief which I must incidentally advise everyone against, for this quantity is in fact rather variable).

However, one can then draw up a separate theory about this quantity k: instead of a given constant, k becomes a dependent variable explained in the model by one or more new equations. These may relate to the way in which households and business react to disturbances of the monetary equilibrium; they can describe what effect this has on the stock exchange and the interest rate level. It may also be assumed that people make allowance for expected price changes: if they expect a price increase, they will want to have less money about the house. This opens the way to the prospect of a further developed monetary view; and in fact Milton Friedman and his followers are looking in this direction for it. You could also say that they are trying to find out what determines the demand for money.*

*M. Friedman, 'The Quantity Theory of Money – A Restatement', *Studies in the Quantity Theory of Money*, 1956.

3 · THE MONETARY EQUILIBRIUM

In the preceding section we encountered the concept 'monetary equilibrium', which was introduced into economics in the thirties by the Swedish economist Gunnar Myrdal. It is as well to consider this concept more closely, because it can cast a light on the great controversy between the monetarists and the Keynesians. We have seen that monetary equilibrium is different from the equilibrium with which the Keynesians concern themselves; the latter relates to a situation in which the effect of the multiplier has worn off ('income equilibrium'). Monetary equilibrium is concerned purely and simply with the money supply. This must be such that people and business together find the supply of money present 'right'; the money does not then exert a disturbing influence on economic life. If we formulate the definition in such approximate terms, everyone can more or less feel what the intention is. But if we start to get more specific, we encounter all kinds of difficulties, which is why the concept 'monetary equilibrium' has given rise to such difference of opinion. What follows now is a specification which is not regarded by all the writers in this field as the best one.

It is a matter of giving substance to the expression: the supply of money that people and business consider to be just 'right'. What I mean by this is that it is useful for a household or a business to maintain a stock of cash, but that one can also have too much money about the house. Anybody who keeps his wealth largely in the form of money loses interest, and moreover runs the risk that other goods (shares, houses, machines, stocks of goods) meanwhile increase in price – a gain that passes him by. Conversely, too small a stock of cash is not very pleasant either, since it restricts your freedom to make sudden purchases. These considerations suggest that from the macro-economic point of view there is an optimum money supply.

This optimum amount of money depends on a number of quantities. In the first place national income, which determines the need of money for transactions; in the second place the interest rate level, for that determines the income that the investor sacrifices by keeping his wealth in liquid form; in the third place the yield of capital goods, since the higher this is, the more inclined entrepreneurs will be to maintain smaller stocks of cash and more capital goods. These relationships lead to the concept of demand for money; the quantity of money desired by business and households depends on the variables mentioned. This demand function has attracted the special attention of the monetarists; Milton Friedman in particular sees the heart of monetary thought in this function.

Monetary equilibrium means that the actual quantity of money is equal to that demanded. If there is too little money, monetary theory expects that people will try to attract money, as a result of whi h the prices of goods or of investments (shares and bonds) will fall. Or there is too much money, and then the opposite happens: price inflation. It is characteristic of the monetary school that it likes to seek the cause of such price movements, if in fact they occur, in shifts between the various kinds of investment, of which money is one. This is called the portfolio approach. Substitution of assets is the mechanism around which everything revolves.*

The reasons why money becomes scarce or abundant may then lie in turn with the government, which has created too much or too little money (usually too much, through reckless financing of budgetary deficits) or with the Central Bank, which has issued too many or too few banknotes, or with the commercial banks, which have loaned too much money, or with the influence of foreign trade – a surplus on the balance of payments leads to domestic creation of money and a deficit on the balance of payments leads to domestic destruction of money. This brings us to money as the driving force in society: the monetarist view.

Keynesians think differently about this. They do not deny that there is such a thing as an optimum money supply, that is, one that tallies with what people and business want. But the Keynesians regard a deviation from this monetary equilibrium as something that will be remedied. A shortage of money will usually not lead to falling prices of goods and securities, but to recourse to the money-creating banks. And an excess of money

*Particular proponents of this are K. Brunner and A. H. Meltzer, 'Money, Debt and Economic Activity', *Journal of Political Economy*, 1972.

will lead to less borrowing from the banks. In other words, the amount of money will adapt to the need for money – after all, that is what we have a modern banking system for. Of course, situations may occur in which the banks cannot keep up with the demand for money (for instance, because they are restrained by the Central Bank) and the Keynesian reasoning does not exclude the possibility either that too much money pours out of the government money factory, but those are extreme situations. Of course, monetary theory is applicable to the German inflation after the First World War and Latin America's monetary chaos after the Second World War; in such cases the monetary system is in complete confusion. But the Keynesian surmises that within wide bounds monetary equilibrium will continue to be more or less maintained because the banks serve their clients flexibly. As monetary equilibrium is usually attained, we do not have to labour the point.

Needless to say, the Keynesians do not think that it is in this way that an equilibrium of circular flow in society is maintained. Monetary equilibrium may not present any problems, but an inflationary gap or a deflationary gap can just as easily occur. In the depths of the depression the money supply can tally exactly with what households and business want, but that does not get rid of the depression. Vigorous overspending may be going on, accompanied by a wage-price spiral, while monetary equilibrium is maintained. The causes of these disturbances are not to be found in the money supply – the latter adapts itself, and therefore is at most an accomplice. The causes lie in the interplay of incomes and spending. In the Keynesian view, money plays a passive role; the word accommodation conveys it well. The quantity of money can therefore be left out of the model after all.

The monetary view is opposed to the latter way of thinking. It considers that money plays a decisive role. The following section serves to elucidate this controversy further.

4·KEYNESIAN VERSUS MONETARY
MACRO-ECONOMICS

In section 2 we cast the monetary version of macro-economics in the form of a two-equation model in order to render possible a comparison with Keynesian theory. The resemblance is a striking one: in both cases Y is the variable to be explained, in both cases a point of intersection occurs, which on the one occasion is called income equilibrium and on the other monetary equilibrium: the curves look like one another, especially if we include the Keynesian $C+I$ in one curve. The two views cannot but lead to the same result, because after all there is only one national income that in fact comes about.

The differences are equally conspicuous. In the Keynesian model everything depends on consumption C and investments I (possibly together with government expenditure G and exports X). The quantity of money M does not occur in the Keynesian story. It is a moneyless model. Things are exactly the opposite in the strictly monetary model. The only relevant variable there is the quantity of money M, and $C = I$ can nowhere be explicitly discovered. A multiplier occurs in both models, but the income multiplier links Y to spending impulses, whereas the monetary multiplier links Y to injections of money. These are two obviously opposite views.

The monetary school naturally has serious objections to the moneyless model. These objections amount to the following: in such a model injections of money can take place without their having the least effect. Suppose that the government finances a budgetary deficit with newly created money. That can occur because the state places Treasury bills with the commercial banks or the Central Bank. This process is bound to have some influence on the circular flow! But nothing can be found of that in the pure Keynesian theory. The moneyless model is therefore a too drastic reduction of reality.

To this the Keynesians can reply: that is so, and therefore the model has to be expanded. In the consumption function and the investment function variables have to be included to reflect the influence of the money supply.

161

This defence of the Keynesian view leads to a synthesis between Keynesian and monetary thinking, which we shall discuss in more detail. It seems to me that monetary criticism can be counterbalanced in this way.

Keynesian criticism of the monetary model consists in two arguments. The first concerns the lack of stability of the income velocity or monetary multiplier k. This is a soft quantity, which adjusts to the needs of monetary dealings. Suppose that business wishes to invest more widely than corresponds to the function $Y = k . M$. Instead of having recourse to the money-creating banks, it can try to draw on existing stocks of cash. If it does not have this cash lying around idle in its own vaults, it can set out to look for others who have ample resources. A certain increase in the interest rate may be required to mobilize the liquidities, but ultimately this succeeds. There are always investors who have money lying around – perhaps because they do not trust the market prices. These speculators who expect the market to fall (also known as 'bears') are sensitive to the interest rate level, and if this goes up they will divest themselves of their surplus resources. While capital investments get started the Keynesian multiplier begins to yield savings, as a result of which the financing tension lessens again. The quantity k is not a parameter but a variable.

This criticism is backed by empirical observations. In Britain the income velocity increased considerably between 1955 and 1965: from 1·7 to 2·3. Between 1965 and 1975 it decreased to 2·1. In the United States the figure stood at 2·4 in 1955, at 3·4 in 1965 and at 4·0 in 1975. There is little constancy.

The second argument of the Keynesians against the monetary view lies in the money-supply function. This was drawn fairly horizontally, in the vicinity of monetary equilibrium. But suppose that the banking system works so effectively that it can easily satisfy the demand for credit. If businesses want to invest more than corresponds to savings, the banks attend to the missing finance. If households want to procure more consumer durables than their income permits, the banks give consumer credit in a pleasant way. Indeed, modern banking no longer concerns itself with the specific expenditure that people want to finance; they can be in the red if they want to. Of course it is not entirely Liberty Hall in the monetary world, because the banks have long been obliged to maintain a certain cover of the cash in circulation in order to meet the requirements of proper banking policy. But on the other hand, the cash in circulation comes from the Central Bank, and the latter tends to float along with the inflation. The government too creates money as the need of money for transactions increases, if only because budgetary deficits are more difficult to cover when there is a strong increase in nominal national income. This results in the creation of money which does not occur autonomously but under the influence of the needs of transactions. Instead of a more or less horizontal curve, the latter displays a positive elasticity in the vicinity of the point of intersection. As a result the point of intersection becomes loose. Should the elasticity of $\emptyset(Y)$ be equal to one, both curves in Fig. 6 largely coincide. Monetary equilibrium is all over the place – in other words, the theory has gone to ruin.

Another way of formulating this Keynesian criticism is to say that the monetarists put forward the wrong relations. They think that the income velocity of circulation of money and the autonomous components of the creation of money are strategic quantities; the Keynesians believe that income velocity and the creation of money adapt to the needs of income equilibrium. Monetary equilibrium adjusts to income equilibrium.

In the case of a controversy of this kind there is an obvious way of finding out who is right: empirical research. In this case we have to see which quantity is stronger: the Keynesian expenditure multiplier or the monetary multiplier. This test has been performed by two monetarists, and they found, not surprisingly from their point of view, that the changes in the money supply for the United States over the period 1897–1958 gave a much better explanation of the fluctuations in spending (especially consumption) than the fluctuations in autonomous spending.* But this result was not very convincing, among other things because autonomous spending is so difficult to identify stati-

* M. Friedman and D. Meiselman, 'The Relative Stability of Monetary Velocity and the Investment Multiplier in the United States 1897–1958', *Stabilization Policies*, 1963.

stically – by fiddling about a little with this concept Keynesian critics found quite different results. Nor is that surprising. In this chapter we shall further see that the monetary multiplier may have a much lower value in one period than in another. The Hicks-Hansen synthesis (section 5) teaches us that. In times of depression a liquidity trap may occur that reduces income velocity, while this quantity may be found to be high precisely in times of great activity. With all that the empirical debate has so far been undecided.

5 · THE CONFUSING HISTORY OF MONETARY THOUGHT

In the above I have repeatedly contrasted monetary macro-economics with the Keynesian version. However, this contrast may give rise to a strange misunderstanding – namely that John Maynard Keynes was a Keynesian. That is not so. He was against classical thought, he was against Hayek's monetarism, he was no adherent of Robertson's monetarism, but he himself thought to a considerable extent in monetary terms. The money-less model comes from the Keynesians, not from Keynes. The latter statements will be explained in this section.

When the *General Theory* was published, monetary thought predominated. It was under the influence of the Swedish author Knut Wicksell (*c.* 1900), who had concerned himself above all with the inequality of *S* and *I*. The interest rate attends to the equality of these two quantities, as we have seen in the classical model (Chapter IV). However, the bankers disturb that natural equilibrium. They set a bank rate that is lower than the natural rate. The entrepreneurs eagerly accept it, and as a result the circulation of money is disturbed. The banking system upsets circular flow. Around 1930 this theory was further elaborated by Friedrich A. von Hayek, the later Nobel prizewinner. He pointed to the distortion that the Wicksellian process brings about in the build-up of the machinery of production. The banks support the investing entrepreneurs, while the consumers would have preferred consumer goods. A struggle is waged for the scarce factors of production; this struggle is initially won by the investors, because they have the backing of the banks. But at a given moment that backing will disappear – namely when lending comes up against the limits of the amount of money in circulation. The banks have to maintain certain cash percentages, and lending comes to grief on this brake. Then it suddenly proves that the investors' ambitious projects cannot be further financed. Half-finished factories are not completed. There is no money for that. The interest rate soars and makes new investments impossible. Then the consumers draw the factors of production away from the investment goods industry. The distortion of the production structure is done away with. This is the punishment for over-investing; a depression is created which must restore a healthier relationship between saving and investing. It is a kind of Greek drama, with iron laws, an unhappy ending and many corpses.

This view of Hayek's is absolutely un-Keynesian, and in my opinion unrealistic too. Even the 1929 depression, to which Hayek's reasoning is tailored, cannot be explained in that way. True, in a depression projects are abandoned half-way, and the increased interest rate may play a part in this, but the decisive factor is a lack of sales – an element that does not fit into Hayek's theory. It is worthwhile establishing this, because later in this book we shall be talking about the crisis of the seventies – and it is occasionally claimed that those events too have a Hayek-type background, but I do not agree with that.

One thing that is certain is that in Hayek's theory the creation of money plays an enormous role – the boom and the depression are explained in monetary terms. It is Wicksell with a dramatic turn. The remarkable fact is that Keynes, one year after Hayek, published a book that was also entirely Wicksellian in structure. It was called *A Treatise on Money* (1930) and explained in two substantial volumes how the circular flow is completely under the spell of differences between I and S. The new element is that a surplus of I over S with the entrepreneurs leads to incomings on which they had not counted – windfall profits that further encourage production. There is a note here of the later multiplier but the book remained entirely in the monetary tradition which, for that matter, was flourishing greatly in Britain. R. G. Hawtrey was of the opinion that the monetary factor sneaked into the system above all via the sensitivity to interest of the dealers who maintain large stocks (an exaggerated view of things: it is precisely the fixed assets that may entail heavy interest charges). D. H. Robertson wrote a particularly nice book, *Money* (1922, with very many impressions between 1922 and 1940), in which the banks were implicitly described as the nervous system of macro-economics. Another strategic factor is what people *do* with their money, whether they spend it or hoard it. *Hoarding* is a key word in this discussion. Monetary theory has many faces but basically the idea is: inflation, crisis, depression – they all come from money.

The General Theory of Employment, Interest and Money was published in 1936. At once the difference between S and I as the driving force of economic life disappeared – to the alarm of all followers of Wicksell and Hayek. But it can be seen from the title alone that the *General Theory* was a monetary tract. The moneyless model, the pride of the neo-Keynesians, does indeed occur in it (in concealed form). It is, however, supplemented by a number of relationships that are dominated by money. This has the following appearance. The quantity of money is fixed by the monetary authorities. But people have their own liquidity pre-ference. This can be reduced to three motives: the transactions motive, which entails that business and households have to have money in the form of cash in order to perform normal payments; the precautionary motive, a kind of addition to the transactions motive (for unexpected payments); and the speculation motive. The latter is encountered among investors who do not trust the market prices and prefer to await a fall in prices. (We have already encountered these 'bears' in this chapter.) The three motives together lead to a liquidity preference which, together with M, determines the interest rate level. The latter, according to Keynes, influences investments as I depends on the marginal efficiency of capital, i.e. the imaginary interest rate at which the present value of the future net return of a capital good is equal to the initial price of that capital good. This fictitious interest rate is compared with the market interest rate. Through this compari-son the decision to invest comes about. It cannot therefore be maintained that Keynes had a non-monetary view of the circular flow!

The moneyless model is in fact an invention of the later Keynesians, who have thus completely turned their backs on Keynes in this respect.* The tie with the *General Theory* can be cut in two ways: by assuming that investments are insensitive to interest (a somewhat dogmatic hypothesis), or by assuming that banks attend to an elastic money supply, in the sense described in the preceding section. The latter operation is more plausible than the former one. Once the *General Theory* had been published, attempts were made from monetary quarters to bring Keynes right back into the old camp. One method is as follows: a difference in time is constructed between I and S. National income is formed, and then is $C+I$; it flows to households and then becomes $C+S$. Between income determination and income spending there is one period, and I may be greater than S. That was the case in the period analysis in Chapter IV. This difference must be bridged by the banks or by dis-hoarding. While the Keynesian multiplier process is in operation, the creation of money therefore takes place. The income multiplier and the monetary multiplier work hand in hand. This view has been propagated above all by D. H. Robertson. Formally there is little to cite against it, and the reasoning also clearly shows that income growth must be accompanied by a growth in the money supply. The disadvantage of this representation is that monetary macro-economics and post-Keynesian macro-economics are difficult to distinguish from each other. The view of the strategic forces in the economic process is obscured; we no longer know what is important and what is not. This is not the synthesis to be recommended.

A more interesting approach is known as the Hicks-Hansen synthesis.† The Keynesian part of the model is simply $Y = C+I$,

---

* A related position is taken by A. Leijonhufvud, *On Keynesian Economics and the Economics of Keynes*, 1968.

† J. R. Hicks, 'Mr Keynes and the Classics: A Suggested Interpretation', *Econometrica*, 1937; A. H. Hansen, *Monetary Theory and Fiscal Policy*, 1949.

$C = C_o + c \cdot Y$ and $I = I_o - i \cdot R$. The latter equation states that investments have an autonomous component and further depend with a regression coefficient i on the interest rate R; the monetary sector enters with this R. This is because R depends on the given money supply M_o (a typically monetarist idea – the monetary authorities determine M!) and the demand for money L.* The latter quantity is divided into the demand for money for transactions, which depends on Y, and the demand for money for speculation, which depends on R (with negative sign). Thus $L = a \cdot Y - b \cdot R = M_o$, in which a and b are regression coefficients. This model leads to the final equation:

$$Y = \frac{1}{1 - c + i \cdot a/b} \cdot \left(C_o + I_o + \frac{i}{b} \cdot M_o \right).$$

Here everything is neatly in place. There are three autonomous components, which one for one can lead to an impulse on national income: C_o, I_o and M_o.

The multipliers are different. For spending the multiplier is $1/(1 - c + i \cdot a/b)$; a monetary influence is incidentally incorporated in this, since i, a and b occur in it. For the quantity of money the multiplier is $i/b \, (1 - c + i \cdot a/b)$, i.e. i/b times as high. Whether the monetary multiplier is greater than the expenditure multiplier depends on whether i/b is greater or smaller than one, or whether i is greater or smaller than b. If the influence of interest on investments is greater than the influence of interest on the demand for money, then the monetarists are right. In the opposite case the Keynesian view of reality is more realistic.

This approach appeals to me. It enumerates things and puts a finger on a number of strategic parameters, quantities that we really ought to know in order to test the reality content of two rival views. But at the same time it points to the weakness of economic insight: parameters i and b are not exactly known. They may vary to some extent, depending on circumstances.

The latter emerges very clearly from the variant of the Hicks-Hansen model that is to be found in most textbooks. In this the

---

*Thus this L does not represent the amount of labour here, as elsewhere in this book.

demand for money is not a linear function of national income; in a depression demand is relatively low, in a boom it is high. Consequently, when demand for goods is deficient, injections of money will stick in the capital sphere. They will not stimulate the level of spending. However, shortage of money will restrain a high demand. This is realistic. We can also easily put it in graphical form. But this curvilineaïity means that a, b and i are not fixed; for each point on the curve they have a different value. These parameters are therefore even more difficult to establish than in the linear model described above. Viewed in this way, monetarism is empirically confronted with superhuman tasks.

And in addition, the quantity of money is given in the above. That is primitive. If M adjusts to the needs of transactions, monetarism collapses. Friedman and his partisans do not want this accommodation of M. They urgently advise the monetary authorities to control the creation of money. The commercial banks must be kept in check. We shall come back to the political aspect of this advice, but it is as well to realize that control of M does not just have a political side – the theoretical model must also be saved by it!

6 · AN EMPIRICAL SYNTHESIS

I have tried to show the crucial differences between the monetarist and the anti-monetarist view. By accentuating the clash of opinions we may get a lively picture – but the practitioners of empirical research have chosen a middle road. They try to incorporate the influence of money in their models. By so doing, the ideological struggle disappears into the background. These models are basically of a Keynesian nature: they start with $Y = C + I + G + X - M$ and specify a consumption function, an investment function and so on. But the models are open – that is, we can feed almost any hypothesis into them. If a monetarist tells us that money is important, we can invite him to make suggestions about the place where the monetary variables should be introduced into the relationships that determine expenditure. He will perhaps answer that he is being invited to have his theory swallowed by Keynesianism – and then he is right. But the alternative – monetarism swallowing Keynesian theory – is simply impossible. The monetarist models are too small and too restrictive to be able to integrate all the intricate relationships of modern economics.

Let us review the various components of expenditure. It is clear that consumption can be influenced by unusually large cash holdings by households. True, this case is not normal; a recipient of income who is not a buyer of securities will usually have little reason to maintain a large cash holding. He gets his money on the last day of the week or the month, and then gradually spends it. But sometimes the situation is different. In times of an abundance of money and a shortage of goods quite a considerable supply of money can occasionally accumulate in the possession of the ordinary recipients of income. Perhaps this goes so far that the recipient of income almost looks like a bear. But this animal quality is only temporary. One fine day he will want to spend his money. Consequently, an over-liquidity of the joint recipients of income is a factor which tends towards a temporary future increase of the propensity to consume. A lot of money in the hands of the consumer does not in itself mean inflation; but it does mean a possibility of inflation for the future. Since the lot of money is usually the product of a more or less inflationary situation – for instance after a war – this potential inflation often comes on top of an actual one.

Something similar can happen with capital expenditure. Here too the presence of liquid assets among the entrepreneurs of those from whom they borrow money may lead to increased spending. We have seen that the classical view that the size of I is determined by the funds available for financing purposes is one-sided; but it is not entirely devoid of reality. The financing question certainly plays a part, and for some firms (small shopkeepers, for instance) a very considerable one. A high liquidity facilitates investments. A low liquidity position, especially of banking, may have an adverse effect on the volume of investments. In that case there is no money to form a temporary bridge between I and S.

As regards exports, here too a lack of available credit may exert a restraining influence. In the case of larger transactions the exporter often has to finance in advance. Not only must he first make his product before he can supply it; he often has to wait for payment afterwards. In large non-recurrent orders for capital goods it is nearly always required of the exporter that he gives credit to his customer. He must therefore cover a temporary financial requirement, for which liquidities are needed.

For the government the situation is somewhat different. If necessary it can create the money that it cannot borrow. Whilst a permanent financing deficit is hardly conceivable in private expenditure, the government can permit itself greater latitude in this field. It has in reserve the Central Bank to cover the deficiency between expenditure on the one hand and taxes and long-term loans on the other. But sometimes the Central Bank is unwilling. In many countries it is formally or factually independent of the government, a position which it may use to lend force to demands for careful financing. Often this warning voice does not help very much, at least as far as the central government is concerned. But in most countries authorities on a lower plane – cities and counties – can run dry. An amazing example is the near-bankruptcy of the City of New York in the seventies. And so, in extreme situations, there is a certain tendency for liquid resources to influence government expenditure, too.

These simple relations can now be introduced into the Keynesian model without the latter's essence being changed. All we have to do is not only to make consumption, investments, exports, and government expenditure dependent on the factors mentioned in earlier chapters, but also to recognize a certain influence of the quantity of money. Not a predominant influence; a certain influence. The econometrists will tell us the exact extent of this influence amid the other determinants.

Now I realize that the econometrists are being burdened with a difficult piece of work by this attempt at a synthesis between the Keynesian and the monetary theory. It is not so difficult to prescribe that the regression equations of consumption and investment (and perhaps of exports and government expenditure) must contain a variable which represents the liquidity of the buyers of securities, the banks, and the recipients of income; however, it is no easy task to put this idea into practice right away. Firstly, it is not easy to find a suitable variable to represent

171

liquidity. For we are concerned not only with the quantity of money (which can be measured), but also with the demand for money by the investors. If this demand is a large one, money is retained without this leading to additional expenditure. Also, the bears' liquidity preference is a fairly capricious factor; first an investor decides to be a bear, then he wants to be a bull or a sheep. It is extremely difficult to crystallize this disposition in a quantitative relation. And, finally, liquidity is not a factor that is always in operation; between certain limits it has little or no effect on expenditure.

Consequently, it is perhaps best not to include the quantity of money itself as a variable in the I and the C function, but only to consider excess liquidity and too little liquidity. The basic idea here is that there is such a thing as a normal liquidity ratio (relation between liquidity and national income) and that departures from this influence expenditure.

In this way a greater effect of the quantity of money on expenditure might perhaps be found than if the quantity of money were included directly as an explanatory variable. The latter has been done by Klein and Goldberger and by Zellner; they have found only modest values for the influence of money.* This ties in with the above argument, but perhaps it does not do justice to temporary, unusual situations.

Since the early work of these pioneers, many models have been built that include monetary variables. The results do not support the monetarist view and there is even a clear tendency to return to Keynesian systems without a monetary sector. A good example of the latter is the Cambridge Economic Growth Project Model, also known as the Stone Model.† In its 1976 version the Treasury Model (to be discussed in Chapter XI) contains a consumption function which takes the volume of personal bank advances into account; the regression coefficient is low. But the investment is supposed to depend on changes in output (that is the accelerator)

*L. R. Klein and A. S. Goldberger, *An Econometric Model of the U.S.*, Amsterdam, 1955; A. Zellner, 'The Short-Run Consumption Function', *Econometrica*, 1957.

† G. D. N. Worswick and F. T. Blackaby (eds.), *The Medium Term, Models of the British Economy*, London, 1974.

and on company savings plus capital grants. In other words, the Treasury Model does not allow for an influence of the rate of interest, bank credits, overliquidity or underliquidity on private investment. Not even stock-building is affected by such monetary factors. The monetary school will not be satisfied with this set-up.

7·MONETARY POLICY: ESSENTIAL OR NON-ESSENTIAL?

The expression 'monetary policy' is used by economists in a broad and in a narrow sense. In the broad sense they mean by it all the influence which the government exerts on the flow of money. In that case the government's expenditure policy and its tax policy are the principal instruments; Functional Finance, i.e. the manipulation of the budget, interpreted in that way, is a form of monetary policy. However, a narrower definition is more practical. Monetary policy would then mean the policy of the government and the Central Bank with regard to the creation of money. That is thus the issue of banknotes by the Central Bank and of circulating money by the state, but it is also government policy with regard to the money-creating banks. Monetary policy in this narrow sense stands side by side with the manipulation of the budget. Monetary policy and budgetary policy supplement one another. As to their mutual importance, there is a certain difference of opinion connected with the background of monetary theory described above. Some consider monetary policy a dominant part of financial and economic policy; this is to my taste a somewhat old-fashioned idea, and it often happens that those who follow it are adherents of 'old' money theories. Others – the Keynesians – consider monetary policy less important; they prefer to rely on budgetary policy for the maintenance of a balanced circulation. To grasp this difference of opinion it is necessary for us first to check what form monetary policy may assume.

It comprises various elements. The most obvious one concerns the creation of money by the state. However, it is only in exceptional cases that new coins and currency notes are made in large quantities; it is not normal for the government to try to cover its financing requirements in this way. The quantity is rather attuned to the needs of the community for cash.

The situation with the creation of government bills is different. The latter can quite definitely expand and contract accordingly as the state has to finance expenditure for which no tax revenue or long-term loans are available. In that case the state can borrow the money from the Central Bank and the latter creates the bills if required.

But, even without the state having expenditure to incur, the Chancellor of the Exchequer can influence the quantity of money in circulation, namely by influencing the national debt. He can borrow money from the public, not because he needs it, but because he wants to drain an excess of liquidity from the capital sphere. (This was practised in the Netherlands around 1960.) The government can also change the form in which the national debt is kept. There are four forms possible: long-term debt (bonds), short-term debt (bills) placed with private persons, short-term debt placed with banks, and debt with the Central Bank. The last two have the creation of money as the counter-entry; by reducing or augmenting the amount of this debt the government can cause the quantity of money to increase or decrease. Even without something changing in government expenditure or in tax revenue the Chancellor of the Exchequer, by converting one form of debt into another, can influence the quantity of money. This part of monetary policy is called 'Debt Management'. One of its variants is the open market policy; the Treasury buys or sells government bonds or bills, and thus increases or decreases the quantity of money. In this way the capital sphere – for it is in this sphere that these operations take place – can be saturated with money or be partially drained of money. In the Depression the monetary authorities hoped that they could revive the economic situation by saturation with money – an often vain hope. By applying the open market policy one merely removes obstacles from the path of financing capital expenditure, but if nobody expects a profit from these investments, this does not help. Perhaps the rate of interest will fall, but we have seen that this is not a vital factor in the buying of capital goods. The change in the composition of the national debt is therefore a powerful means of changing the supply of money, but not necessarily of changing expenditure. The open market policy is more effective if there is an excess of liquidity. In that case it can make a valuable contribution towards the stability of a national economy because – as we have already seen – an over-supply of money does not leave expenditure alone in the long run.

There are still more methods of changing the stock of money. These consist in influencing the creation of money by the banks. The government (and the Central Bank) can try in four ways to check or to encourage the creation of credit (that is to say the creation of money) by the private banks.

The first way is that of the supply of cash. Bankers need cover for the credit they grant, and this cover consists in the coins, currency notes, and banknotes issued by the Treasury and the Central Bank. By keeping down the quantity of this kind of money, the banks are ultimately hindered in their creation of bank deposits. The open market operations can therefore be used for this purpose.

The second way is to lay down reserve requirements. This is usually done by the Central Bank. It tells the banks that they can give as much credit as they like, and to whom they like, but they must take care that at least x per cent of this credit is covered by cash. By manipulating this percentage, the Central Bank influences the possibility which the banks have of creating money. This is especially practised in the United States, where the Federal Reserve System (the Central Banks) possesses considerable powers in this respect. Something similar is done in the Netherlands by the Netherlands Bank.

Then there is a third method. The Central Bank does not prescribe a minimum reserve ratio, but concerns itself with the nature of the credits. It says to the banks that they may grant no credits, or only a limited number, on deposit of securities as collateral – for it suspects that this money will be used for speculation on the stock exchange (buying 'on margin'), and it is anxious to prevent this. Or the banks have to give priority in their credit policy to certain industries, and restrain the others. (This is a modern French practice.) Such methods are called qualitative credit control, as opposed to the quantitative described above.

And finally we have the fourth method which the Central Bank uses to try and harness the private banks to monetary policy: Bank Rate policy. This is the oldest method. It is again based on the fact that the money-creating banks need cover and that the latter consists in banknotes or, in particular, credits from the Central Bank. If a bank's liquidity becomes too low, and the bank consequently threatens to lose the freedom of manoeuvre in its credit policy, it borrows from the Central Bank – or, in the U.K., from the discount market, which in turn borrows from the Bank. The latter asks for interest in return; this is the Bank Rate or Discount Rate. By raising this the Central Bank tries to frighten off its clients – the discount houses and the private banks. It will do this if the creation of money goes too far. The banks then get expensive credit from the Central Bank, and will also increase their own rates of interest. It is then hoped that this will restrain the businessman's demand for credit, and so have a moderating effect on the supply of money.

Thus monetary policy possesses a series of devices which in the course of time have been developed into a delicate piece of machinery. Much could be said about the technique of this, but we are concerned more with the question of whether these instruments, for all their aspects, are particularly effective in controlling the circular flow. It goes without saying that those who use these instruments, and thus think entirely in monetary terms, often have a favourable opinion of the effectiveness of monetary policy. I shall have more to say about this in Chapter XII, where we shall see that this policy is subject to many limitations. It does not always prove possible to achieve the desired effect in the short run and for this reason some monetarists have abandoned an activist form of intervention. They do not want a situation in which first credit restrictions are announced and then injections of money have to be given again. The growth of the quantity of money must be coupled in the long term with the trend in the demand for money. According to a strict interpretation of this objective, the quantity of money must grow along with real national income, no more and no less. That is called the 'fixed money–growth rule'. In that case the price level is constant. If we put this real growth at 4 per cent, the norm for monetary policy is set: 4 per cent. This point of view has been defended by some adherents of Friedman, who for that reason are called 'four percenters'.

The discussion of monetary policy is characterized by a certain asymmetry. Though the Keynesians emphasize budgetary policy, they do not spurn regulation of the money supply. Some monetarists rely entirely on monetary policy and think that budgetary policy has a destabilizing effect. In a political respect monetarism can therefore sometimes lead to a dogmatic view of the world. In practice, of course, a combination of all policy instruments occurs. They all have their specific advantages and disadvantages. These will be discussed in Chapter XII, which is also meant to damp down excessive confidence in simple monetary rules.

CHAPTER VIII

The Price Level

1·THE IMPORTANCE OF THE PRICE LEVEL

Until now we have taken the price level P as given. Y, the national money income, was written as PQ, in which Q stands for the national product. So $P = \dfrac{Y}{Q}$. If P is constant, Y and Q move parallel. In that case we can put P (which is calculated as an index number) at 100, and write $Y = Q$. This is how simple Keynesian models deal with the problem. The price level exercises no influence at all; its movement in time is not explained.

This treatment is of course unsatisfactory in times of steadily rising prices. Since 1945 there has been price inflation throughout the world. In the fifties most Western nations experienced a yearly increase in the price level (to be written henceforth as p) of 3–5 per cent. In the sixties p itself increased, and became 5–10 per cent. The mid seventies brought another acceleration in the rate of inflation – in Britain the startled public were confronted with an annual increase in the cost of living of no less than 20 per cent. At the end of the seventies the British price level stood at more than five times the price level of 1950. Or, in other words, the pound had lost 80 per cent of its value within thirty years.

These dramatic events should be explained, and that is what we shall try to do in the next three sections. But even more important is an answer to the question: what are the consequences of this continuous price inflation? Most people feel that price inflation is a bad thing. But there are various views on the degree of harm that is done. Here are two extreme ideas:

The first argument says that price increases are a direct attack on a nation's real income. If prices double, the standard of living is halved. If Y is given – the higher P, the lower Q. In this view the shrinking of the pound is an utterly alarming thing – it explains Britain's economic troubles.

178

But this view is completely fallacious. If P goes up, Y is *not* a constant. Every increase in prices is reflected in an increase in somebody's income. This becomes obvious when we look at the diagram of the flow of incomes and expenditure. The more likely relationship is therefore: if P goes up, Y goes up, and Q is unaffected. There is one clear exception to this rule: if P goes up because imports have become dearer, we have to pay the foreigners more than before. This is what economists call a deterioration of the terms of trade, and it means a loss in real income. This happened in the seventies. Some of the strong price increases were caused by higher import prices – but certainly not all of them. We shall come back to this.

The other extreme view is much more reassuring, and fortunately also more realistic. It says that the price level P is unimportant. This was ventured as a first approximation by John Stuart Mill, the classical economist of the mid nineteenth century. If all prices double overnight and all incomes are adapted immediately; if everybody then had twice as much money as before; if nobody had any debts and any claims to money; if production went its own way – in that case the value of money would be irrelevant. This is the case where Q is unaffected by price inflation. The classicists concentrate on this situation, not because they believe it to be a perfect description of the real world, but because it is instructive: *real* economics – that is, the analysis of quantities like Q (being determined by L, K and the production function), income distribution (being determined by marginal productivities) and growth. The price level is just an afterthought, added to translate all these 'volumes' into money values.

This train of thought is indeed much more helpful than the alarmist idea that price inflation spells certain ruin. It teaches us that we should watch real quantities and that price increases are important only in so far as they affect these volumes. But the view à la Mill is of course too extreme if it makes us believe that volumes are not affected at all. In the words of the model-builder: the price level P (and perhaps its increase p) should enter into some of the equations of the model – and then it may well be that the real quantities like Q, K and L are affected.

The first equation in which the price level pops up is that which explains exports. Given the rate of exchange, a country's competitive position is determined by its price level (and the quality of its products). In a strictly classical view the rate of exchange reflects the price level – every drop in the internal value of money leads to the same drop in the external value of money, and then P becomes irrelevant again. But in practice the rate of exchange and the price level may move in less than perfect symmetry, and that is why the two variables should be taken into account when the movements of exports are analysed. A country with rapidly rising prices may become the victim of stagnation – X is hurt and additional damage may be done via the multiplier.

The second place in the model where P appears is in the demand for money, if such an equation is present (which is the wish of the monetary school). The higher the price level, the more money is needed to let the economy run its course. If the banking system and the monetary authorities do not comply with the needs of the private sector, an increase in P will check itself. This is an equilibrating force, known as the Pigou effect. But most models do not take this subtle relationship into account.

More complicated are the effects, not of P, but of p, the rate of price inflation. They enter into dynamic models. The (nominal) rate of interest is essentially a sum of two components: a real remuneration for the lender plus compensation for the loss in value of his capital. The latter equals p. In other words, to find the real rate of interest we should deduct the rate of inflation from the nominal rate of interest. A nominal rate of 12 per cent and a rate of price increase of 9 per cent (these are roughly the British figures for 1978) lead to a real rate of interest of 3 per cent. If p is very high, the real rate of interest may become negative – a not uncommon phenomenon in the seventies. (In Britain, the year 1977 showed a price increase of almost 16 per cent and a rate of interest of about 13 per cent.)

In the same way the increase in real wages can be found by subtracting p from the increase in money wages. All these effects are relevant to the distribution of income – it is well known that this distribution is affected by strong price inflation. These effects will concern us in the next chapter. They may have important feedbacks to real quantities because, in the course of price and wage inflation, profits may be squeezed, and this will certainly have an adverse effect on investment, production and employment. The problems involved in the dynamics of the wage-price spiral are complicated and constitute a white spot on the map of economic theory.

The point is, however, that the impact of the price level on economic activity and real volumes is mainly roundabout. This is not to say that the impact is unimportant – but it is a far cry from the naïve idea that price inflation spells direct doom for the economy. This is true only when p becomes so high that the monetary system no longer functions. Galloping inflation may undermine the foundations of a nation. Gloomy speculations on this subject – for instance by J. Rueff – may be of a compelling nature, but they lack precision and even conviction. The theoreticians of disaster do not specify the value of p at which doom sets in. Nor is the character of doom specified. Is it 5 per cent? Or 10 per cent? If so, Western society would have collapsed before 1970. In my opinion, price inflation of more than 5 per cent is a nuisance, and two-digit inflation may become harmful to the working of a free-enterprise society – but these are vague feelings. Economic theory does not give precise and well-documented answers to the important question as to the critical level at which p becomes disruptive. Also, much depends on the causes of the inflationary process; some are more dangerous than others.

On these causes there are three schools: the quantity theory, the Keynesian approach and the cost theory. They will now be discussed.

2·THE QUANTITY THEORY

The basic idea of the quantity theory is that the value of money is determined by the quantity of money. The more money there is in circulation, the more prices will rise. In some older variants of this theory the two quantities were even assumed to be proportional; the price level rises and falls in proportion to changes in the quantity of money. We recognize the monetarist view discussed in the previous chapter; it says that national income and the money supply are proportional. Indeed, the quantity theory is the core of monetarist thought.

Of course, this 'naïve' quantity theory does not give a proper picture of reality. For if the national economy grows, and trade becomes more intensive, more money is needed. This additional money does not lead to higher prices. It may also be that wealth-owners wish to keep more money in cash than before; in that case, too, the quantity of money may increase without anything happening to the prices.

To escape these difficulties a new variant of the quantity theory has been brought to the fore, which is connected in particular with the name of the American Irving Fisher (1867–1947). This proceeds from the idea that it is not so much the stock of money itself that determines the value of money as the flow of money. Money moves. This is expressed by multiplying the quantity of money by the velocity of its circulation. The product of the two factors is the total sum of expenditure during a given period. In this connection the quantity of money is called M – elsewhere we have used this letter for imports, but this does not really matter; only in this chapter does M mean money – and the velocity of circulation V. The product of M and V is called the effective quantity of money. MV has become a much-used shorthand expression for total demand. It belongs to the vocabulary of the monetary school. (A Keynesian would prefer the shorthand expression $C+I$. However, these two quantities, MV and $C+I$, are not equal. $C+I$ refers to the final sales of consumer and capital goods; MV also embraces all intermediate transactions and is many times greater than $C+I$.)

Fisher confronts this MV with the total flow of the things that are bought for money. He calls the volume of trade T. These turnovers have to be multiplied by the price level P. The product PT is the flow of turnovers in a given period, expressed in money. It will be clear that this PT must be equal to MV, since the total flow of money on the market is equal to the total flow of goods. In this way Fisher arrives at the 'equation of exchange' $PT = MV$, from which P can be solved; $P = \dfrac{MV}{T}$. Prices rise accordingly as the quantity of money and the velocity of circulation of the money increase; prices drop accordingly as the volume of trade rises at a given money flow. This is the modern version of the quantity theory that is to be found in all the textbooks on economics.

The correctness of this equation $P = \dfrac{MV}{T}$ is to the best of my knowledge disputed by nobody. MV must be equal to PT; the flows of money and goods keep each other in equilibrium. If the flow of goods increases, prices drop, at least as long as MV remains the same.

It is not the accuracy of the equation of exchange that is attacked, but the use made of it. The equation suggests that M, V, T, and P are independent of each other. This suggestion is misleading. For if M increases, it may be that the velocity of circulation V decreases; not by chance, but because the extra money has been injected into the capital sphere which, as we have seen in the previous chapter, sometimes tends to function as a kind of money trap. It is also quite possible that an increase in the quantity of money, if it takes place in the income sphere, evokes an increase in production and therefore in the volume of trade T. This can be seen in a depression; an increase of M does not then lead to higher prices, but to a higher total expenditure and greater employment. Only when these quantities begin to approach their ceiling do prices rise. This increase in prices may assume serious proportions as soon as total expenditure on goods and services exceeds productive capacity. The latter in itself suggests that the quantity theory, although based on the right equation, perhaps does not after all cast a clear light on the actual factors determining prices. For it is silent on the production ceiling, on the presence or absence of what we previously called a 'Hayek situation': the struggle between the consumer goods sector and the capital goods sector for the scarce factors of production.

Reasoning further along these lines, we encounter a real objection to Fisher's quantity theory. It may be that the price level rises without the cause for this being in the supply of money or the velocity of circulation, or in the volume of trade. Just suppose that wages rise. The unions have demanded a general wage rise and have got it, for instance because it was thought that prosperity should be distributed in another way. These higher wages lead to higher prices. P rises, and now changes will have to occur in M, or V, or T, or all three; for the equation $PT = MV$ continues to hold good. But it does not explain the level of the prices; anyone who wants to know why the prices rose should not consult Fisher's equation of exchange, but need only glance at wage policy. Here we come across a fundamental one-sidedness of Fisher's theory; it is born of the wish to derive the value of money from the quantity of money. Why is this necessary? The value of money can quite well be governed by other elements of the economic model. More will be said about this in the following sections.

Other criticism of Fisher's theory is also possible. I consider it a difficulty that the price level from the equation $PT = MV$ is so comprehensive. For these prices relate to everything that can be bought for money. If any article should be excluded, it is no longer true to say that the total flow of money must inevitably be equal to the total flow of turnovers. Viewed in this way, however, the turnovers comprise not only the sale of consumer goods and capital goods, but also the turnovers of intermediate products and even of factors of production. Every wage payment is included in the product PT; T therefore also comprises employment and P the wage level. There is still more; the stock market is included in the equation. A rise in the market price of shares is included in the factor P, and larger turnovers in securities increase T.* And, worse still, the flow of payments MV also includes the payment of taxes; it is hardly possible to make a breakdown into a price and a volume component. Both P and T prove to be complicated conglomerates of highly divergent elements, and no splitting-off of limited sectors is possible.

There is another difficulty. The velocity of circulation of money is rather difficult to grasp. If money moves more quickly, there may be various reasons for this. Perhaps the recipients of income

---

*Since this is extremely unsatisfactory, some economists have taken pains to banish stock exchange transactions from the theory. For instance, J. W. Angell supposed, for the sake of discussion, that securities are bought solely with money not used before; an expedient which strikingly illustrates what far-fetched means have to be used to save the quantity theory.

are spending their incomes somewhat more quickly. Perhaps businessmen are holding smaller quantities of cash in proportion to their turnovers. Perhaps, too, wealth-owners have decided to transfer the wealth that they have kept in liquid form to the income sphere. Perhaps the government lets the money flowing into the Treasury flow out again somewhat more quickly. The velocity is a complex concept; it does not lend itself easily to a breakdown into different components. The same holds true for its reciprocal, the 'cash balance'; a concept introduced in Cambridge by Pigou and later by D. H. Robertson.

Yet this breakdown has been tried. The concept of cash balance draws attention to the human decisions which influence the demand for money. Since the mid fifties M. Friedman (Chicago) and his school have tried to analyse the factors behind this demand. Quantitative research points in the direction of the rise in prices being an important variable; it explains the behaviour of the velocity of circulation in hyperinflations. Friedman's work has led to a revival of the quantity theory. However, the main drawback of this approach remains that money, not income, is the starting point of the reasoning. This seems an unnecessary limitation.

3 · THE KEYNESIAN THEORY OF THE PRICE LEVEL

We have seen that the monetary explanation of prices is old and venerable, and yet at the same time modern and controversial. However, there is an alternative that can also make a strong appeal to tradition. Since Marshall we have had in micro-economics a way of explaining prices that is generally accepted. It is the theory of the market price, in which a supply and a demand curve together determine the price. So why don't we simply take over that model when we are concerned with inflation?

The reason is that we are concerned with macro-economics. In micro-economics a higher price leads to a lower-demanded quantity. This is the 'law of demand', and although 'law' is a heavy word, this relation usually applies. Technically speaking, the demand curve has an obviously negative elasticity. There are exceptions to that rule – sometimes the demanded quantity remains what it is, despite the increase in price – but they are rare. And the supply curve has a positive elasticity, since entrepreneurs will supply more at higher prices than at lower ones. There is usually a clear point of intersection between the two curves, and that is necessary, for otherwise the theory does not hold water.

Macro-economically, things are different. If the price level is higher, this does not mean that the demanded quantity decreases. After all, prices are at the same time incomes; we see that with one glance at the circular flow, and one of the reasons why the circular flow is so close to our heart is that precisely this way of presenting things elucidates the relation between prices and incomes. In macro-economic terms, rising prices lead to rising incomes, and there need be no question at all of a decreasing demand. In other words, the macro-economic curve is inelastic from the Keynesian viewpoint.*

The same holds good for the supply curve. In the short term productive capacity is given. Thus at a low price level the entrepreneurs will nevertheless want to produce. What is more important is that a low price level as a rule also entails a low cost level – this is the mirror image of the thesis that costs are incomes. Here too it is true that things have two sides to them in macro-economics. We therefore have two curves that are both inelastic. Supply and demand stand stiffly and vertically side by side. That leads to one of three things. Either the demand is greater than the supply. In that case the prices rise, without any prospect of equilibrium. Or the demand is less than the supply, so that prices fall; the end of the fall is not in sight. Or the curves more or less coincide – and then the price level is detached, which means that we have no theoretical explanation of what is happening.

* We have already established that the monetarists think differently about this. They point to the real cash effect that gives the macro-demand for goods a negative elasticity. This effect occurs only when the money supply does not adjust to the higher prices. The latter condition causes pure Keynesian eyebrows to be raised.

Now how do we get out of this dilemma? Well, there is a solution which we may call Keynesian. This drops the idea that the price *level* has to be explained. Instead we consider the *movement* of prices. In symbols: not P but p (the percentage increase or decrease in prices) becomes the variable to be explained. And this p is then made dependent on the inflationary or deflationary gap. This Keynesian variable is therefore fed back into the model. If Y is the national income, and $Y^\star$ is the income that just generates sufficient spending fully to occupy productive capacity, then $p = f(Y - Y^\star)$. The relation could very well be a curvilinear one, since prices more easily rise in overspending than they fall in underspending. This equation can thus assume all kinds of forms. But it very clearly suggests that the price increase is nil when spending is in equilibrium. (We shall encounter this equation again, in slightly disguised form, in the chapter on wages – there it is known as the Phillips curve.)

Compared with quantity theory, this way of reasoning has a disadvantage: not the level of but the change in the price level is explained. That is less elegant, for after all we are concerned with the level. This level will adjust; the theory referred to here is concerned only with the process of adjustment, not with the ultimate equilibrium. And yet the approach has advantages too: in year-on-year models it is precisely the changes in economic life that we wish to understand. In that case the level is the accumulation of all changes in the course of time. In addition we must of course make a start somewhere, but the theory can easily accept that a price level from the distant past is taken as given.

Compared with quantity theory, we see another clear advantage: we no longer need interpret the price level as one indivisible whole. The $M \cdot V = P \cdot T$ variant of monetary theory must throw together in one heterogeneous heap all goods, and labour, and securities, in short everything that money can buy or rent. If desired, the Keynesian view can draw up a price equation for consumer goods, for investment goods, for houses; a disequilibrium can exist on each of these markets. It is highly important that the price of labour can be introduced as a separate variable – the wage increase then depends on the tension on the labour market.

If we explain price increases by too great a claim to productive capacity, we throw light on an aspect of inflation that some observers consider extremely important: the fact that people want more than there is available. Consumers want too much. Wage-earners want too much. Investors want too much. Providers of capital want too much. The government wants too much. Tax-payers want too little. The strange thing is that most economists, who nevertheless have long been alive to scarcity, do not put much emphasis on this view. Perhaps they consider it a truism. It is the sociologists who are attracted by it – they point to the infectious nature of ambitions. Inflation is the result of interaction of social groups. This is fine, as soon as an inflation model appears with quantifiable parameters. We haven't seen one yet. There are also moralists who are of the opinion that by pushing ambitions into the foreground they have exposed something very deep. From this one can embark on a critical commentary of modern life, point to the frustrations of a hurried life, condemn advertising and encourage moderation and accommodation. I am not against this. Actually, I am in favour of the bicycle, the carrot, the piano, and against the car and the aeroplane. But these opinions have little connection with science. For the verifiable hypotheses that proceed from this view are none other than those of the Keynesian price equation, which contains spending as the principal explanatory variable. The latter equation is verifiable; the moral judgement that all of us are too greedy is much less verifiable.

This Keynesian theory of price inflation has a striking shortcoming. It predicts that if spending conforms with productive capacity ($Y = Y^\star = Q^\star$) no price increases will occur. In a strict variant it even predicts that in the event of underspending the price level will fall. This is at variance with reality. In the United States the sixties were not characterized by persistent overspending; production usually remained somewhat below the growing trend of $Q^\star$. But prices kept on rising. In extreme cases the price level can rise during a period of stagnation: that is called stagflation. In Britain prices rose strongly in the second half of the seventies simultaneously with a weak labour market and under-occupied machines. Y was much smaller than $Y^\star$, but

p was 10 to 20 per cent. This phenomenon is at variance with the Keynesian hypothesis.

This indicates that other causes are at work. Everyone knows them: rising import prices, rising tax rates. Wage inflation also plays a part (although some may feel that the increase in money wages should be explained by a Keynesian model). In order to understand the interplay of wages and prices – the notorious spiral – we do not strictly need expenditure analysis. This in no way means that the Keynesian theory is worthless. In a macro-price equation a stress term can very easily be included that represents the influence of the inflationary gap. But in addition other explanatory variables must be introduced. One category is self-evident: costs.

4 · THE COST THEORY

The idea that prices may be explained by the costs of production was the one generally prevalent in the nineteenth century. However, objections were also always made to it. Paintings are often expensive, without great costs having been involved in their making. The same goes for antique furniture. In these special instances the cost theory does not work, but that does not particularly matter for our case, since we are talking about the price level, and such *curiosa* carry little weight in that. What is more important is that the cost theory cannot explain the complete price; for the price contains not only costs but also a profit margin. We shall therefore have to go more deeply into this matter.

The price level is determined in part by the cost level. This is doubtless a correct proposition. But it is not exact enough. We can make it more accurate by remembering that it is not in the first place the total costs incurred by the firm that are important, but the costs per unit product. For this wages are important, and also depreciation, interest, the costs of raw materials. We must know what portion of wages is included in the unit cost, and what portion of raw material costs. It seems to me that it is easy to realize that these cost factors weigh less heavily according as the productivity of the factors of production concerned is higher. If wages remain the same, and the productivity of labour rises, the wage factor in the cost price becomes proportionately smaller. If wages rise just as much as the productivity of labour, the wage costs per unit product remain the same. This idea may also be applied to the other factors of production. In this way we find the rule that the level of unit costs is equal to the wage level divided by the productivity of labour plus the level of interest and depreciation divided by the 'productivity of capital' plus the rent divided by the productivity of land. When imports play a role, their price and their 'productivity' should also be taken into account. This gives the factors determining the level of cost prices; they are the prices of the means of production and their respective productivities.

As I said earlier, this does not give a complete impression of the price level; for costs are not in themselves prices. The difference between the two is the profit margin. We must draw up a separate reasoning for this.

The profit level depends in general on two things: on the one hand on the degree of competition and on the other hand on the development of sales. If competition is fierce the profit margins are usually less than in monopolistic situations. The latter is particularly evident when we see what happens in the case of a decrease in costs, for instance as a result of the rise in productivity. If there is lively competition between the entrepreneurs, lower costs will be passed on in the price. The consumer profits from it. If competition is overshadowed by price agreements, or if businessmen are scared of what they consider to be cut-throat price decreases, prices remain rigid; falling costs lead to a higher profit margin. The same can happen if the prices of raw materials drop; with inflexible prices this means that the gain is not passed on to the customer, but disappears into the pockets of the suppliers.

The increase of sales is also important for profits. If the total demand is small, the entrepreneur must be satisfied with a small profit total. If sales increase, so does this total. And this happens in particular if excess demand develops. An increase in demand which exceeds the production potential of a country may lead to higher profits. In this situation profits swell, not only through the increase in sales ('in breadth') but probably also via larger profit margins ('in depth').

The theory that accounts for the price level by costs must be supplemented by observations, in the spirit of the above paragraphs, concerning the profit margin. This brings us back to the Keynesian approach to price inflation, and indeed the cost theory and the Keynesian theory supplement each other.

It is consequently not surprising that this form of reasoning is particularly applied by the practical man. If a businessman wonders how the price level will behave, he studies the markets within his range of vision; he asks himself whether wage increases are in the air, and he makes an estimate of how demand will develop. If he thinks that demand will remain at a reasonable level, he assumes that wage increases and other established or expected increases in costs can be passed on to the consumers, with constant profit margins. If he expects a drop in the market, or increased competition, he will suspect a lower profit margin, and vice versa.

The same method, but in a somewhat more elaborate form, is followed by the econometrists who are building a quantitative model for a whole national economy. They need a 'price equation' which can help them to explain – and forecast – prices. This price equation usually has roughly the form as given above. This therefore means in practice that the model-builders, who must make an assumption in their reasoning regarding the price level in the following year, first investigate how wages, import prices, and such 'large' cost categories will probably develop. They then have a look at demand; they estimate the extent to which the market will allow the shifting of the rise in cost to the buyers. They must of course take into account the degree of competition and government policy (to which we shall return). The government sometimes puts a stop to the passing-on of cost increases; this was repeatedly tried in the Netherlands, and more recently in Britain.

The fact that practicians and econometrists follow the cost theory – somewhat supplemented by elements of the encounter theory – naturally does not automatically imply that this theory is a first-rate one. It may very well be that other theories lead to a deeper insight into hidden relations. But this much is certain, that the cost theory and the encounter theory together form a sufficient aid for a simple and practical approach to the problem of the value of money. In my opinion their combination is to be preferred to the quantity theory, which, whilst well thought out and capable of inspiring scholarly observations, encounters a series of practical objections and is also too closely connected with the typical monetary approach.

The cost theory has a further advantage. It reminds us that the prices that the consumers pay find their way in the form of returns to the entrepreneurs, who spend them again on the factors of production. Someone who forgets this may reason as follows: if prices rise, people can buy less, and in that case the real national income drops. This would be true if the money income of the factors of production remained the same, in spite of the rising prices. But that is illogical. Higher prices lead to higher incomes. Primarily these may be higher profits. However, they may also be higher wages, or higher rents. This is a matter of distribution, which will be discussed in the next chapter. It is therefore not correct to think that 'higher prices' are identical with 'lower real incomes' and less prosperity. Somewhere somebody's income must increase as a result of the price increase.

But the real *raison d'être* of the cost theory lies in the fact that the price of three cost factors comes about in a special manner, outside the internal supply and demand mechanism. The first of these is the import price level – an important variable, given for the national economy and susceptible to sharp increases. The shocks to which the British economy was exposed in the seventies came in the first instance from outside: prices of raw materials had been rising since 1970, and the price of oil since 1974, and, further, the European Communities were exerting an upward pressure on import prices. This explains part of the British price inflation – but only part, for the total price increase in 1975 and 1976 was much higher than in the rest of the industrialized world.

The second special-price category is formed by tax rates. Sales tax and income tax, together with social security contributions, exert an upward pressure on prices – but the rise in these rates is not explained by supply and demand. It is a political datum – that is, a strong argument for the cost theory.

The third price level that forces up costs is formed by wages. In Britain these now constitute 80 per cent of national income. They are rising quickly, under the influence of collective wage agreements. Neither the quantity theory nor the Keynesian theory nor an ordinary supply and demand theory has a grasp on this wage inflation. In the following chapter we shall see what this wage push depends on.

However, one thing that is certain is that the increase in money wages, which we call w, reacts to the price increase p; for unions want to protect the real wage. Since p also depends on w, we encounter a double relation: the wage-price spiral. This can go its own way, irrespective of whether Y is greater or smaller than $Y^\star$.

Anyone who is alive to this spiral discovers countless mechanisms that work in exactly the same way. Wages push up other wages. The professions follow, or lead. Inflation also pushes up the nominal interest rate – this makes its effect felt in the prices. Because prices and salaries go up, the government raises taxes. Everybody tries to pass on cost increases – this becomes a general parlour game. The extent to which passing-on proves successful determines the rate of inflation.

To understand this process we need a spiral model. This competes with the monetary and the Keynesian model.

Such a spiral bloc is to be found at present in every econometric model. It can be supplemented by elements of the Keynesian approach to the price level. For instance, we can make a distinction between cost-push and demand-pull inflation. There is nothing mysterious about that. Many people think that economics does not understand inflation, but that is not true.

Or is it? Here my scepticism emerges. The spiral is based on the passing-on of cost increases. This sometimes proves quite successful. If money wages increase by w and labour productivity by h, then the cost increase is $w-h$. If the share of wages in the price is λ, then in the event of perfect passing-on $p = \lambda(w-h)$. In reality the passing-on is not always perfect. In that case $p = a\lambda(w-h)$. Here a, the shifting elasticity, is less than 1. In order fully to understand the process, we must know a. It should preferably be a constant.

Alas, this a is not constant and we do not know it. I have made calculations for the Netherlands in the seventies in which a lies somewhere between 0·9 and 0·5.* This means that the spiral was halted at the expense of profits. But the estimates of a are highly uncertain. A small difference in a is of strategic importance to the development of profits. In the sixties a was nearly 1 in the Netherlands – all cost increases were passed on. This means that we do not exactly understand the dynamics of the spiral – in particular the shifts in income distribution caused by it cannot be expressed by constant parameters.

Here economic theory fails, for profits are fed back via investments. The spiral sometimes affects investments, and sometimes does not. Stagflation is sometimes aggravated by its own dynamics, and sometimes it is not. We can establish that this depends on a, but a itself eludes us.

Consequently we also do not know for sure how bad inflation is. The cost push can affect production, but this need not necessarily happen. Everything depends on whether profits maintain themselves – then the spiral is fairly innocent. However, we know much too little about this development of profits – I shall repeatedly come back to this point.

5 · THE GOVERNMENT'S PRICE POLICY

As the reader will be aware, the governments of the various countries of Western Europe and the United States now and again try to influence prices. They do so above all in the case of an inflationary gap, which might lead to the leapfrog process outlined above: cumulative price and cost inflation. This is a harmful process; it favours the debtor, forces people with fixed incomes to join the ranks of the underprivileged, harms a country's competitive position on foreign markets and undermines confidence in

*'Wages, Profits and Employment in the Mid-Seventies, the Controversial Case of the Netherlands', *Pioneering Economics, International Essays in Honour of Giovanni Demaria*, Padua, 1978.

money. Needless to say, the government counters this by aiming at price stabilization.

Price policy follows two lines of approach. The first is that of the government subsidy to the entrepreneur or to the consumer. This can be an excellent method if the aim is to keep a certain good cheap so that everybody, irrespective of his income, can buy it. However, this has nothing to do with combating inflation. On the contrary, the subsidy increases the real value of purchasing power, stirs up the circulation, and encourages overspending. A government that tries to combat rising prices with steadily increasing subsidies is heading inevitably for an inflationary gap.

The second method of price stabilization is to influence the decisions of the entrepreneurs who fix their prices. This influence may assume the severe form of a price freeze – in which every price increase is forbidden – or the less strict form regulating the costing procedure to be followed or forbidding entrepreneurs to pass on certain cost increases. In a weaker form the government can try to persuade entrepreneurs not to increase their prices. Sometimes this 'psychological' line of behaviour is supplemented and backed up by the possibility of special price regulations in strategic sectors as a silent threat. Also attempts are often made to promote competition, to counter monopolies and price-fixing agreements, and thus to increase price flexibility. This policy of encouraging competition is therefore indirectly aimed at price determination. The exact form chosen – the severe, the psychological, or the indirect – differs from country to country and sometimes from industry to industry.

The potentialities of such a policy are regarded differently, depending on the macro-price theory to which one adheres. A proponent of the quantity theory will be easily inclined to underrate the success of such attempts. For to his way of thinking the price level is determined by the quantity of money (which in turn is determined by the creation of money by the banks) and the velocity of circulation of money. Viewed in this way, rising prices are a symptom of fundamental disequilibrium. Keeping prices down is 'artificial'; it does not help, for the money will find a way out. The government can save itself the trouble.

The cost theory, combined with the Keynesian theory, views this differently. Prices are determined by the level of money costs and by the profit margin. If expenditure rises, prices threaten to rise more strongly than costs: the profit margin increases. If this happens the entrepreneurs acquire an extra possibility of profit. The additional profit will be passed on in the form of large incomes. Higher profits invite wage claims, and so a cost inflation may develop. But costs are at the same time incomes. If the incomes of enterprises and households increase, investments and consumption will rise. A price increase – i.e. an increase in the money flow – can exert a stimulus in the interaction of prices, costs and expenditure. This process is not necessarily checked by higher prices; it may even be incited by them. And then there is some point in price policy; it pours oil on troubled waters.

Of course the importance of such a price policy should not be exaggerated. There is no question of driving out an inflationary process starting with excess demand by keeping prices stable. An inflationary gap forms a basic factor which must be combated by a government policy, for instance in the form of Functional Finance. Price and wage policy fails to bring about this fundamental adjustment. But it is true that a policy which is directed towards balanced expenditure can be aided by a stabilization of prices. And furthermore a government that wishes to combat inflation by means of budgetary and monetary policies can suffer a severe setback from rising prices and wage claims. Price increases can cut across the balancing efforts. Price stabilization is then the prerequisite of a more fundamentally directed policy.

This important matter (important because it recurs regularly in practical politics) can also be illustrated from another angle. The quantity theory, and more generally older monetary theory, is too inclined to regard prices as more or less mechanically determined quantities. The price level is, as it were, fixed by the economic laws of the market. It goes its own way, and no government can do anything about it. However, this view overlooks the fact that prices are often not so much 'formed' by the market as 'made' by men, in this case entrepreneurs. They are 'administered' by big firms. Of course, in their price policy, the suppliers cannot detach themselves from the market. Sales possibilities set limits to what they can ask for their product. But these sales possibilities do not form fixed data. In turn they are connected with the price level; for if prices are high and the incomes which are paid to the factors of production from these prices flow on briskly to the households, sales will not need to suffer any adverse effects from a price increase. From the point of view of the equation of exchange we may say that the quantity of money or the velocity of circulation will tend within certain limits to adjust to the interplay of wages and prices. The influence goes not only in the direction of M and V to P, but also conversely.

If this is true, and prices and wages possess a certain degree of independence of monetary and market data, determined as they are by influential entrepreneurs, why should the government not try to have its own say in this matter? If excess spending causes increased prices and increased prices provoke cost inflation, and cost inflation in its turn brings about increased expenditure, why should the government have to submit in advance to this price determination and have to confine its influence to the budgetary and monetary fields? This is not evident *a priori*.

The situation is quite different, however, when prices are pushed upwards by increased wages and import prices. If these increased costs are not fully shifted and profits are squeezed, a general price policy loses its sense. This is the typical situation of the seventies. The dynamics of the spiral threatens investment, production and employment. Price inflation is too low, not too high. This rather startling conclusion is not sufficiently appreciated by most political commentators. It adds new material to the controversies on economic policy. The debate will go on.

CHAPTER IX

The Wage Level and Unemployment

1 · WAGE PROBLEMS

Keynes's theory has led to new insights in various fields of economics. We have already been able to note this with regard to the relation between saving and investment, with regard to the determination of the national income, with regard to the balance of payments, and above all with regard to government finance. We have also seen that the theory of money and prices has developed in a new direction under Keynes's influence. However, the significance of Keynesian theory for wages seems to me to be even more important. To be able to define this significance somewhat more accurately, a survey will first be given below of the various wage problems which confront the economist.

The first problem, which has been attracting attention for centuries now, is what determines the level of wages. This is of course a major problem of economic and social welfare. The wretched condition of workers in Europe during the nineteenth century gave rise to numerous pessimistic views and forecasts. In 1803 Malthus saw no other prospects for the workers than famine, disease, and misery, as the inevitable consequences of over-vigorous multiplication and of the shortage of food. His contemporary Ricardo, together with Adam Smith the founder of the classical school, did not have a much more favourable view of the situation. Continuous overpopulation would permanently keep wages down to the subsistence minimum; the wage level would be just sufficient to keep people from dying. A temporary rise above this level would soon lead to such an increase in the surplus population that the old level of poverty would be restored. In the middle of the nineteenth century Marx based his sombre view of the future of capitalism on a similar wage theory, which Lassalle called the 'iron law of wages'.

These gloomy views, which seemed to be confirmed by actual

events of those days, were not without their opponents, however. Adam Smith himself had offered more pleasant prospects in 1776. Increasing production would lead to more prosperity, probably for the workers as well. The Frenchman J.-B. Say, known to us for his fundamental law of markets ('supply creates its own demand'), already pointed out in Malthus's day that wages are determined by the productivity of labour; the employer will be compelled by competition to pay the worker a wage reflecting what he has produced. Rising productivity leads in the long run to rising wages.

However, this productivity theory could not get a firm footing as long as economics was not in a position to solve the problem of how output, proceeding from the cooperation of a number of factors of production (labour, capital, land, entrepreneurship), had been 'created' by each of these factors of production. As long as this problem had not been solved, the economic contribution of each separate factor of production was an open question. This point became urgent around 1870, when a new doctrine of value developed in Austria and elsewhere. Economists began to realize that the value of everything that is produced is based in the final analysis on the satisfaction of the consumer's wants. The value and the price of the factors of production are determined in turn by the value of the final product. But how is this value to be imputed to each of the factors of production? How is the value of a table to be broken down into the value of the cabinet-maker's work and the wood?

The 'imputation problem' was solved at the end of the nineteenth century by a number of economists, including J. B. Clark. They investigated what happens to the volume of production if one unit of labour is added to the labour already employed. The increase in production thus created is called the marginal product of labour. Now the basic idea is that with every addition of labour to an existing production process an increase in the quantity produced can be achieved, but that this accretion becomes increasingly smaller with successive additions of labour. The marginal product decreases as the quantity of labour increases, assuming that all the other factors of production – machines, land, and enterprise – remain the same. As long as the marginal product of labour is greater than the wage, it is profitable for the employer to hire more workers. He therefore keeps on demanding extra labour until the wage and the marginal product of labour are equal. In the state of equilibrium, therefore, equality of wage and marginal product prevails. This wage level theory is called the marginal productivity theory. It is applied not only to work, but to every means of production, and thus forms a starting-point for a general theory of the distribution of the national income.

This marginal productivity theory has been the subject of considerable controversy since its discovery about seventy-five years ago. It has repeatedly been attacked, touched up, changed, reformulated. Up to the present day it has had its critics and its proponents. Most economists are more or less in agreement with the idea that wage and marginal product of labour are equal. But they ask themselves whether it is true that the marginal product determines the wage. It might also be that wages are not so much the result of competition between employers as of collective agreements between employers and unions; and in that case the employers adjust to this wage level the quantity of labour which they can profitably employ. The marginal productivity might then be the guide to the level of employment, since in this situation it is not marginal productivity that determines wages, but wages that determine marginal productivity. This sequence of reasoning stresses the power factor, and in this case the concept of marginal productivity has less importance than in the view held by J. B. Clark, who says that productivity determines wages. Yet it may be said that roughly speaking a certain correspondence exists between wages and productivity. If productivity rises, so do wages. *Real* wages, that is. This correspondence is one of the most basic facts of economic life. We can even say that, roughly speaking, the increase in the average real wage rate in a country is determined by the increase in average labour productivity. This means that under normal conditions of economic growth real wages increase by 2 or 3 or 4 per cent per year. In times of stagnation, when production and productivity display zero growth, real wages also stagnate; we shall return to this sad situation later.

In discussing the macro-economics of these things we should bear one distinction in mind: that between money wages and real wages. Whilst real wages are determined by real quantities, like production and productivity, the money wage level is a much more volatile quantity. Money wages may be pushed up by 10 per cent a year, or 20 per cent, or 100 per cent – but that leads to price increases.

The wage-price spiral frustrates the naïve hopes of those who believe that the working class can be made well-off by distributing large sums of money to the households. An increase in real wages of 2 per cent can be realized at a money-wage raise of $w = 5\%$ and a price increase of $p = 3\%$, but also at $w = 15\%$ and $p = 13\%$. The former seems a more civilized road to prosperity than the latter, but unfortunately the latter figures give a more realistic description of what happened in the seventies. A combination of high growth rates of nominal values and low growth rates of real values often turns up at critical moments in the history of a nation. France in 1968 is a good example: high hopes ending in frustration. Portugal in 1975 is a more tragic case – the abolition of authoritarian rule was accompanied by the desire for rapid prosperity, with a violent wage-price spiral as the result. Britain has also seen that doubling money wage levels (between 1972 and 1976) does not bring prosperity if *as a result* prices are driven up – the real wage increase in this period was only a few per cent, which tallies with the rise in labour productivity. We cannot avoid these hard and fast relations between real wages and productivity by letting great waves of purchasing power flood across the country.

What I shall now do is this. In section 2 I shall give a formal account of the classical theory of wages and employment – that is, a modern version of the ideas of John Bates Clark. In section 3 this is compared with the Keynesian view. Section 4 is about money wages – what determines their level, and their rate of increase? In section 5 we re-encounter the wage-price spiral. It also discusses the way in which this spiral may be suppressed – that is, by an incomes policy. It boils down to the simple prescription that increases in money incomes should be kept within the limits of productivity growth.

2 · THE NEO-CLASSICAL THEORY OF WAGES

The reasoning for this is as follows. The amount of capital in a country is given, and so is the production function. By inserting various values of L in $Q = F(L, K)$ we find a curve representing the marginal productivity of labour. This is dQ/dL as a function of L: a downward curve, on account of the old Ricardian law of diminishing returns. By assuming that entrepreneurs will engage an additional worker only if his marginal product is higher than his wage, we arrive at the conclusion that this curve indicates what quantities of labour will be demanded at a varying given wage. If there is to be full employment, only one real wage rate is possible. We can find this by inserting a given K and a given L in the production function, and then determining the derivative dQ/dL.

This view does not exclude a situation in which real wages work out higher, for instance through union action. But in that case the employers will demand less labour than corresponds to full employment. We can also formulate this as follows: the employers are incited by the wage increase to shake out labour until the marginal productivity of labour has again become equal to the higher wage rate. The amount of capital per worker has then increased. Viewed in the longer term, if the stock of capital goods is not constant, this process can assume the form of accelerated substitution of capital for labour. This is a normal process, but it can be stirred up by real wage increases exceeding the normal increase in labour productivity. Say's Law still works in that case – the whole product is sold – but there is no full employment. The labour market is disturbed. Classical theory thus gives a certain view of the cause of unemployment: too high wages. In this it differs from the Keynesian view, which will be discussed in the next section.

Classical theory does not stop at the explanation of real wages. It also explains the share of labour in national income, to be called λ below. This explanation is particularly elegant and surprising for this λ proves to be equal to the percentage by which production rises if we allow the amount of labour to increase by 1 per cent. This quantity is also known as the labour elasticity of production.*

The thesis that the share of labour is determined by the labour elasticity of production has far-reaching implications. It means that the distribution of national income between labour and capital depends on a technically determined quantity. The production function, and not the power of the unions, mainly determines the distribution. The unions can exert influence only if they manage to change the labour elasticity, and that isn't easy. Power is therefore dashed to pieces against iron structures.

The latter is particularly striking when this production function is of a certain kind known as the Cobb-Douglas function. A short digression on this may be useful. In the twenties two American researchers, C. W. Cobb and P. H. Douglas, sought an empirical answer to the question of what the growth of production depended on. They concluded that this was such that an increase by 1 per cent of L led to an increase of Q by approximately 0·6 per cent, while an increase by 1 per cent of K led to an increase of Q by 0·4 per cent. This relation proves to be described by a production function of the shape $Q = L^\lambda K^{1-\lambda}$, where $\lambda = 0·6$. That is the Cobb-Douglas function.†

This function became tremendously popular – not so much as a key to growth, but because under this function distribution is in fact completely fixed. In other words, if the amount of capital per worker increases, which constantly happens in the course of history, λ does not change. The Cobb-Douglas function thus leads to a constant share of labour in the course of time.

If we consider this result more closely, the insensitivity of

*The proof goes like this (see also p. 53). If the wage is dQ/dL, the total wage bill is L times this quantity; to find the share of labour λ we must also divide by Q. Therefore $\lambda = dQ/dL . L/Q$. If we take a good look we also see here $dQ/Q/dL/L$; that is the relative change of Q that proceeds from a relative change of L, i.e. the labour elasticity of production.

†That exponent λ is really identical with the elasticity of production follows from the proof on p. 53.

income distribution proves to reduce to the following. Under the Cobb-Douglas function labour and capital can easily replace one another. If the stock of capital goods grows more quickly than the population, real wages will rise and the real return on capital will fall relatively. The scarcity relation between L and K shifts, and this shift is reflected in the relative prices of the factors of production. An increase of 1 per cent in the amount of capital per worker leads to a decrease in the price relationship between capital and labour likewise by 1 per cent. In the language of economics, the elasticity of substitution between labour and capital is equal to one here. This is one of the most characteristic properties of the Cobb-Douglas function. The specific value of this elasticity leads to the share of labour in national income being insensitive to an increase in the amount of capital per worker. And moreover the unions can do nothing about the distribution between capital and labour, for, if they were to push up real wages above their equilibrium value (i.e. the marginal productivity in full employment), then just so much substitution of labour for capital would occur that the old distribution, as indicated by λ, would be restored. The completely determinate picture of distribution has therefore come unstuck on the elasticity of substitution, which under the Cobb-Douglas function is equal to one.

A Cobb-Douglas world is a hard clear one, completely accessible to the human mind (no wonder, because it is a world that has been devised entirely by the human mind). This explains the great attraction that this special form of the production function has always had for economists. In addition, for a long time the empirical material seemed to tally quite well with the hypothesis of such a function. And it is still true to say that the Cobb-Douglas yields a usable first approach to certain problems.*

But nevertheless too many awkward facts were discovered in macro-economics that refuted the theory, especially in the fifties when doubt arose about the reality content of the Cobb-Douglas function. The reason for this was that labour's share in national income did not prove to be constant. In almost all

---

* We have already mentioned Tinbergen's work on the distribution of income among persons with different levels of schooling.

Western countries it displayed a striking increase: instead of the 60 per cent plus that Cobb and Douglas found for the twenties, for the post-war years percentages of 70 and later even 80 were found. The share of capital proved to decrease over longer periods. The shift is clearly illustrated for Britain by a λ of 63 per cent in 1938 and a λ of nearly 80 per cent in the seventies. Under the Cobb-Douglas this decline could be explained only by technical changes in the nature of the production function; the engineers could be claimed to have increased λ. This is not impossible, but it does not appear a very convincing explanation.

To understand the shift in income distribution recourse was had within neo-classical theory to production functions other than that of Cobb-Douglas. They were devised by R. M. Solow, among others.* These new functions have the property that the elasticity of substitution between labour and capital need not necessarily be equal to one. A lower value is also possible, and probably more realistic. Empirical research quite often suggests values in the vicinity of 0·6, but this parameter is uncertain. Such a lower substitution elasticity than one has far-reaching consequences for our subject.

In the first place, accumulation of capital at a low substitution elasticity will lead to a rapid decline in the return on capital. By 'rapid' I mean that the decline in the rate of return is relatively greater than the increase in the amount of capital per worker. Real wages increase so much, and the remuneration of capital decreases so much, that the share of capital in national income falls. That is the paradoxical situation that occurs in reality: as production becomes more capitalist, distribution becomes more labourist. The paradox becomes understandable when we use production functions of the Solow kind.

In the second place a low substitution elasticity means that the unions can increase the share of labour. They can force up money wages; this leads (perhaps) to an increase in real wages. The latter increase is not entirely compensated for by substitution. At a low substitution elasticity a net growth of labour's share remains. In fact the increase in the share of labour in Britain,

* 'A Contribution to the Theory of Economic Growth', *Quarterly Journal of Economics*, 1956.

above all in so far as this took place in the sixties, is attributable to the shift in both scarcity relations and relative power. The respective proportions of these two causes cannot be precisely calculated.

In this situation, in which the human mind is in a certain twilight state, new flashes of insight appeared. In the seventies econometricians began to experiment with new production functions. Capital goods are not viewed in these functions as a homogeneous stock, but as being built up from vintages. Every year part of the stock is formed, and this vintage has its own labour productivity. The amount of labour per machine is fixed. Substitution, the characteristic mechanism of the classicists, is not possible within a vintage, but indirectly, namely by changing the age of the average stock. That can be done by accelerated scrapping. In this view entrepreneurs react to the wage push by getting rid of old machines at a high rate. Since the latter have a high labour intensity, jobs disappear at a high rate. At the same time capital is rapidly invested in new, labour-saving machines. The net effect on employment is bad. Moreover, if new investment does not take place as a result of the profit squeeze, employment decreases even more quickly.

On the basis of such a model (a 'fixed proportions vintage model', also known as a 'clay-clay'), a number of Dutch econometricians managed to turn around public opinion in the Netherlands. In 1974 the Central Planning Bureau published an extremely sombre study of the accelerated scrapping and the shake-out of labour.* The cause lay in the wage push, and above all too in the increased burden of social security contributions and taxes. This tax variable also seems responsible for the rapid depreciation of old machines. The (Labour) government became so impressed by the computer runs that, for the first time in history, it advocated the recovery of profits. A restriction of the social programme was initiated: a victory for hyper-classical thought. But at the same time a flood of criticism was launched against the specification of the vintage model. The latter is indeed vulnerable; many parameters, including the technical progress

* *Investment, Wages, Prices and Employment* (a publication of the Central Planning Bureau), The Hague, 1974.

embodied in each vintage, are difficult to estimate. The discussion was a violent one and was directed particularly against the conclusion that an increase in government expenditure that is covered by taxes has a tremendous negative effect on employment (anti-Haavelmo effect; see Chapter VI). For the time being this debate remains inconclusive, but one thing that is certain is that the influence of wage inflation and the increasing tax rates is now viewed much more gloomily than in the sixties.

In this section I have indulged in a rather difficult explanation in order to give the reader an idea of the intellectual strength of neo-classical thinking. Strict logic and empirical research go hand in hand. And at the same time a *view* of social relations is built up. Everything fits together into a fine structure of the human mind.

But at the same time it is evident from the above that a number of things are uncertain. The parameters of the production function, and in particular the value of the elasticity of substitution between labour and capital, dominate distribution – and these numbers are controversial and uncertain. Econometricians dispute the correct specification of the production function. Quantitatively speaking, we do not have great certainty as regards the classical wage theory. And this certainty will become even less after reading the next section.*

3 · THE KEYNESIAN VIEW

There is enormous confusion about the intellectual heritage of Keynes where wages are concerned. Some Keynesians work with

---

*For the connoisseur it may be added that the neo-classical theory supplies us with an exact value of the elasticity of the demand for labour. This is easiest to derive under a Cobb-Douglas. Call the real wage V. Then $V = \lambda L^{\lambda-1} K^{1-\lambda}$. It follows from conversion that L depends on V according to $L = \left(\frac{1}{\lambda}V\right)^{\frac{1}{1-\lambda}} K$. This is the demand for labour function. The elasticity is $\frac{1}{\lambda-1}$: a dreadfully high value, because if the share of labour is 0·75, the elasticity stands at -4. This means that if the real wage is pushed 1 per cent above its equilibrium, employment falls by 4 per cent. Note that real wage is concerned. If the unions push up the money wage nothing need happen to employment, provided that this wage push is fully passed on in the prices.

models in which the capital coefficient K/Q is constant. In that case substitution between labour and capital is impossible, marginal productivity is nil and the distribution theory, as described in the preceding section, does not apply. Other followers of Keynes, notably Mrs Joan Robinson, go further by rejecting the marginal productivity theory most wrathfully. They regard dQ/dL as a dangerous swindle. Their arguments boil down to the thesis that the stock of capital goods cannot be valued in terms of money before the distribution is known, so that classical theory entails circular reasoning, and further that the marginal productivity theory is aimed at defending capitalist exploitation.* This Cambridge School forgets that Keynes himself was not averse to marginal productivity.

In my opinion the key to modern Keynesian thinking about wages is as follows: while classical theory is interested in real wages, Keynes spoke mainly of money wages. He took these as given – he did not find their explanation interesting. Keynes was concerned with the question of the influence that money wage increases exert on employment. And the answer, which is implicit in the Keynesian model, is: hardly any influence at all.

The Keynesian theory must be compared with a naïve view found among some entrepreneurs. This is of micro-economic origin and runs as follows. If wages, the price of labour, rise, it becomes more expensive for the entrepreneur to keep workers in employment. He will have to ask more for his product. A more expensive product is more difficult to sell. Higher wages may therefore mean lower sales; lower sales mean lower production and less employment. Labour, therefore, is subject to the same rule as all other things: the higher the price, the smaller the quantity sold. Unemployment is a sure sign that wages are too high. The depression is mainly the fault of the unions. Wages must be reduced; sales and employment will then increase again. By reducing wages sufficiently unemployment can be eliminated completely.

That there is something wrong with this reasoning is already

*I don't agree with any of this, but here is not the place to go into the controversy. For the Battle between the Two Cambridges see my *Income Distribution*, Pelican, 1974, p. 416.

apparent from the fact that the converse argument can also be defended. Whilst the classical school was at its heights, opposite views were occasionally heard. At the end of the last century J. A. Hobson asserted that unemployment was the result of a lack of purchasing power among the mass of consumers. The rich have purchasing power, Hobson said, but they use it insufficiently for the purchase of consumer goods; the poor would like to do so, but they do not have the money. As a result, consumption stagnates. Sales and employment could be stimulated by a more uniform distribution of the national income; increase wages, and employment increases too. The reader, having followed Keynes's theory in the preceding pages, will recognize in Hobson a forerunner of Keynes, and the *General Theory* does in fact mention this stagnation theory in approving terms.

The view that higher wages lead to greater purchasing power and thus to larger sales keeps on popping up. In the twenties it was the German union leaders who brought it to the fore – the theory is of course a godsend to the unions. But to others as well. Henry Ford defended a similar argument, and definitely not on abstract grounds only. 'I give my workers higher wages than other employers,' he said, 'and that makes them feel happier and work better. With their greater purchasing power they buy my cars. This makes these cars saleable in large quantities, and they can be produced cheaply. Despite the high wages, the costs of production go down and profits go up. But the most important thing is that a large market is opened up. High wages promote mass consumption and are therefore a prerequisite of a developing national economy.'

The theories of Hobson and Ford spotlight a weak side of the naïve view. But they are not complete. If wages go up, many things may happen; it is not certain that total income will increase by the same amount. It may well be that profits, or interest payments, decline. In that case, total income may go up less than the wage bill. But, on the other hand, classical economics wrongly proceeded on the assumption that the national income and therefore the total demand for goods remained constant despite the change in wages. This ties in with the main classical idea: national income is given by productive capacity, and by

Say's Law. Classical theory stresses the cost aspect of the wage, but neglects the purchasing power aspect, so that incorrect conclusions are drawn, or conclusions which hold good for a single industry or a single firm, but which cannot hold water on the macro-economic plane. On the other hand, the purchasing power theory is macro-economic in set-up, but, like classical theory, it is one-sided. In some variants it confuses wages with national income. National income does not necessarily have to rise just because wages do; it may be that profits, or interest, decline, so that the total purchasing power does not so much increase as shift from one recipient of income to the other. A very weak spot is the confusion of the wage level and the wage bill; if one goes up, the other may remain constant because of a decline in employment; the wage bill may even go down. And Ford's view is highly coloured by the fortunes of the young automobile industry in Detroit. Ford was right regarding his own industry in those years, but it is dangerous to apply those experiences to a whole national economy.

In the thirties, when unemployment formed a burning problem, the two one-sided theories coexisted. The economists of the day insisted that wage cuts would be beneficial. Great economists such as L. Robbins and L. von Mises attributed unemployment to too high wages. Less official views claimed the opposite. It was difficult to say which of these theories was more correct.

Meanwhile some had already attempted a synthesis. The Dutchman J. Goudriaan had already expressed the opinion at the beginning of the thirties that the cost aspect and the purchasing power aspect of a wage increase cancelled each other out, so that ultimately employment would be changed neither by a wage increase nor by a wage cut. This was more or less proved in the mid thirties, when M. Kalecki investigated events in France.* It does not often happen in the social sciences that a combination of circumstances is such that one can almost speak of a theoretical experiment. This was by way of exception the case when, under the Blum Government, the French wage level was increased in a short span of time by a large percentage. Prices went up, but

* M. Kalecki, 'The Lesson of the Blum Experiment', *Economic Journal*, 1938.

employment did not decrease. It did not increase either. The considerable unemployment continued, barely affected by the marked movement of wages.

This result is what one would expect from Keynesian theory, namely that employment is determined by national income and income is determined by spending. The level of money wages does not appear in this primitive model. In Keynes's own view the matter was a bit more subtle: higher wages would lead to a higher propensity to consume, because workers save less than capitalists do. On the other hand, a lower rate of profit might decrease investment. The two opposite reactions might cancel each other out. The demand for labour would therefore be insensitive to the wage level.

Actually the situation is more complicated than that. Neoclassical theory points out that sharp rises in the wage level make it profitable to replace labour by machines. This process is called capital deepening. It is good for productivity and for real wages but, in the long run, it may be bad for jobs. If the wage push – that is, an increase in money wages exceeding growth in labour productivity – goes on and on for years it will have this creeping effect on employment. The level of unemployment will remain invisible for a long time, because the required investment creates income and jobs – the Keynesian effect, which counteracts the classical effect. Their balance is uncertain and difficult to predict. But if a recession sets in, for whatever reason, the accumulated expulsion of labour may reveal itself in the form of stubborn ('structural') unemployment. On top of this an even more treacherous mechanism may be at work: the profit squeeze. The decline in the rate of profit (profit per unit of capital) has been a well-established fact in the United States, Britain, the Netherlands and other Western European countries since the middle of the sixties.* It corresponds to a shift in the distribution of the national income: the share of labour increased from about 60 per cent after the war to 80 per cent or even more in the

* See, for the U.S.A.: William D. Nordhaus, 'The Falling Share of Profits'. *Brookings Papers on Economic Activity*, 1974. And for Britain: Mervyn A. King, 'The U.K. Profit Crisis: Myth or Reality?', *Economic Journal*, 1975. The movement of profits in figures is more significant than their absolute

seventies. British company profits, as a percentage of national income, declined from 15 per cent in 1960 to less than 7·5 per cent in 1975. The rate of return on business capital was also halved: from 14 per cent in 1960 to 7 per cent in 1976. In the meantime, the interest rate doubled – from 6 per cent to 12 per cent! Rates of return and interest rates moved like the blades of a pair of scissors, cutting down investment.

The causes of the profit squeeze are complicated and it is by no means true, or even likely, that the wage push is the main causal factor behind it. Yet it is almost certain that wage inflation is in some way responsible. This creates a peculiar dilemma. If money wages are forced upwards in order to accelerate the growth of real wages there are two possibilities. The first possibility is that the wage push is shifted forward to the consumer and other incomes (profits, rents, rate of interest) adapt themselves in an upward direction to the new wage level. In that case the wage push leads to sheer price inflation. There is no additional increase in real wages, apart from the existing real wage growth corresponding to the growth of labour productivity. There will be no effect on employment – again, a Keynesian model.

But there is another possibility: the wage push is not fully shifted to the consumer and real wages are increased at a faster rate than productivity growth. Now other incomes are harmed. If these are incomes of passive investors, like bondholders, the rate of interest goes down and this stimulates capital deepening. This process can go on for years without employment being seriously affected, as we saw before, but if the wage push goes on it will bite into profits. Then we may expect a brake on capital investment – just the opposite of what the neo-classical theory predicts. Now two bad influences on employment combine: the total amount of investment becomes smaller and capital deepening goes on. The multiplier works in a downward direction. If the profit squeeze really begins to bite it may lead to a paralysis of economic life. In this case Keynesian and 'structural' unem-

---

level. The latter depends on the way the figures are calculated: before or after tax, depreciation on replacement basis or on the historical cost of the machines, etc. The decline in profits is not conspicuous in France, Italy and Sweden.

ployment go hand in hand. One reason for this unholy combination may lie with the wage push, although this is not the only reason.

According to some this reflects the situation of Western economics in the mid seventies. Wage inflation has led for decades to price increases and to capital deepening – two things that neutralize each other in the sense that their effect on employment is contrary. Structural unemployment was always veiled by a high level of spending, and the real rate of interest bore the burden of the increased share of labour in the national income. But in the meantime a decrease in the level of profits developed, which has led to a vulnerable financial position of business and eventually to a recession. Some outside shocks – increases in oil prices, for instance – have been sufficient to throw the economies of the Western world over the edge of a depression. In this sense wage inflation certainly has had an influence on employment.

What we learn from this is first of all that the wage push seems to pose a rather clear-cut dilemma. Either it leads to higher prices or it leads to unemployment. Which of the two will occur is a matter of shifting. The two disagreeable outcomes are alternatives – in the economist's language, there is a trade-off between them.

Unfortunately, the economist's problem is less simple than just pointing to the trade-off. He has to specify which of the two cases will occur and this means that he has to come to grips with the shifting process. In other words, what he needs is a theory of profits. What determines their level and why have they tended to decrease since the end of the sixties? Now such a quantitative theory of profits is lacking. We can enumerate the causes of profits – technical progress, being one up with regard to one's competitors, monopoly positions, and, above all, the volume of sales – but their macro-economic mix is unknown. This is one of the holes in economic theory.

The obvious answer to this type of theoretical uncertainty is model building. Indeed, older research, for instance by H. J. Witteveen (*Loonshoogte en werkgelegenheid*, 1947), pointed in the direction that employment is fairly insensitive to wage changes, at least on a short-term basis. But the realities of the post-war decades have not yet been caught in the nets of the econometricians. The wage push is a fact of life; its responsibility for the profit squeeze and for unemployment have not yet been established beyond doubt. There is a general feeling that wage inflation is not as innocuous as the older Keynesians thought, but the quantitative relationships between money wages and profits have not yet been estimated. These relationships are different for different branches of industry; in some sectors of the home market wage increases are shifted far more easily than in others, whereas some industries may even profit from them. A special case is the export industry – wage increases here merely raise costs and not sales. In this latter case the wage push has a definite adverse effect on employment, but for the economy as a whole such statements are dubious and depend on the particular situation at the time.

Under such circumstances very different and contradictory ideas may circulate in political circles. Trade unionists are not impressed by the arguments of those who blame wages for a low level of profits and employment; they blame business for inventing too few opportunities or for channelling them in the wrong direction. Businessmen blame the unions (and, of course, the government) for the profit squeeze. The forces of the market do not point to a determinate wage equilibrium either – after all, decades of wage inflation were compatible with near full employment. This has profound implications for the balance of power in society. Before we go further into this we should first consider the question we discussed very provisionally in the previous section: What determines the wage level?

4 · ONCE MORE THE SPIRAL

The empirical models of today always contain price equations and wage equations that in interplay yield a spiral. In this section, which is an extension to section 4 of the preceding chapter, I want to show you how explosively that can work out.

Let us first assume that the price equation is of the simple cost-push type. The price increase p is then determined by the wage increase w in so far as the latter exceeds the increase in productivity h, and by the increase in the other incomes, which we shall call z. This z is therefore roughly the percentage increase in the gross profit margin. Further, in realistic models the increase in import prices is also included, along with the rise in tax burden on consumer goods, but for the time being we shall leave the last two influences out of consideration. We are therefore talking about a purely domestic cost push. If income distribution between labour and capital remains unchanged (the share of labour λ is constant) and further capital productivity is constant (this more or less fits in with reality), $p = \lambda(w-h)+(1-\lambda)z$. This is simple cost push, without monetary influence and without any influence on underspending or overspending.

The equation for the increase in money wages w can likewise start in the first instance from a constant share of labour. We have seen that in this case real wages rise just as quickly as labour productivity, or money wages rise with prices and labour productivity; therefore $w = p+h$. From the combination of the price and the wage equations it follows that $p = z$. This means that the two conditions – a perfect cost-push inflation and a constant share of labour – can be realized at any level of p and w. The spiral can therefore continue unchecked, *provided that the gross profit margin grows along with prices* or, which is the same thing, the percentage mark-up remains constant. The result may then be a price inflation of 5 per cent, or 10 per cent, or 50 per cent. Anything is possible. We can also put this in another way, viz. that at a given share of labour and perfect passing-on of wage inflation, the spiral model does not elucidate what actually happens. The price increase is determined by something else – the monetary school would know what that was, namely the quantity of money.

Does this mean that we can forget the spiral model? No. Even in this simple form, it teaches us right away what is going to happen if the unions want to increase the share of labour while businessmen keep the relative profit margin constant. Then the equations enter into conflict – very high rates of inflation break out. Galloping inflation can therefore be caused by a very simple interplay of social groups battling for income distribution.

But these are only speculations on what is possible. We can most certainly explain the actual inflation of the seventies by means of a spiral model, but in that case it must be set up more realistically than the incomplete mini-model (two equations with four unknowns) that we have been considering so far. Allowance must be made for import prices – they were fairly constant during the period 1960–70, after which they began to rise, and after 1973 the increase became extremely high (the oil crisis). The gradual rise in the rate of taxation will also have to be taken into account. A more extensive price equation of this kind must be combined with a wage equation, in which the increases in money wages depend on the rise of the cost of living (indexation), productivity and perhaps on the labour market situation (Phillips curve). Moreover, the model must be dynamic in set-up, i.e. must include time lags. Such equations show us how an initial impulse, for instance among import prices, can have considerable consequences. The spiral maintains itself. Anyone who ponders such models at length is not surprised that the price increase in Britain grew to nearly 25 per cent in 1975 – what is instead surprising is that a few years later (1978) the price increase had been reduced to approximately 10 per cent. There was no explosion.

It is therefore possible to break out of the vicious circle. That is because the impulse from import prices may decrease (as it did after 1975) and also because some income categories do not manage to maintain their position. They act as a buffer. In the seventies these categories were interest (the real rate of interest became almost nil and occasionally negative!) and profits. The assumption of the explosive model is a constant relative profit margin ($z = p$), but business was unable to achieve that target. The cost increases were insufficiently passed on. The result was a profit squeeze, as described above. This is favourable from a viewpoint of inflation but unfavourable for investments, employment and growth. The wage-price spiral was therefore partly to blame for the stagnation – not because the price increase was too high, but because it worked out too low.*

* This means that those authors who always attribute price inflation to profits are wrong. The most extreme representative of this trend is C. Levinson, *Capital, Inflation and the Multinationals*, 1971. This view is just

Perhaps the reader has gained the impression that the spiral model explains inflation quite well. That impression is a correct one, as long as we describe what happens in words only. But if we demand genuine quantitative information – that is, genuine science! – we ought to remember what was said in the preceding chapter. The results of the model, i.e. the wage and price increase, are strongly influenced by the coefficients showing the influence of w on p and, we may now add, of p on w. Above all the passing-on of cost increases is a strategic factor. If this passing-on coefficient is one, we get something quite different from what we get at $0 \cdot 8$ and $0 \cdot 6$. The results are highly sensitive. And now it so happens that we do not know these passing-on coefficients very well. Nor are they constant in time. In the seventies, with their low spending, they were probably lower than in the sixties, when the general situation was a thriving one.

This lack of insight means that we do not know for certain why Britain has a fiercer wage-price inflation than other countries. In 1975 the price increase in Britain was nearly 25 per cent, in the United States 9 per cent, in the Federal Republic of Germany 6 per cent. Why the differences? Probably they are due to the values of the passing-on coefficients. But where do these values come from? That is speculation, not empirical science.

All this is a reason for intellectual modesty. But one thing that is certain is that the wage-price spiral is dangerous because it can affect real quantities, such as production, investments and employment. Moreover, inflation is unfair to people with fixed incomes. The spiral model suggests a simple political solution for these problems. It may be deficient empirically, but from a viewpoint of economic steersmanship it is in a strong position. We do not need the exact values of the parameters and yet derive a political recipe from the model.

This solution consists in a wage policy on the strength of $w = h$ and a profit policy on the strength of $z = 0$. Wages are

---

as untenable as the other extreme, which states that inflation is caused exclusively by the 'wage grab'. A highly suggestive article along these lines may be found in the *Economist* of 5 December 1975, under the title 'The Doom Syndrome'. In my opinion the *Economist* is somewhat closer to the truth than Levinson, but they both forget the interaction of the spiral model, linked to productivity and relative profit margins may not increase. By concentrating this rule on various kinds of labour – miners, dockers – and making teachers and policemen keep in line with the rest we get an incomes policy that suppresses the spiral.

As the reader knows, much has been said in recent decades about such a policy. It has been tried out again and again, particularly in Britain – with little success.* I shall revert to the difficulties of an incomes policy (Chapter XII), but I should like to spotlight one objection at this point, because it proceeds directly from the spiral model. To avoid the wage push we need $w = h$; but to keep labour's share constant we need $w = p+h$. To break out of the spiral the unions must therefore start by accepting a temporary reduction of λ. They don't like this and the same applies to every special group of workers. It is difficult to find a beginning for this moderation. Consequently an incomes policy must always begin gradually – after you, is the polite cry – which in practice boils down to its not beginning. Meanwhile, inflation continues and everybody complains about a phenomenon which we all keep alive together.

*An example: in 1977 the British Government wanted to keep wage increases down to 10 per cent. In that same year the firemen put forward a demand for 30 per cent and the miners one for 90 per cent. In the light of this, the final result – an average wage increase of 15 per cent – might have been much worse. But in that year the increase in productivity was at most 2 per cent. The difference between w and h, i.e. 13 per cent, is the wage inflation – a solid basis for the spiral in the following year.

CHAPTER X

Economic Growth

1 · THE TOPICALITY OF GROWTH THEORY

As long as economics has been in existence it has displayed interest in economic growth – that is to say in the increase of the national income per head. But the intensity and the focal point of interest have kept on changing. The mercantilists wanted to develop industry and trade to make the state strong and rich, and they regarded restrictions on imports as one of the most suitable ways of doing this. Adam Smith believed that a free development of the productive forces would best serve progress. The accumulation of capital, technological progress, and the increasing division of labour would gradually cause the production per head to grow. Ricardo had a much gloomier view of this: an increasing population would lead to low wages, to a shortage of land, and thus to high rents; profits would suffer from this and growth would, as a result, stagnate. Such pessimism continues to ring through the nineteenth century, and gave economics its name of the dismal science. In Marx's theory, too, 'development' means decline, at least under capitalism; his macro-economics rather resembles that of Ricardo, but has a dramatic conclusion: the collapse of the capitalistic system.

Adam Smith's optimistic view, which has proved much more realistic, also keeps on turning up, for instance in John Stuart Mill and later in J. Schumpeter, who pushed forward the entrepreneur as the man who, by 'new combinations', keeps growth on the go. But the neo-classical theory of the twentieth century begins to display a certain interest in the Stationary State: an economic movement which keeps on turning in the same circle and in which all quantities are at rest. There are no savings, no investments. Economic life has entered its final stage. A. C. Pigou, for instance, elaborated on this strange idea, and the problem of growth disappeared from view as a result.

Moreover, in the thirties the old pessimism returns in a new form: that of stagnation and the perpetual depression. In the Keynesian world of ideas economic growth remains in the background at first. The conquering of deflation was too urgent an aim to allow of an intensive study of a development of income over longer periods. Although reflections on the distant future are not entirely absent from the *General Theory*, as a rule Keynes takes productive capacity and the state of technology as given. He observes the income effect of investments, and not the capacity effect. This is an obvious one-sidedness, in fact exactly the opposite of the one-sidedness which we encountered among the classicists in section 3 of Chapter II.

After the war new interest was aroused in growth, which since then has assumed unprecedented proportions. There are various reasons for this new interest. In the first place the economic renaissance of Europe, and more particularly the increased growth rate, encouraged a study of the phenomenon that was being enacted under the noses of the investigators. Whilst the percentages by which the national income per head in Europe rose over long periods – for instance a century – were about 1 or 2, and really only displayed higher figures – 3 to 4 – in the twenties, the post-war growth rates increased to 4 and 5 per cent. The fifties were good and the sixties even better. Some countries, like Japan, managed to reach figures well above 10 per cent a year. This New Golden Age required an explanation. Moreover, some countries did not do so well – Britain, for instance, was constantly lagging behind the rest of Europe.* These differences in growth rates between countries formed a challenge to the explanatory power of economics.

In the meantime, the problem of growth derives its greatest urgency from the realization that the grinding poverty in three-quarters of the world is intolerable. Much of growth theory there-

---

*From 1955 to 1973, the period before the recession, output per head in U.K. manufacturing rose by an annual average of 3·2 per cent. The figure for continental Western Europe was 5 per cent. The difference looks slight, but its cumulative impact is substantial: the increase in the level of output per head was about 75 per cent in Britain, and 150 per cent on the Continent. Such are the laws of growth: the small difference counts.

fore concentrates on the problems of underdeveloped countries. These problems are tremendous and demand a rather different approach – a more sociological one – from the one which we have in mind in this book. The reader will forgive me if I pass over this side of the matter.

Finally, at the end of the sixties new criticism of growth broke out. Formerly, distinguished minds had occasionally commented that there was really something vulgar about increasing real incomes for all and sundry – but this conservative and romantic criticism had never made much impression. Most people wanted better houses, more education, more transport (above all to exotic countries), more recreation – and economists noted these unmistakable wishes. However, the new criticism means that these desires cannot be met. We shall grind to a halt because of pollution, shortages of natural resources and an energy crisis. This view has become a topical one above all through the first report of the Club of Rome, *The Limits to Growth* (1972). There is now a flood of new literature on this subject. I shall consider it briefly, but this chapter is mainly concerned with the familiar contrast: that between the classical and the Keynesian view.

2 · THE CONSTANT IN GROWTH

It seems as if everything changes in the course of growth. Formerly there was no television and still earlier there were no cars. Once there were no unions and social laws – now there are. The government sector has spread to a formidable extent. Agriculture has relatively shrunk, industry first became larger and then relatively smaller, and the service sector is rapidly expanding. The computer is changing life. By thinking about these things one easily arrives at the conclusion that no constants can be discovered in the growth process – if this is the case, economists can shut up shop and make way for the historians.

But the point is that rather unwieldy relations are quite definitely to be found in the trends. Let me mention five possible candidates.

(1) The growth rate q. This is almost always positive. (The exceptions are the 1930s and 1975.) Over long periods – say two

centuries – we see a strikingly gradual movement. The classical theory would even have us believe that fundamental forces keep q on a fixed growth path. That yields an interesting theory – see the next section – but empirically it does not hold water. The growth rate fluctuates in time. It was high in the sixties, and low in the seventies. There are very clearly Keynesian influences at work that depressed q in the seventies. It is often claimed that these forces making for stagnation also include a fatal process of weariness of Western civilization; some observers act as if from now on q will be negative. However, it is difficult to see why the seventies should yield such a tremendous breach in the historical structure. The growth rate will therefore remain positive. Perhaps the flourishing figures of the sixties were the exception that has to be explained, and not the other way round.*

(2) While the growth rate of production q is not constant, the growth rate of labour productivity $q-1$ displays a much more stubborn character, especially if we take averages of, for instance, three years. Even in slow years in which production does not increase very much the rise in productivity continues – which then results by definition in a declining number of jobs. The unemployment of the seventies can be explained by this in part. And yet the growth of productivity over longer periods is again not entirely constant; there are times when it goes more quickly. There are also differences between countries (see the preceding section). This is concerned with technical progress.

(3) Technical progress is the mainspring of growth. We define this quantity as that part of the growth of production which

---

*If q is constant, we speak of exponential growth. The formula $Q_t = Q_o e^{q \cdot t}$ applies to this, in which Q_t is the real income in period t and Q_o the initial level (period 0). The growth rate is q, exponent t indicates the time and e is a number about equal to $2 \cdot 718$. The formula entails that Q doubles in a period that is equal to 70 divided by the growth rate. For instance, a quantity that grows by a modest $2 \cdot 5$ per cent a year has a doubling time of about twenty-eight years. By thinking about this a person can enter into a very jolly frame of mind (even before retirement he will become just as prosperous as someone now earning twice as much) or become extremely depressed (if production doubles the number of oil disasters and road accidents will increase by the same extent, and perhaps even more). Exponential growth has been depicted by the partisans of the Club of Rome as a very nasty thing.

cannot be ascribed to the growth of capital and of labour. The symbol for this residual value is q'. We shall later see that classical theory has found a magic formula for this q', which also more or less tallies empirically. This formula is $q' = \lambda(q-1)$. In ordinary English this means that technical progress is equal to the share of labour times the growth of labour productivity.

Like other such relations it applies only approximately and over longer periods. I suspect that technical progress is somewhat more constant than the growth of labour productivity. Perhaps q' will prove to be one of the parameters of the growth model. We shall return to the question of technical progress.

(4) The capital coefficient or capital-output ratio, defined as the stock of capital goods divided by real national income, comes near to a constant, viewed historically. Figures of 3, 4 and 5 are often mentioned. The theories of growth are therefore built up on this quantity. We shall see that the classical theory regards the immobility of this coefficient as the result of a process of equilibrium, while the Keynesian growth theory regards the capital-output ratio as a pre-set quantity – a real parameter. Whichever of the two approaches one chooses will determine the nature of the growth process – this statement will be explained in the following sections.

A constant capital-output ratio implies a constant capital productivity. Growth has manifested itself as growth of labour productivity. This is a very fortunate circumstance for the human race, since it is labour productivity and not capital productivity that determines the real income per head. This thesis which will seem strange at first sight was explained in Chapter II.

(5) Income distribution between labour and capital is not constant but changes slowly. In the short term the share of labour λ and the share of capital κ may be taken as given – that too is an important element of growth theory. We saw in the preceding chapter how classical theory explains the fixed nature of λ and κ.

From these five elements a coherent theory must now be built up. This theory must in the first place explain the height of q. In addition other problems arise that are connected with the stability of growth. The classical view – the reader will not be surprised to learn – regards the process of growth as a balanced one. The Keynesian approach predicts instability. Let us examine that now.

3·THE CLASSICAL GROWTH FUNCTION

Classical theory explains the level of production by using a production function $Q = F(L, K)$. The growth rate q is therefore explained by the growth rates of the working population l and the capital stock k. Now the question is: if the production function is given, what does the growth function $q = f(l, k)$ look like?

The answer is given by marginal productivity theory, as set forth in the preceding chapter. There the elasticity of production with regard to labour was set out; this is the percentage increase in Q which follows from an increase in the labour force by 1 per cent. Call this elasticity ε_L. In the same way the elasticity of production with respect to capital is ε_K. Because q, l and k are percentages, the growth function cannot be anything else but $q = \varepsilon_L l + \varepsilon_K k$. That is, if the production function stays where it is; then all growth is explained by growth of labour and capital. The growth function, as described here, is not the last word that classical theory has to say on the subject. The next step is this. Under conditions of perfect competition the elasticity ε_L equals λ, the share of labour in national income. And $\varepsilon_K = K$, the share of capital. We therefore have $q = \lambda l + \kappa \cdot k$, or, because $\lambda + \kappa = 1$, $q = \lambda l + (1 - \lambda)k$. This can be reproduced in words as follows: the percentage growth of production is equal to the percentage growth of the amount of labour times the share of labour plus the percentage growth of capital times the share of capital. Or, to put it differently, the percentage growth of production is equal to the weighted sum of the growth percentages of the factors of production, the shares in the national income being used as weightings. This fundamental growth equation holds good only if technology does not change; if the production function shifts, q is larger than the growth function indicates.

But even if the reader finds this too erudite, he can still grasp the meaning of the growth function. The contribution that for instance capital makes to growth depends on investment and on the importance of capital in the whole production process. The same applies to labour. This may be explained by means of the following example in figures. Let us assume that the working population of a country increases annually by 1·5 per cent, and that the investors cause the stock of capital goods to grow by 6 per cent a year. The share of labour is for instance two-thirds, and in that case the share of capital in the broad sense (including rent and profit) is one-third. Production then grows by $\frac{2}{3}$ times 1·5 per cent plus $\frac{1}{3}$ times 6 per cent = 3 per cent. And if we are especially interested in the growth of production per head of population (or in the growth of the productivity of labour; as long as the population and the working population grow at the same rate, this amounts to the same thing), this percentage can also be easily calculated: of the 3 per cent growth in production 1·5 per cent must be deducted for the population growth, and 1·5 per cent growth remains for increasing prosperity.

This calculation also clearly demonstrates how population growth exerts a negative influence on income per head. While the population increases by 1·5 per cent, as a result production grows by only 1 per cent, and the income per head thus drops 0·5 per cent. In our specimen calculation this is more than made up for by the formation of capital, but the prosperity would have been greater if the increased stock of capital goods had been combined with a population growing more slowly or remaining stationary.

The neo-classical theory of growth starts from the growth function as defined here. It works with the concept of factors of production that can be combined in different relationships; in other words, labour and capital can replace each other. That distinguishes the genuine neo-classical theory of growth from the more neo-Keynesian one that will be discussed in the following section: the theory of Harrod and Domar, which starts from a fixed relationship between the amount of capital and the amount of final product. This fixed relationship has strange consequences, as we shall see below, and it is probably not a realistic description of reality. The neo-classical theory will have nothing to do with a fixed coefficient of this kind. It studies the case in which the amounts of labour and capital smoothly adjust to one another.

That, too, is perhaps not quite realistic; it sounds too good to be true. And classical theory completely abstracts from the sales disturbances that may occur in the process of growth. As we know, that is a consequence of Say's Law, which the classicists adhere to as a kind of simplification. Through this abstraction the neo-classical authors concentrate their attention fully on the supply side of production. In their view investment is fully determined by the relationship between wages and interest; a sales deficit that paralyses the growth of capital has been excluded from the model. An intellectual concentration of this kind may yield useful results and in fact the neo-classical theory of growth has, since the second half of the 1950s, been developed into a remarkable construction, full of surprises and incredible conclusions. Unfortunately, it is too complicated to be dealt with here in its full majesty, but some of its principal properties may be explained. The most important one is this: the neo-classical theory of growth concentrates on equilibrium. In this case not a stationary state but a well-balanced growth equilibrium. Of the various 'growth paths', that one is selected for further study which shows certain regularities.

This leads to special attention for what is now called the State of Steady Growth. This is by definition a constant growth percentage through the course of the years, that is to say a given q. Now it can be proved that a constant q implies that q is identical with k. In other words, growth is steady only if production increases as quickly as the stock of capital goods! The proof is simple. Assume that the savers start to save more than before, so that k increases and becomes greater than q. In that case, by definition, the fraction Q/K, i.e. the productivity of capital, drops. The effect of the increased accumulation is reduced by the lower productivity of capital. This decline of Q/K continues as long as k is greater than q. The productivity of capital does not reach equilibrium again until capital and production grow again side by side.

Bearing the equality $k = q$ in mind, all kinds of equations can be drawn up. This equality may be entered into the growth function to see what the result is. I shall leave the algebra to the reader, and advise him also to work out the equation for the growth of real income per head $(q-l)$. He will find that, in the State of

Steady Growth, $q-l$ is equal to zero. Production increases just as quickly as the population and real income per head is constant. Now this is one of the surprising tricks of neo-classical thought; we started by assuming a constant growth of production, and this simple idea gives birth to a system in which, production, capital and population increase at the same rate! By some peculiar intellectual trick the State of Steady Growth has been turned into something which resembles the Stationary State!

Something else emerges which is perhaps even stranger. The propensity to save has no effect on the rate of growth. If the recipients of income allow s to increase, so does S and, as a result, I and also k, but in that case the growth rate is no longer steady. The productivity of capital decreases and forces the system back to the old rate of growth. The savers cannot influence the balanced growth rate. They may succeed in throwing the system off the equilibrium growth path, but that only temporarily. The growth rate returns to its 'steady' value. Even the savers are powerless *vis-à-vis* the iron laws of classical economics! I can imagine that gradually the reader is beginning to feel that his leg is being pulled. That is so, but I am simply giving the neo-classical theory a say.

Incidentally, the conclusion that $k = l = q$ also seems likely to irritate people. Because in that way the amount of capital per worker remains constant, and prosperity does not increase. Now, the reader will say, that's a fine thing ... in reality economic development displays exactly the opposite. Over the last two hundred years both K/L and Q/L have increased, and a good thing too. A 'theory of growth' that abstracts from this is not worthy of the name.

But now I must nevertheless defend the classical theory. In the first place, in the circumstances described, production per head may increase, viz. if there is technical progress (defined as an increase in output with given inputs); in my opinion, the merit of the neo-classical theory is that this element comes to the fore as the decisive factor in economic development. That checks with empirical research (S. Fabricant, M. Abramovitz, E. F. Denison), in which it was found that 80 to 90 per cent of the increase in the productivity of labour over a long period must be ascribed to a shift in the production function.* In the second place the neo-classical theory does not claim that the actual growth rate will always be steady. It does not claim to give a picture of what actually happens, but of an underlying mechanism. In the real world there exist disturbances of equilibrium that temporarily cause production to grow more quickly, but in the end – that is the contention of classical economics – the system tries to return to the steady growth rate. With the reflections outlined above, the classical theory has thrown a new light on some of the forces that restore equilibrium, i.e. among others the movement of the productivity of capital. And in the third place the neo-classical theory, with its arresting equations, is an excellent subject for students, and others who are eager to learn, to get their teeth into. It is an aspect of economics that gives us faith in the ingenuity of economists, and that is worth quite a lot.

But here again the danger threatens that we shall proceed to overrate these intellectual constructions and that we shall come to believe that reality follows the models of steady growth. In that case we shall arrive at the view that l (the only autonomous quantity in the system), together with the progress of technology, fully describes the process of growth and that all the rest adjusts to these. This view is summed up in the saying that growth is governed by God (in the birth of children) and engineers. Some people proclaim something similar to this in all seriousness. The actual world is just a trifle more complicated.

This is above all so, because in fact growth is not a steady process. The disturbances are caused among other things by under- and overspending, which may lead to severe growing pains. To understand these we require Keynesian macro-economics. But the latter approach must then be coupled to a theory that may be described as classical to the extent that it considers the increase in the productive capacity. An analysis that starts from a given capacity is of course completely useless as a theory of growth – that is in fact the serious reproach that may be addressed to the older

---

* For this, see for instance E. F. Denison, *Why Growth Rates Differ*, 1967, which gives an enormous number of growth figures, and makes an attempt at quantitative explanation.

Keynesian analysis. We must therefore try to arrive at a kind of synthesis. Something similar is discussed in the following section, regarding which the reader must note from the beginning that the growth function from this section is then abandoned. There is no flexible combination of factors of production, but a rigid relationship. In that case the growth of capacity is governed by investment, provided that there is always enough labour to man the machines. In this way we get an approach which, while it includes the capacity effect of investment (and is to that extent classical), turns out quite differently from the genuine neo-classical theory from this section. It might be called the neo-Keynesian view. In the recent literature both approaches to the process of growth struggle for precedence. As a result the discussion between Keynesians and neo-classicists reaches new heights.

APPENDIX

The Golden Rule of Growth

The classical theory concerns itself with steady growth – a course of events in which the growth rate q is constant and moreover $q = k$, which means that the capital coefficient is constant. This is all very special, and we have made it even a little more special by working out that L too grows at the same rate – only technology breaches the zero growth of productivity.

However, it can become still more special, though that seems almost impossible at first sight. This brings us to the absolute zenith of classical logic.* We can examine a particular case of steady growth, namely that in which the stock of capital goods grows at a well-determined rate; the growth rate k is identical to the real interest rate. (Population growth will just have to adapt itself flexibly to that – how it does so we shall leave out of consideration.) This equality of the growth rate and the rate of interest is called the Golden Rule of Accumulation. The case is not as strange as it appears. It occurs, micro-economically, in the case of someone who leaves his money in the savings bank to

*See for this E. S. Phelps, 'The Golden Rule of Accumulation: A Fable for Growthmen', *American Economic Review*, 1961.

grow with interest; he lives on his earned income. Macro-economically, too, the case occurs if, with steady growth, all unearned incomes are invested and all earned incomes are consumed. The highly surprising consequence of the Golden Rule is that in that case the growth path of consumption becomes higher than all other growth paths.

This is so surprising because one would think that a high rate of investment initially calls for a sacrifice of consumption that later bears rich fruits. In other words, it looks as if a growth path that begins low may very well end high. Growth paths intersect. However, the theory of the Golden Rule shows that there is one special growth path for which the consumption curve 'dominates' the others, and that is, as said, the growth rate that is identical with the interest rate or – which amounts to the same thing – the growth rate at which unearned incomes are invested and earned incomes are consumed. It is not difficult to prove this thesis.*

The Golden Rule is just a little more than a joke. It is a perfect example of what classical deductive theory can achieve. It points to underlying relations that the untrained eye does not perceive. A harmony between capitalists and workers also shines forth on us which is even more wonderful and beneficial than the usual association of interests in which real wages increase through capital accumulation.

But at the same time the Golden Rule does not describe reality. The growth that is in fact observed is not even steady, and the variable q is not necessarily equal to the real interest rate. Furthermore, it is not so that a large stock of capital goods calls for an (absolutely) high level of investments (as is the case under the Golden Rule). Things may go quite differently: a high K may

---

*The proof is available in a number of variants. The simplest variant is $C = Q - I$. Write all three variables as functions of K, i.e. $C(K) = Q(K) - I(K)$. Evidently $C(K)$ is maximum if the derivatives of C and I are equal to one another. The derivative of the production function $Q(K)$ is the real interest rate, and that of $I(K)$ is the growth rate k. Further, we can multiply the real interest rate by the capital coefficient; we then get the share of capital in national income. We can likewise multiply k by the capital coefficient; we then get the propensity to save. Consequently the propensity to save must be equal to the share of capital in national income if consumption is to be maximized.

induce us to reduce the growth rate because we are rich enough, and then k therefore becomes lower as K is higher. As an optimization rule 'real interest rate = growth rate' is therefore anything but convincing. Politicians need not trouble themselves about the Golden Rule.

4·THE NEO-KEYNESIAN GROWTH EQUATION

Investment increases both productive capacity and money income. If there is to be balanced growth, both effects must be in accordance with each other. This is the basis of a synthesis between classical and Keynesian theory made by R. F. Harrod and E. D. Domar,* which throws a strange light on the rate and the stability of the growth process. The reasoning can be drawn up most simply. All that is needed is to introduce a new quantity, viz. the relationship between a certain addition to the national product (or the national income at constant prices) and the necessary addition to the stock of capital goods. This relationship is called the capital-output ratio. It is not as new in our reasoning as it perhaps appears; in fact it is the reciprocal of the (marginal) productivity of capital which we encountered in Chapter II. This quantity is represented by g. Depending on the stage of development of the country, it may assume very different values; as a rough guide, it will lie between three and eight. For special industries it may be somewhat lower or higher. In Western Europe national figures of three to five have been found. The lower the capital-output ratio is, the better; less investment is then required to arrive at a certain percentage of growth. Though the ratio is not one of the great Constants of Nature, the Harrod-Domar type of growth theory treats this figure as *given*.

By definition $g = I/\Delta Y$ (capacity effect; ΔY is the increase of Y). So as not to complicate matters, let us ignore X, M, G and T. In that case national income will adjust to that level at which $I = S = s \cdot Y$ (the multiplier or the income effect). Therefore:

*R. F. Harrod, 'An Essay in Dynamic Theory', *Economic Journal*, 1939, and 'Towards a Dynamic Economics', 1948; E. D. Domar, 'Expansion and Employment', *American Economic Review*, 1947.

$g = s.Y/\Delta Y$. By a small conversion: $\Delta Y/Y = s/g$. This is the growth equation, which has become very popular.

Its popularity is not surprising. For if we examine the equation, we see that it establishes a connection between the growth rate of national income and two simple quantities: the propensity to save and the capital-output ratio. If production increases at this rate, the product is sold and the new capital goods remain in use. In this sense growth is balanced. If the actual growth rate differs from this quotient, disturbances occur which have been the subject of most alarming reflections. It has been concluded that the growth must be extremely unstable. We shall come back to this instability in the next section. Reference may now be made to another useful employment which can be made of this very small equation, and which explains its popularity.

For it can give a quantitative impression of the degree of expansion which a national economy will display. Let us assume that the propensity to save is 20 per cent, a figure that for a country in the West is neither extremely high nor very low. Let us then assume that the capital-output ratio in that particular society is 5. The growth percentage that follows from our equation is 4, a reasonable figure for a Western country. However, a higher percentage is possible; this is evident from recent experience. Both the propensity to save and the capital-output ratio may be more favourable; for instance 25 per cent and 3; this implies a growth percentage of 8. Such simple arithmetic has something very attractive about it, and it has the advantage of drawing attention to strategic factors in development. It therefore goes without saying that the capital-output ratio has met with great interest and that considerable empirical research has been done into this figure. It has been found that the underdeveloped countries are faced with a high capital-output ratio. In combination with a low propensity to save caused by poverty, this gives an unfortunate result. Put s at 10 per cent and g at 7. The growth figure is then $1\frac{1}{2}$ per cent. Not much for a country aiming at accelerated development. Definitely too little if the population increases annually by 1 per cent. And so small as to be catastrophic if the population increases by 2 per cent. We have here one of the many variants of the low income trap: the income per head remains stuck at a low level. It may even decline. Part of the tragedy of the under-developed countries is already clearly manifest here.

The calculations look attractive, and perhaps they have convinced the reader so greatly that he has already made his choice: for the neo-Keynesian calculation and against the classical method of computation given in the preceding section. In that case it is time to throw a spanner in the works and to remind the reader that the method of Harrod and Domar is based on a very special assumption, viz. a constant capital-output ratio. Every increase of capital leads to an equal percentage increase in production. On further consideration this amounts to the fact that there is always enough labour available to keep the new machines running. The labour force must adjust to the new capital goods. As we have seen, that is precisely the opposite situation to that in which the theory of steady growth applies: in the neo-classical case the formation of capital adjusts to the autonomous given population growth.

The difference between the two views may be further illustrated by another numerical example. Put s at 20 per cent and the initial value of the capital-output ratio at 5. According to Harrod-Domar the increase in production works out at 4 per cent. The growth of the stock of capital goods is of course also 4 per cent. If we were to apply the neo-classical growth function to this case, a 4 per cent growth of capital would yield a rise in production which does not amount to 4 per cent, but only to κ times 4 per cent, i.e. for instance 1 per cent (for convenience's sake κ has been put at $\frac{1}{4}$). This seems much less than in the theory of Harrod-Domar. But note that in the neo-classical calculation we assumed that the amount of labour used in production remains the same: $l = 0$. If the working force were also to increase by 4 per cent, as the theory of Harrod-Domar tacitly assumes, then according to the growth function labour adds a further contribution to production of $\frac{3}{4}$ times 4 per cent $= 3$ per cent, and the neo-classical theory arrives at the same result as the growth equation of the neo-Keynesians.

And so, the reader might say, it's six of one and half a dozen of the other. No, definitely not. The classical view is much wider and much more flexible (strangely enough; when we were discussing

Say's Law earlier, we had to conclude that the Keynesians have a general theory and that the classical theory deals with a special case!). Take, for instance, the case in which $k = 4$ per cent and $l = 0$ per cent; the classical theory then produces the answer $q = 1$ per cent. The neo-Keynesians, with their fixed relations between capital and labour, are at a loss with this case, at least if they start from full employment. For then the new machines cannot be manned, and the growth of capital serves no useful purpose. Thus q becomes 0 (while with the neo-classicists at least $q = 1$ resulted). And, as a consequence, this whole situation does not fit into the neo-Keynesian scheme of things, for now the capital-output ratio has suddenly become variable! After all, the stock of capital goods has grown, production has not, and the relationship between the two has changed. This illustrates the special character of the neo-Keynesian theory of growth. It is a fairly limited construction.

Furthermore, when using the neo-Keynesian equation s/g it must always be borne in mind that it is not meant to describe the actual growth rate so much as the growth rate at which the stock of capital goods is fully used. The actual growth path may differ from this, both upwards and downwards. Investments may be smaller and larger than corresponds to s/g, and so, therefore, may be the rise in production. However, this results in violent disturbances. These are discussed in the following section; it will be found there that the theory of Harrod and Domar has melancholy implications for stability of economic life. That, too, is a point to keep in mind when a choice must be made between the neo-classical and neo-Keynesian approaches to the process of growth.

5 · STABILITY AND THE GROWTH PARADOX

The tenor of the previous section was that s/g is the percentage of growth of national income at which the capital goods are fully utilized. We shall now see that investment must therefore also increase by the same percentage every year. If this does not happen – if for instance it stays at the same level for a time – disturbances of a paradoxical nature occur.

For just see what happens if in a given year investment fails to reach a growth figure of s/g, for instance because the entrepreneurs take a rather pessimistic view of things (stock exchange quotations are down, strikes are expected, there are rumours of war or of disarmament). In that case the productive capacity does not increase as much as s/g. But through the effect of the multiplier a depressive effect on the national money income occurs, as a result of which the capital goods will not be fully utilized in the near future. Too low investment leads to unutilized capacity, or, to put it differently, a slower growth than s/g leads to over production! That is the growth paradox.

It requires little imagination to see how serious this can be. Unused machines have an extremely discouraging effect on investing. Consequently, in the following period the level of investment will fall still further below the required level; and this will lead to a further overcapacity. Accordingly as less is invested, and growth proceeds more slowly, a greater part of the capital stock stands idle, and the forces hampering investment become stronger. To put it another way, a small downwards deviation of the growth rate s/g leads to a cumulative deflationary gap and in fact to stagnation and depression.

And conversely, too, the equation creates the impression that growth is extremely liable to explode into inflation. If a little more is invested than corresponds to s/g (for instance because autonomous investments increase), more extra income is created than corresponds to the growth of productive capacity. Despite the high investments, the machines cannot keep up the pace of demand, so that still higher investments are encouraged. Too rapid growth of productive capacity leads to underproduction – it seems incredible, but it is strictly logical.

Anyone who gives some thought to these processes cannot but come to the conclusion that balanced growth is practically impossible. The smallest departure from the narrow path of balanced growth leads to cumulative disturbances of equilibrium. The original Keynesian theory, which we have developed in the preceding chapters, was not as pessimistic as that. It showed that inflationary and deflationary gaps are possible, that the true equilibrium is a special case, and that economic life may freeze in a state of disequilibrium. The reasoning of Harrod and Domar is much more disquieting in this respect: it predicts wild, cumulative movements in spending and income.

And in another respect, too, this philosophy is not very encouraging. Growth seems to depend on the degree of utilization of the capital stock; employment does not figure in the story. Even if the equilibrium growth rate s/g should be achieved, full employment is still not yet ensured. You could therefore make up an extremely sombre story about a community in which full capacity growth and full employment differ.

Of course, all this evokes criticism. For actual economic life is not as unstable as all that. The reasoning is reminiscent of the case of the centipede that had always been able to walk well until somebody proved that this was really impossible with all those legs. The story goes that from then on the creature kept on stumbling; but it should instead have decided that there was something wrong with the theory.

Now such criticism may increase our insight. It concentrates on the constancy of the capital-output ratio, and it shows how important this rigidity may be for the economic process. A fixed relationship between investment and additional production implies that additions of labour to an existing production machinery do not summon forth any greater production. (In technical terms, the marginal productivity of labour is zero.) But relationships in production are not that rigid. To see this we may set against the theory of Harrod and Domar the classical theory of growth, which is based precisely on flexible relationships between the factors of production.

When we were discussing the classical system, we saw that prices occupied a central position in it. Prices control sales, and they also control the proportions in which the means of production will be applied. For it is possible to make a product in various ways: with a lot of labour and little capital or with less labour and more capital. These two factors of production can replace each other, and the extent to which the substitution is profitable for the entrepreneur is determined by the relation between the prices of capital and labour. The classical theory of growth deduces from this that balanced growth and full employment have a good chance of being realized. For if at a given moment too little should be invested to satisfy the demand for final products, the demand for labour increases. Wages go up and this stimulates investments because the entrepreneur prefers to avoid this expensive labour. In this way a stimulus is engendered for the formation of capital, which is less unstable than the process of Harrod and Domar described above. Conversely, unemployment will lead to falling wages, which makes it profitable for the entrepreneurs to replace capital by labour. Growth then means that the stock of capital goods increases only slowly, whilst the additional product is produced above all by additional labour. The capital-output ratio then falls. In this classical train of thought a flexible capital-output ratio adjusts to the requirements of the situation instead of repeatedly throwing the economy out of balance.

This classical growth theory, which has been interestingly described by R. M. Solow,* cannot be denied a certain realism. The 'input mix' is definitely not as rigid as the constant capital-output ratio suggests. The price system plays a part in directing the growth process. But on the other hand we may not rely on so great a flexibility that growth will always be balanced. Input substitutions make the razor's edge of growth less difficult to tread than the pessimists think on the basis of the small equation; but the possibility of cumulative disturbances, or at least of accelerations and retardations of growth, is definitely there. This is clear to see from the variations which growth figures have displayed in the Western world in the course of the years; and it is also a fact that this instability makes stringent requirements of government policy. It renders the task of Functional Finance more difficult.

There can be little doubt that in the course of a given period – say Britain after the war – classical and Keynesian forces have been at work. It is their mix that is debatable. In the fifties and sixties growth in the United Kingdom was reasonably steady. There was almost continuous full employment, and the stock of capital goods was sufficiently utilized to warrant a reasonable level of investment. The growth rate of production was relatively low, but it was almost always positive. There were certainly no wild swings in the level of national income. The trouble was mainly

* 'A Contribution to the Theory of Economic Growth', *Quarterly Journal of Economics*, 1956.

with inflation and the balance of payments – not with the process of growth as such. A classical theorist, looking at Britain in this particular period, might have been strengthened in his conviction that the underlying mechanisms were those described by his favourite theory.

The hyper-Keynesian view, as described by the Harrod-Domar model, was falsified in this period. For though there were certainly fluctuations in the rate of growth, they did not throw the economy off its growth path. They did not turn into wild swings in the level of activity. Growth proved to be much more stable than the Keynesian theory predicted.*

The seventies present us with a more uncertain case. Here classical and Keynesian views on growth and stagnation compete. The mix of the two mechanisms is a moot point. I shall come back to this topical issue in Chapter XI.

6 · TECHNICAL PROGRESS

This chapter began with smooth, attractive formulae like $Q_o e^{q \cdot t}; \lambda \cdot l + \kappa \cdot k; s/g$. However, it gradually became less clear. Nevertheless, one of the greatest uncertainties has only been incidentally mentioned so far. This is the steady shift of the production function, which is called technical progress. Many macro-economic problems accumulate here.

In itself the definition that macro-economics gives of this quantity is very exact and remarkable. The extremely complex process, in which steam engines are replaced by internal combustion engines and electric motors, and in which the computer makes its appearance in the engineering industry, book-keeping and space travel; this whole sweep of events, which is so difficult to follow, is represented by one figure per period of time. I called it q' above. It is the relative increase of Q that cannot be explained by the increase of L and K. In the classical growth function $q' = q - \lambda.l - \kappa.k$. This is a sharp definition, and one

---

*Of course, a Keynesian might reply that this relative stability was the result of deliberate government interference – inspired by Keynesian theory. But this certainly implies an overly optimistic view of the efficacy of British stabilization policy.

which is rather fruitful for econometric research. The results of this research came as a shock to many economists.

In the fifties a number of econometricians tried to explain actual growth rates by the contributions of capital and labour. This had little success. The researchers found large residues, which always indicates that there is something wrong with the theory. The first one who came across this in 1956 was M. Abramowitz,* after whom the unexplained 'residue' is therefore called. Only half the growth in production was attributable to population growth and capital accumulation; when the growth productivity was considered, the residue even increased to more than 80 per cent. R. M. Solow† and others arrived at similar disturbing results. It proved that saving and capital formation were less important than economists had previously thought, and that quite different things propelled growth – things that the textbooks had preferred to take as given. By regarding technology as autonomous the economists had shut themselves off from a large area of reality in which all kinds of things happened that they did not understand, and which descended on them with full force since Abramowitz and Solow. For technical development, as macro-economics defines it, is not only given but is also a kind of dustbin – everything that does not follow from L and K belongs in it, and that is quite a lot. Not only the work of the engineers, but also that of the managers (better organization), not forgetting the whole of education! For a better quality of labour is not measured by the quantity L, which comprises only individuals, without weighting them in some way or the other. From the quantitative viewpoint alone, education is already a tremendously important industry, to which some pure economists kept their eyes tightly closed. Abramowitz's residue was therefore a sign that there was still something to investigate, and since then work has started on this.

Before we take a look at these new ramifications of research, a few remarks should be made in defence of the classical theory.

* 'Resource and Output Trends in the United States since 1870', *American Economic Review*, 1956.

† 'Technical Change and the Aggregate Production Function', *Review of Economics and Statistics*, 1957.

The shock caused by Abramowitz *et al.* knocked some economists off balance. As a result a simple application of the formula for balanced growth was occasionally forgotten: an application that *predicts* the strong influence of technical development. The classical growth equation is $q = \lambda l + \kappa \cdot k + q'$. If we assume, entirely in line with the classical tradition, that $\lambda + k = 1$, and also that Q and K grow equally (i.e. a constant capital coefficient), then $q = l + \dfrac{q'}{\lambda}$ or $q - l = \dfrac{q'}{\lambda}$ follows. This may look forbidding but it states that the growth of productivity is equal to technical progress divided by the share of labour. If we put the latter at for instance 0·8, this means that the growth of productivity is 1·25 times technical progress. Anyone desirous of explaining the historical growth of productivity will find 80 per cent technical progress and 20 per cent of capital intensity. Now that is precisely what happened to Abramowitz, Solow *et al.* Consequently, there is no reason for surprise. On the contrary, there is slight reason for satisfaction among adherents of the classical theory. The deductive manner of reasoning does not prove all that fruitless!

Nevertheless, many unsolved questions remain with reference to q'. Efforts have been made to reduce the dustbin nature of this quantity by making a quantitative division into forms of technical progress. This research has been initiated in particular by E. F. Denison.* In the first place he has tried to isolate the influence of education. Extensive information is available on increased schooling, above all for the United States. When Denison had examined the period 1950–62 in that country, education already supplied him with a quarter of economic growth. Independently of this he tried to draw up an index for technical knowledge; this can be calculated in various ways, and the result was another somewhat weightier factor.† The influence of the increase in scale was also separately estimated; this influence was about 10 per cent of the growth of production.

---

* *Why Growth Rates Differ*, 1967.

† One way is quantifying a country's expenditure on research and development. Another is estimating the difference in productivity between advanced and backward firms. This is statistically a field full of pitfalls, but something can be made of it.

Although these estimates are highly experimental, they nevertheless point in the direction in which quantitative research could move. But we are far from saying that we understand q'. Product innovation, the readiness to accept new techniques, managerial drive – these are all things that are difficult to quantify.

But even if we understood these things, we would by no means have wormed all the secrets out of technical progress. Another moot point is that production function shifts; it may be that this shift is 'neutral', that is, the curve retains its shape, but moves to a higher level. However, it may also change shape. This means that, at a given volume of production, technology demands more labour, or more capital. Much has been written about this nonneutral technical progress. The main question is what influence technology has on the demand for labour. There are strong rumours circulating about this. Many people fear that the computer will make all work superfluous. The machines and the robots will attend to production and there will hardly be a place left for people. This fear is probably highly exaggerated for mechanization and computerization are fundamentally nothing more than an increase in labour productivity. This process has already been going on for a while – since the Middle Ages and in any case since the invention of the steam engine. And yet there was still full employment in 1970. Of course, laboursaving technical progress may lead to a rapid shake-out of labour in certain sectors (office work, chemical industry), while new jobs are not easily created elsewhere; the result is frictional unemployment, and that can be irksome enough. But general unemployment emerges only when productivity increases more quickly than production; in other words, when sales are not enough to utilize the increased productive capacity. We recognize the Keynesian problem of underspending. As long as sales grow sufficiently, people keep their jobs, despite technical progress.

In the seventies this last condition has not been satisfied. The delay in the growth of world trade and the weak domestic situation created unemployment in Britain which was aggravated here and there by the increase in productivity. But this places the country in a remarkable dilemma. In the short term a combination of labour-saving technical progress and as lack market is bad for employment. In the long term technical progress is probably good for the growth of the markets. The lagging innovation and the limited rise in productivity (as we have seen, over the period 1955–73 this was only 3·2 per cent a year, as against 5 per cent for continental Western Europe) have probably impaired the competitive position of the United Kingdom. Real wages could only increase slightly. The unemployment situation deteriorated.

It would not be a good policy to halt technical progress *in the general sense* so as to save jobs. Of course, this does not mean that special cases may not occur where things are different: if considerable local unemployment exists somewhere, without any prospects of some kind of expansion, the computerization of a large regional firm may have a harmful effect. In such a case we are concerned with frictional unemployment, though this can be persistent and very bad. In economic policy very tricky questions can arise between furtherance of technical progress in general and halting technical progress in special cases. As elsewhere, there are no simple solutions here.

7 · THE DANGERS OF GROWTH

Can production keep on rising? At first sight it can, because the formation of capital continues, technology makes ever greater strides, new products continue to appear and human needs tend to adjust to a larger supply of goods and services. And yet some economists already pointed at a very early date to the possibility of a certain saturation and to the desirability of an austere life. In his *Principles of Political Economy* (1848) John Stuart Mill advocated a stationary situation, within which distribution ought to be improved and people should devote more energy to pleasures of the mind. Mill regarded industrial growth as a passing phase, necessary for reaching a certain level of prosperity; thereafter the passionate cry of 'more, more' would have to be stilled. Similar recommendations may also be found in Keynes (*Essays in Persuasion*, 1931) and in J. K. Galbraith (*The Affluent Society*, 1958). So it is not true that economists have venerated growth as a kind of sacred cow. But it *is* correct to say that many of my professional colleagues are alive to the scarcity that still exists on essential points; they believe that this can be alleviated by economic growth. More and better housing, better medical care, more education – everyone really wants these. And in the developing countries an increase in production is vital – everyone knows that.

But there is a hitch here. The production and consumption of most goods entail waste, and this is beginning to accumulate. In part it is decomposed by nature, but in part this by-product is poisoning the natural environment. It is precisely the poisonous forms of waste, such as mercury, residual DDT, chlorine and radioactivity (a by-product of the generation of atomic energy), that are increasing with particular rapidity. Biologists and nature-lovers have long been warning us of the great dangers that this entails for man. Above all, they have pointed to the vulnerability of the food chains. An alarming vision of the near future may be found for instance in Rachel Carson's *Silent Spring* (1962), in which the great extinction is evocatively described.

Economists have in the main reacted to these problems as follows: harm to the environment forms a cost factor which unfortunately is not reflected in the price of the product. This is called an 'external effect', and it is a fault of the price mechanism that it makes no allowance for these effects. As a result the volume of production of such pollutants is too great. Price determination should be corrected by the government; a tax must be imposed on the injurious product equal to the harm done to the environment. This creates an incentive to replace the polluting product by a clean one. The engineers will also perfect air and water treatment plants. If the corrected price mechanism does not form a sufficient incentive, the government will have directly to order treatment or ban production. Industry will then certainly start searching for new techniques, and human inventiveness will put development back on the right track.

This belief in the corrective effect of substitutions and new technologies was seriously undermined in the sixties. In the first place, governments proved extremely lax in taxing external effects; they allowed huge quantities of poison to be dumped into the sea and emitted into the atmosphere. Physical prohibitions, too, have been maintained most inadequately. Even in emergencies such as those created by smog, governments continue to play a waiting game. In the second place, heavy taxes on specific pollutants proved barely to check the latter's growth; an example is the motor car and petrol. In the third place, the suspicion is growing that substitutions are not an adequate remedy, because nearly all products have an adverse effect on the environment: treating plants must first be built, and moreover demand energy; the production of energy is one of the big polluters. The same applies to the recovery of metals from waste (for instance the dangerous mercury); this recycling also calls for equipment and a great deal of energy. The production of energy presents particularly frightening problems: the heating of the atmosphere and water, and the radioactive waste of nuclear power plants. In the fourth place, it is feared that, even if industry and government follow a faultless policy, this does not in itself offer a guarantee against disasters, e.g. in the transporting of injurious and poisonous substances. A number of accidents with oil tankers have nurtured this fear. For this reason alone an exponential growth in pollution is to be expected! And in the fifth place, we are still saddled with worldwide population growth, which even with constant *per capita* production still results in an increasing burden on the environment.

Under the influence of these ideas and of the highly progressive pollution of air and water, pessimism about growth increased in the sixties. The stench and the decay, the dead fish and the undrinkable drinking water have naturally received considerable publicity. Minor or major catastrophes are regular occurrences. During the past few years disquiet has become universal. Economic growth, which used to be welcomed as beneficent, has increasingly come to be regarded as a threat to life on earth.

The worries on this score have been spelled out by a number of economists, including E. J. Mishan. In *The Costs of Economic Growth* (1967) he advocates an exact calculation of national income, in which the losses of natural environment and human lives (for instance in road accidents) are deducted as costs. His argument is that such a calculation will demonstrate that the costs of growth are higher than the proceeds, in other words that in the West today no real economic growth still occurs. His argument has sometimes been challenged, but since the calculation of the external effects has never in fact been performed, the discussion has remained rather inconclusive. Attempts to express harm to the environment and the costs of traffic jams and road accidents in terms of money have since been undertaken, but they have not yet proved a success. One may even doubt whether the extinction of certain birds can ever be expressed in money terms – I don't think it can be done – and when one human life is lost, economists must confess that their figures are falling short of reality. Consequently we do not know for sure whether an increase in prosperity is still going on in Western countries. Personally I believe it is, but at the same time I do not think that this will be the case much longer, unless we radically change our production and consumption habits.

Growth pessimism was given a tremendous boost by the publications of a couple of research scientists of the Massachusetts Institute of Technology, J. W. Forrester and D. L. Meadows. The former devised in his *World Dynamics* (1971) a model that investigates the interplay of a number of highly aggregated variables, viz. world population, industrial world production, the food supply, pollution, and the natural resources still remaining. This model has been further elaborated by Meadows, and in particular his report *The Limits to Growth* (1972), commissioned by a number of alarmed industrialists and bankers (the Club of Rome), has made a deep impression. It acquired enormous publicity and has probably formed a turning point in thought on the future of mankind.

The basic idea in the work of Forrester and Meadows is simply that continued growth leads to infinite quantities that just do not fit into a finite world. The remarkable result of such processes was already discovered by the king who promised the inventor of chess a reward of one grain of corn on the first square on the board, two on the second, four on the third, etc. There was not enough corn in the whole country to reach the sixty-fourth square. At a growth rate of 4 per cent production doubles within twenty years – the earth cannot keep that up for centuries to come.

This basic idea has been elaborated into a complicated model which cannot easily be described in equation form but must preferably be dealt with by the computer. This is because the many relations between the different variables are not rectilinear; the multipliers in question depend on the level of the variables. Take for instance the state of affairs in the oceans; it is not just that more mercury, more DDT, more radioactive waste result in proportionally higher pollution. For, as the oceans are increasingly poisoned, the absorptive capacity of the sea will decrease; the period within which decomposable substances become harmless lengthens as pollution grows. This lengthening of the pollution absorption time ('Polat') gives a curvilinear relation between pollution and production. That is not just a complication for the model; at the same time it forms a deadly threat to life in the ocean and thus ultimately to human life on earth.

The result of Forrester and Meadows' model is particularly alarming. As the population grows it will be possible to produce sufficient food only if tremendous quantities of artificial fertilizers and insecticides are used that strongly attack the environment. Moreover, natural resources (mercury, oil, natural gas) are becoming exhausted. If in addition industrial production should continue to rise, that too will, according to the model, give rise to catastrophic pollution. A shortage of food occurs, the factories can no longer operate for lack of oil, anyone who falls in the water becomes ill, and babies are malformed by radioactivity. It is possible to postpone these disasters, but if the population is allowed to increase unchecked, this means that the blow is all the harder when it comes. The MIT scientists have not made one particular prediction, but have worked out a very large number of possibilities, strategic variables being changed in each case. The actual time of the ultimate catastrophe proves to be fairly insensitive to such changes, unless they all occur at once. Depending on the assumptions, a pronounced decline of prosperity will be enforced within a period varying between 50 and 100 years. To put it in another way, if we go on like this, somewhere in the twenty-first century the light will go out and the new famine stalk the land.

But the authors do not believe that these disasters are inevitable. They do, however, warn that partial solutions will not help. Both capital formation and population growth will have to be checked, and even entirely stopped. This conclusion is, however, practically on a par with the inevitability of great disasters, if only because it excludes for the developing countries any prospect of a substantial rise in their standard of living. They will have to choose between continuing famine and disastrous pollution of the oceans, above all because so far it has proved practically impossible to check population growth in the developing countries, let alone stop it.

The calculations of Forrester and Meadows are easy to criticize. Thus it is clear that their variables are too 'big'; the whole world is compressed into a few quantities. The measurements are extremely sketchy – a variable like 'pollution' (worldwide pollution!) can hardly be reproduced in one measurable quantity. Meadows had to guess about the behaviour of the Polat (see p. 246). Some have disposed of the calculation as: 'garbage in, garbage out'. Worse still, this model makes no distinction between polluting and barely polluting production; feedbacks from pollution and exhaustion to production methods are conspicuously absent from their model. By introducing a new clean-up technology much kinder results could be achieved. The model has been violently attacked on the latter point in particular. A biting critic in the *Economist* speaks of 'The Limits of Misunderstanding'. But others have made an article of faith of the new doomsday philosophy.

This discussion will continue – the end is not yet in sight. However, agreement has been reached on some points. The first is that the bottlenecks in various parts of the world are different. In the poor countries the worst threat is the terrible shortage of food. Overpopulation and a low productivity of agriculture are the most obvious causes – behind these lies a complex of social and political factors. In the rich countries constant pollution threatens, which becomes visible above all in oil disasters at sea (but is of a stealthy character), and an energy shortage. The latter is recognized by everyone, but the solutions differ. The debate concentrates on atomic energy, which according to some is deadly dangerous, and the desirability of zero growth – according to some salutary and to others a source of tension and conflict. The debate is overshadowed by great uncertainty regarding future technology. Can technology save us? That is no simple question for simple economists, who have long taken technical progress as given and beneficial. Economists will have to listen to scientists discussing atomic fission versus fusion, the adsorptive capacities of the ocean, pollution leading to high or to low temperatures on earth – and he may be glad if he can understand, more or less, what the scientists are talking about. His own opinion hardly counts.

But in the midst of these uncertainties a policy must nevertheless be followed. Some remarks are made on this in Chapter XII.

CHAPTER XI

Fitting the Jigsaw Together

1 · TWENTY-FIVE EQUATIONS

So far the reasoning has been as follows. We were looking for the factors that determine national income and at the same time indicate the size of other important macro-economic quantities. To track down these relations we have alternately adopted three theoretical points of view: the classical, the Keynesian and the monetary. We have seen that all three of them can contribute to explaining various observed phenomena. But our treatment was fragmentary: each chapter yielded a few equations. It is now time to consider the whole model.

What I describe below is one possibility. I do not say: that is how it has to be, but: that is how it might be. Someone may ask: should we really include marginal productivity, considering how difficult it is to measure? And then somebody else can reply: yes, I still attach quite some value to that concept, because it plays an important part in classical thought. Someone can complain that the model is too complicated (in earlier publications I used to say that ten was a nice round figure, and now I'm going to write twenty-five equations). Another person can point to the much too aggregative nature – oil production in the North Sea will after all at least have to be dealt with separately, and so will the building trade. He or she is right. Somebody may remark that the variable which he or she regards as governing everything (the prices on the stock exchange, money, the energy supply, exploitation) has been given a much too modest place; however, that criticism at the same time entails the obligation to suggest a better arrangement. Sociologists may complain that it is all considered too much from the economic point of view – their proposals for improvement of the consumption equation, the wage increase equation, or anything else, are eagerly awaited. Political scientists will rightly remark that our primitive equation for government expenditure and taxes does no justice to the present state of research into political science – that may lead to important improvements of such equations and, who knows, to the linking of a macro-economic model to a political science model.

I should like to make separate mention of one strategic choice. In the first chapters variables were written as levels: the production level, the price level. Later chapters dealt with changes in level: growth level, inflation level; these are expressed in percentages. In practice we can hardly get away from the changes: the spiral is expressed in the movement of wages and prices and, anyway, everybody is interested in the *increase* in real wages. We therefore always end up with mixed models, in which both levels and changes in levels occur. In that case we have to take great care that we do not write contradictory things. For instance, it is dangerous to allow the level of national income to depend on Keynesian variables (i.e. the multiplier times the sum of the autonomous components) and then to determine the growth of income in the classical way (for instance as the weighted sum of the growth of the quantities of the factors of production plus technical progress). This can yield contradictions, namely if in both cases hard and fast parameters are assumed. In the following survey this matter occasionally emerges; I then indicate that we can take two directions with an equation. This serves more to bring up the problem than to solve it consistently.*

The equations are given below in words, not in symbols. The advantage is obvious: the model is less frightening in appearance. The disadvantage is that a somewhat larger area of paper is covered and also that it cannot immediately be seen whether one quantity influences another quantity positively or negatively. In mathematical notation this is apparent from the sign of the regres-

*However, the possibility of contradiction is always present. The model-builder may not be too tolerant. He may not write a price equation with a constant profit mark-up and later introduce a variable distribution of profits and other income. This 'indeterminateness' plays a part when we discuss the Treasury Model. The reader can examine whether the following twenty-five equations contain inconsistencies – I am not sure that he will not find them.

sion coefficient. To rectify this, the sign is given in brackets behind most quantities. Plus means that an increase in the variable leads to an increase in the quantity sought; minus means the opposite. The exact relationship between quantities (e.g. proportionality) is left open, except in a few special cases where we are obviously concerned with addition $(Y = C+I+G+X-M)$ or division. Well, here are the equations, twenty-five in all.

(1) National income is the sum of consumption, investments, exports and government expenditure minus imports. This is income determination. The equality mentioned is always present. The equation corresponds to a point on the 45° line in Fig. 3.

(2) Consumption depends on national income $(+)$, income distribution $(+)$, the quantity of money in the hands of the households $(+)$ and taxes $(-)$. This is the consumption function.

(3) Savings are defined as national income less consumer expenditure and taxes. They occur in both households and business; the propensity to save will differ in these sectors. Instead of a definition, we can also include behavioural equations. In these, savings are influenced by profits, among other things. Of course, the savings function must be consistent with the consumption function.

(4) Investments depend on: profits after tax $(+)$; the desired stock of capital goods minus the stock of capital goods present $(+)$; savings $(+)$, though not in the classical sense that investments are equal to savings, but availability of savings does help; and finally on the liquid assets in the hands of the entrepreneurs $(+)$. This is the investment function.

Here we re-encounter the flexible accelerator (in which at the same time underspending and overspending are done justice), elements of profit theory and of monetary theory. If desired overcapacity can also be included $(-)$. See for this No. 12. Replacement investments can be specified separately (they may depend on scrapping). Stockbuilding too is sometimes taken separately (depends on price expectations and the interest rate).

(5) Exports depend on the competitive position on foreign markets, represented by the relationship between the foreign and the domestic price level $(+)$; the rate of exchange $(+)$ and, to a large extent, the volume of world trade (the latter quantity

weighted with coefficients that correspond to the importance of the various countries as customers).

(6) Government expenditure is autonomous in most models; but we can also write that it depends on the norm that the government wishes to adhere to for the budgetary deficit (+); on the budgetary deficit itself (−) and on the level that this spending had in the past (+). There are other conceivable variants in which a part of G is endogenized; for instance, the growth of G is partly linked to the growth of the car population. Payment of social benefit increases in times of unemployment.

(7) Imports depend on national income (+), relative foreign and domestic prices (−) and the rate of exchange (+). The first explanatory variable seems to me much more important than the other two.

(8) Tax revenue is determined by national income (+) and the tax burden fixed by politicians (+). This taxation equation is a very rough one. It can be subdivided according to kinds of tax – VAT, profits tax, wage and income tax. The subdivision is necessary in order to find out what part of taxes burdens business. Unfortunately, this is not known (passing-on!).

(9) National income is by definition the product of real national income (see No. 12) and the price level. Of course, we can also reckon on changes here: the growth of national income is the sum of the growth of production and the price increase.

(10) The growth of the stock money supply depends on the deficit on the Budget and the extent to which the latter is financed by the creation of money (+); the balance on the current account of international transactions (+); imports of capital (+); the creation of liquidity by the commercial banks on behalf of business and households (+) and on possible intervention by the monetary authorities through discount policy, open-market policy and more direct measures (+ or −). The quantity of money is by definition equal to that of the year before plus the growth.

(11) The demand for liquidities depends on national income (+), the interest rate (−), and the expected changes in the price level (−). To keep in step with the money creation equation

(No. 10), we must consider here the *changes* in the demand for money.

(12) The national product depends on the inputs labour (+) and capital (+) and on the production function.

Equation 12 is interpreted by the classicists in such a way that labour and capital are given, and the national product follows from this. Keynesians keep open the possibility that production is given (by demand), so that the inputs follow from that. In the latter case the productive *capacity* is greater than production. Overcapacity can be fed back into the investment function.

(13) Productive *capacity* may be specified separately, usually as a growth rate; for instance, as the sum of the growth of the labour supply and the growth of labour productivity (see Nos. 15 and 17).

(14) The real wage level depends on the marginal productivity of labour. This gives us the demand for labour curve. It can easily be written on a blackboard, but it is difficult to pin it down empirically. We can also follow another method: the real wage level is equal to that of the year before plus the change. The latter depends above all on the growth of *average* productivity. Switching from marginal productivity to average productivity is permitted only with constant distribution (see Chapter IX).

(15) Labour productivity is by definition equal to production divided by the amount of labour utilized. Usually this variable is specified as a growth rate. It may be given, but it is perhaps more illuminating to note that this growth rate depends on investments (+), technical progress (+) and the volume of unemployment (+). The last quantity expresses the fact that, in times of insufficient utilization of the productive capacity, rapid increases in labour productivity are possible – this means that unemployment often takes so long to disappear.

(16) Employment. This is by definition equal to production divided by labour productivity. Both variables are determined elsewhere in the model. Employment can also be derived from a vintage model of the stock of capital goods. In that case the number of jobs depends among other things on the age structure of the machines (and indirectly on the real wage rate).

(17) The supply of labour. This can be interpreted autonomously (perhaps as a growth rate); or as a function of the wage rate. Textbook economics prefers the latter, but then lapses into casuistry and does not come up with really verifiable hypotheses. Thus a higher real income can elicit more supply, but can also lead to substitution of leisure time for incomes, as a result of which the relationship works out negatively. According to some the supply function must in any case include something about social insurance $(-)$; if the difference between wage and unemployment or assistance benefit is small, a negative effect on the supply may be expected.

(18) Unemployment. By definition the difference between supply of and demand for labour. A distinction must be made here between unemployment due to underspending and unemployment that is the result of qualitative discrepancy between supply and demand (schooling, place of residence, branch of industry). Our model makes no provision for this division; it is too aggregated for that.

(19) Real interest. By definition equal to the nominal interest rate minus the increase in the general price level. The nominal interest rate is a question of supply and demand on the capital market; there are countless possibilities for the model-builder here (for instance taking large capital imports into account). We can also start from the real interest as the marginal productivity of capital, and find from that the nominal interest rate by adding the price inflation; but in times of sharp price increases the real interest rate is forced down below the 'natural' level, i.e. below the marginal productivity. This equation interests the monetary school in particular.

(20) The amount of capital utilized depends on the accumulated stock of capital goods $(+)$, which consists of vintages of differing labour productivity (the older the machines, the lower the labour productivity). Influence is also exerted by the scrapping of vintages $(-)$ that are economically outmoded and the new investments $(+)$, which are explained by equation No. 4.

(21) The scrapping of machines depends on the autonomous increase in productivity $(-)$ that is embodied in the machines and the increase in real labour costs $(+)$.

(22) The increase in money wages depends on the rise in prices (+), on the growth rate of labour productivity (+), on the tension on the labour market (+) and on a not so clear variable (+) that represents the power and the attitudes of the unions.

(23) The share of labour in national income can be written autonomously. We can also assume that it is equal to the labour elasticity of production, and write that its growth depends on the growth of the capital intensity of production (+) and the substitution elasticity between labour and capital. If the latter is equal to one, the capital intensity has no effect, otherwise it does. The rate of wage inflation also exerts some influence (+).

(24) The price increase depends on the cost increase (+) (wage increases, increase in import prices, increase in taxes; *minus* increase in productivity) and on the movement of profit margins (+), which may occasionally turn out negative.

(25) The profit margin depends on the rate of cost increases (−), on the utilization of capacity (+), on the ratio between foreign and domestic price level because this ratio determines profitability in the export sector (+) and on the real growth rate (+). Total profits are, by definition, equal to the profit margin times the turnover. Because the equation for the profit margin is so weak, we may also take profits as a residual: national income minus costs, and then proceed to find the profit margin by division. Unfortunately, this procedure is also doubtful.

We have here at first sight twenty-five equations. In reality there are more, because under some numbers a definition has also been included, and that too is an equation (for instance No. 15: the definition of labour productivity plus a regression equation). Some definitions are not explicitly stated; we have not written down that the relative price increase is equal to the difference between new and old price, divided by the old price – such things speak for themselves.

The model contains a number of exogenous quantities. They are introduced from outside; if we want to predict we have to estimate these quantities separately. (If we make mistakes when doing so we get incorrect results, but that is not the fault of the model.) Exogenous are above all the volume of world trade, the price level abroad, the rate of exchange, government expenditure, taxation, the creation of money by the banking system, the method of financing budgetary deficits, capital imports, the existing stock of capital goods (with all the old history embodied in it), the supply of labour and the state of technology. That is quite a lot. But what is explained by the model and its parameters is more: national income (in money and real), investments, the balance of payments, labour productivity, real wages, growth, inflation, profit and employment.

If you want to discuss the model you can divide it into blocs or submodels. They correspond more or less to the theoretical approaches. Thus the Keynesian view comes to the fore in the spending bloc – equations 1 to 9. The monetary mini-bloc comprises equations 10 and 11. Classical theory is embodied by Nos. 12 to 21: production function, labour productivity, stock of capital goods, accelerated scrapping. The spiral bloc comprises Nos. 22 to 25 and endeavours to explain inflation. Equation 25 is a stepchild: profits. The blocs of course are interrelated – variables from the one submodel return in another. These are the feedbacks. We could easily have included more of these: unemployment for instance is a loose end in our model, but this quantity affects government expenditure (on social security) and labour productivity (in a strained labour market employers hang on to labour, at a certain unemployment they shake out surplus labour, at high unemployment rates dismissals are halted by social considerations, by union action, perhaps by employment subsidies). Thus there is much to be added or changed.

The model described above belongs on a blackboard. It is not good enough for real empirical research – on the one hand it contains equations that are difficult to estimate and on the other, according to recent views, it is much too aggregative. Let us see what the empiricists are doing.

2 · ECONOMETRICIANS AT WORK

Quantitative research is already very old. Well known is the work of William Petty, who published his *Political Arithmetick* in 1679. But this was more the intelligent collecting of statistical material on the population, taxes and trade than the estimating of parameters – the characteristic of modern econometrics. Pioneers in the latter field were H. L. Moore (*c.* 1900) and H. Schulz (*The Theory and Measurement of Demand*, 1938), who sought demand elasticities. However, their work was micro-economic. One of the first great macro-studies was by Cobb and Douglas: the research into the production function that was discussed above. They estimated in the main one function, so that was hardly a model as yet.

Empirical model-building stems above all from the 1930s. There was a clear link with the economic situation – the Great Depression – and the work of Keynes. Jan Tinbergen was one of the first to put together an econometric income and expenditure model. The first attempts, in 1936, appeared in Dutch publications. They led to an invitation from the then League of Nations; the results of that research were laid down (1939) in *Statistical Testing of Business Cycle Theories*.* Right up to the present day this book determines the nature of the system of equations. Since then there has been considerable improvement in econometric techniques, there is much more statistical material available, the equations have become more complex, Keynesian relationships have been joined by classical submodels, the number of equations has been stepped up tremendously, computers have been called in to help; but the fundamental properties of the research have remained the same. This may appear from the following survey.

In his day Tinbergen used forty equations. The connection between spending and incomes received full attention – it was a Keynesian model. But it was certainly not 'moneyless'. Separate markets for shares, bonds, etc. were described. One of the things that emerged was that investments are not very sensitive to interest, a hypothesis that maintained itself for a long time; another was that the rigid accelerator does not work. Profits make a much better explanatory variable. These are still defensible hypotheses.

In 1945 the Central Planning Bureau was founded in the Netherlands to continue the research under the direction of Tinbergen. Initially the model did not become public. One of the first publications was the thesis of H. J. Witteveen, *Loonshoogte*

*Two volumes. The first is entitled *A Method and its Application to Investment Activity*. Part II is *Business Cycles in the United States 1919–1932*.

en werkgelegenheid (1947). He used Tinbergen's model to estimate the elasticity of the demand for labour; this worked out at a very low level. This is not so very surprising when it is borne in mind that substitution between labour and capital did not occur in the model. The Keynesian hypothesis of an inelastic demand for labour influenced Dutch thinking on wage inflation for decades. Not until the sixties did criticism come from classically oriented economists, who pointed to the harmful effect of the wage push. The wage explosions were then going full blast. However, this criticism was not translated into an econometric model. Not until the seventies, when the Central Planning Bureau's system of equations had been repeatedly changed and expanded, was a vintage bloc introduced, as a result of which the impact of wage inflation on employment via accelerated scrapping came to light. I mention this remarkable development because it is so paradoxical: at a time when Keynesian unemployment reared its head the neo-classical explanation came to the fore in the Netherlands! In British model-building, as we shall see, there is as yet little to be perceived of such a neo-classical reaction.

The more or less official model of the Central Planning Bureau was for a long time the only one that counted in the Netherlands. It was published from 1955 onwards. The Central Bank worked with a small set of monetary equations, but that was not taken very seriously. However, in the course of the sixties and the seventies competitors came forward. Some were thought up by the universities. The Central Planning Bureau started to use various models side by side: for the short term, for the long term. The newspapers wrote about the battle of the model-builders. Parliament intervened. Model-building became an issue of political discussion.

We see the same development in the Scandinavian countries. Norway in particular was in the lead, under the influence of Ragnar Frisch. The impetus often came from government offices which wanted to use the models for policy purposes. This monopoly was later breached. Gradually the diversity of the system increased.

In the United States and Britain the development was different. Initially the Federal Government stood aloof. The American pioneer was Lawrence R. Klein, an independent research man. The Council of Economic Advisers, which has to assist the President in policy-making, did not do much in the way of model-building; if they had a model, they kept it under lock and key. In 1950 Klein published a first attempt, entirely in the style of Tinbergen (*Economic Fluctuation in the United States*). Here too the connections between income and spending are emphasized. The production capacity is not explained. There are only three definition equations and three dynamic reaction equations involved. Attention was concentrated on problems of estimation, the collection of material, in brief on econometric techniques – the underlying theory did not exceed that of a simple textbook. A distinction is made between profits and wage incomes, but the wage bill is explained by (delayed) national income; profits thus form a residue. Investments are related to these profits, with a lag, and (negatively) to the capital stock. Inflation plays no part. There is no profit squeeze. The supply side is poorly represented. In the later attempt (together with A. S. Goldberger) the model was expanded and refined,* but it remained Keynesian. An enormous leap forward was *The Brookings Quarterly Model of the U.S.* (1965), a voluminous publication by J. S. Duesenberry, G. Fromm, L. R. Klein and E. Kuh. It is a system of 150 equations, divided into a large number of blocs. Separate research teams concerned themselves with the submodels. Suppy and capacity equations are present. Non-economic variables are introduced (housebuilding depends on the number of marriages). The regression equations become longer. However, limits are set to the growth of the number of explanatory variables per equation – if the number exceeds five or six, the correlation automatically increases and the testing possibilities become less sharp. One therefore cannot say: toss in a few more explanatory variables. The Brookings model also shows that the inclusion of additional explanatory variables that have in turn to be explained themselves leads to a particularly rapid growth of the whole set-up.

Since then the American econometricians have been very hard

*L. R. Klein and A. S. Goldberger, *An Econometric Model of the United States 1929–1952*, 1955.

at work. All kinds of competing models have sprung up. Every self-respecting economics faculty has started its own research programme. Without doing injustice to others, I may perhaps point to one exercise, performed in the seventies by B. Hickman and R. M. Coen.* Their model is modern and most attractive. In addition to Keynesian and monetary equations it contains a fully fledged classical submodel, with a Cobb-Douglas production function, marginal productivities and demand for labour and capital curves. Wages already influence employment via substitution. A distinction is made between full employment output (at which optimum use is made of capital stock, that is at minimum cost) and potential output (at which capital stock is used to its maximum extent). Profits depend on a mark-up that is not constant but dependent on demand pressures on capacity. Investments depend on sales and on the wage/interest ratio. The results cast light on the discussion between monetarists and Keynesians – thus Hickman and Coen find that the pre-war multiplier was rather stable at the level of three and the post-war one equally so at the level of two. Considerable criticism of specific equations is possible – personally I find the money wage equation, in which employers act as wage-setters, not a very fortunate one – but the Hickman-Coen model is one of the finest attempts now available.

The British got into the game rather late. Keynes himself saw little in the econometric method. Nor did the Treasury. The *Economic Surveys* that the Labour government published soon after the war did at first contain targets and forecasts, but after a few years it proved that these were at variance with the actual achievements. This was grist to the opposition's mill, and so the publication of the figures was stopped. It took nearly twenty years before a new Labour government appeared with similar estimates. All that time the Treasury relied more on superior intelligence and the skilful combination of a few strategic numbers than on formal model-building. The human brain is in fact preferable to a poor model, but around 1968 it was nevertheless concluded in Whitehall that a system of equations is not an unnecessary luxury. Then the Treasury Model was born. The principal reason seems to have been that the Chancellor of the

*An Annual Growth Model of the U.S. Economy, 1976.

Exchequer wanted to know how much public expenditure he could permit himself without squeezing private investments and the balance of payments. Thus fear of overspending was present at the birth of this exercise. The exact nature of the model was kept hidden from outsiders; this led to considerable criticism. In 1975 the Industry Act laid down that the system of equations has to be published regularly. Which is why I can come back to it in the next section.

But meanwhile the universities had already started with their own modelling. In Oxford a group of econometricians was busy in the fifties following the line of Lawrence Klein; in 1961 they produced the first publication of a fully blown system of equations.* In Cambridge Richard Stone was the great inspirer. Around 1960 he set up the Economic Growth Project Model at the Department of Applied Economics. That developed into a formidable undertaking. In the course of the years the system grew into more than a thousand equations (consisting of 700 behavioural and technical relationships and 300 identities). The size of the system was caused above all by the fact that a distinction was made into dozens of sectors; thus there is not one consumer good but more than forty. The inter-industry flows between these sectors again give rise to a very large number of input-output equations that are not included in the above number of one thousand. It is a good job that there are such things as computers.†

---

*L. R. Klein, R. J. Ball, A. Hazlewood and P. Vandome, *An Econometric Model of the United Kingdom*, 1961.

† The properties touched on were those of 1973. They are described in the collection, *The Medium Term: Models of the British Economy* (ed. G. D. N. Worswick and F. T. Blackaby), 1974. This collection of essays also describes the Treasury Model and a third system of equations devised by the Cambridge Economic Policy Group (under the direction of W. A. H. Godley), which is called the 'Par Model' and predicts equilibrium values – a kind of neo-classical steady state system. In the 1960s the National Institute of Economic and Social Research had set up a predominantly Keynesian model. There is also the Southampton Economic Model of the U.K. and a model devised by the London Graduate School of Business Studies. The then Department of Economic Affairs also had its own system of equations. Information on all this research is to be found in K. Hilton and D. F. Heathfield (eds.), *The Econometric Study of the United Kingdom*, 1970,

The Stone model bears witness to impressive skill and sophistication, but is rather naïve on a number of points. The investment equation makes a distinction between replacement investments (these depend on depreciation) and expansion investments. The latter depend on changes in output (rigid accelerator). Neither profits nor taxes have a direct effect on business investment. The price equation is of the cost-push type with a constant profit mark-up. This therefore means that within the model quickly rising import prices or wage inflation cannot affect profits. In so far as net profits were to be depressed in some other way, for instance by rising taxes on profits, this model predicts no influence on investments! The wage push may stalk through the model – this has no effect on employment. Price inflation is also of little relevance – its influence runs via foreign trade (in so far as not compensated for by depreciation of the pound) and the fiscal drag: the progression in income tax (but this phenomenon can easily be attended to by a reduction of tax rates). Owing to the fact that the money wage increase is autonomously introduced, the model is also incapable of explaining why the wage-price spiral in Britain in 1975 was so violent. All this shows that the Stone model, 1973 version, was not very suitable for grasping the turbulent events of the seventies. The Keynesian relations are done justice, but they describe only part of reality.*

There is little point in discussing all systems of equations now under study in Britain, but it is perhaps interesting to make an

---

and above all in the collection *Modelling the Economy* (ed. G. A. Renton), 1975. I can warmly recommend the latter book to the reader, provided that he has a strong stomach.

*In 1974 T. S. Barker, after reproducing the Stone model, wrote that 'a British prices and incomes policy cannot stop world inflation. It can however play a part, along with exchange rate policies and the management of demand, in isolating the domestic economy from the worst effects of world inflation' (*The Medium Term: Models of the British Economy*, Worswick and Blackaby (eds.), London, 1974, p. 56). This is very true, but the quotation proceeds on the assumption that foreigners are the real villains. Less than a year later the U.K. was to have the highest inflation rate of the whole of Europe, and it had become a problem how Europe was to isolate itself against the worst effects of British stagflation. The Stone model does not contain a spiral submodel to familiarize its architects with this side of British life.

exception for the impressive operation that the Treasury is now performing. The strength and weakness of contemporary model-building may be illustrated by it.

3 · THE TREASURY MODEL *

This product of the Civil Service is a battery of some five hundred equations. It is dynamic, quarterly and fully computerized. It is quite considerably aggregative – little distinction is made between branches of industry (one exception: North Sea oil is always dealt with separately). However, a distinction is made between three levels of government (central, local, public corporations), and various categories of government expenditure (all exogenously determined). There are many kinds of taxes and grants. The purpose of the model is of course making forecasts; these are regularly published in the Treasury's *Economic Progress Reports*. But in addition it is the intention to demonstrate what the consequences are of policy measures. It is therefore an aid to planning (for this see Chapter XII of this book).

At first sight the model is forbidding. That is because of the notation – hundreds and hundreds of variables have to be mentioned, so that the simple alphabet is not enough. Consequently letter combinations are used, with a system behind them. Incomes are in general Y. Public corporations are PC. Income of public corporations is YPC. The part of YPC originating overseas is called $YPCOS$. Total personal disposable income is $YPDY$. Personal receipts of rent, dividends and net interest are $YPRDI$. Taxes are T, the corporation tax revenue is $TCCTR$. Prices are P; the wholesale price is PW; wholesale prices of manufacturing capital goods is $PWMCA$. Pages full of such code words seem more complicated than reality itself, but it is not difficult to see through this. The system is predominantly linear. It connects mainly levels and not changes. (The parameters are not elasticities but derivatives.)

Let us cast a glance at a number of strategic equations. The consumption function (which is right at the end of the model) says that the volume of consumption depends on disposable

* My description is based mainly on the *Technical Manual 1977*, H.M. Treasury, London (£1·50).

personal income, wealth and personal bank advances – all *real*, i.e. measured in constant prices. 'Disposable' means that the taxes have been deducted. Of these variables, the income term is of course the most important one. This consists of four segments, viz. pay, grants, profits (including income of the self-employed) and imputed rent. These four income categories have different propensities to consume. This is a traditional consumption function. One fine day the Treasury econometricians will definitely make a distinction between durable and non-durable consumer goods. Perhaps they will meet the monetary school part of the way, but sensational developments are not to be expected.*

The export equation is sophisticated and makes allowance for supply and demand functions. Capacity constraints are imposed. World prices are exogenously calculated. Imports depend on production and on price relationships. That is conventional. The investment equation is more vulnerable. Real investment in manufacturing is divided into replacement and net investment. Replacement depends among other things on depreciation (that is a trend component which is autonomous, and is not dependent on the wage push). Investment depends on the *variation* in output (flexible accelerator) and the real cash flow (= company saving plus receipts of capital grants minus stock appreciation and minus capital taxes). The same equation holds good for the services sector; in the case of agriculture the cash flow is omitted. Shipping and North Sea oil investment are forecast separately. Stocks are related to output, which implies that stockbuilding depends on the rate of growth of output (accelerator). Housing is dealt with separately, as is investment in the health and education sectors.

We can do a lot of things with these investment functions, but not everything.† Profits occur in them (as a part of cash flow); this is therefore an improvement on the Stone model. Wage

* What economics would like to know is how much *satisfaction* people derive from this consumption. The Treasury doesn't know, nor do other macro-economists.

† One possibility is that whole chunks of investment are estimated outside the model, for instance by asking the firms concerned what they have in mind. In this way one circumvents the model. There is a rumour that the Treasury is not averse to this procedure.

inflation puts in only an indirect appearance, to the extent that it reduces profit (but we shall presently see that this relationship remains very obscure in the model). There is no direct, neo-classical impact of wages on investments; the model does not recognize that the wage push leads to substitution of capital for labour. Nor does the wage push lead to accelerated scrapping of old machines.

Now something about profits, that strategic variable. They are found in the Treasury model by deducting from national income a number of income categories, in particular wages. Thus we find a residue – a method of calculation that ties in with that used by the businessman. However, that procedure has draw-backs from the point of view of model-building. All mistakes of estimation are concentrated in the residue. Moreover, with this subtraction sum we do not have a theory in the sense of a variable hypothesis.

The odd thing is that the model does produce such a hypo-thesis at a different place. If prices are explained, it is assumed that there is a constant mark-up on costs. (In other words, on the domestic market. In the case of exports the profit margin is a variable that depends on what the market will bear.) This fixes the profit margin. Total profit depends on sales, and propor-tionally. Underutilization losses are excluded. The wage push has no effect on income distribution. These are serious restrictions (which make the Treasury model inferior to that of Hickman-Coen). Moreover, we cannot have it both ways: determining profit by deducting earnings from independently determined national income and in addition assuming a constant mark-up. They may lead to different results. In other words, the equations threaten to become inconsistent.

In fact there is a third possibility of gaining insight into profits. We can introduce into the model a hypothesis with reference to the development of profits, for instance a well-determined down-ward trend. This quantity is then imposed, and we see what happens with the other variables. However, this way* will yield

* Suggested by A. A. McLean in his discussion of the Treasury Model, *The Medium Term: Models of the British Economy*, Worswick and Blackaby (eds.), London, 1974, p. 19.

little in this model, since profits do not have a strong effect on the other variables. They only help to determine national income, but investments react weakly. The regression coefficient of investments is very small indeed. However we turn, the treatment of the causes and effects of the level of profits remains a weak link in the model.

The way in which the Treasury Model tackles productive capacity is not very convincing either. There is a production function of the Cobb-Douglas type. The capital stock does not occur in it; instead a time trend has been included that determines the growth of capital. This means that the model assumes that capacity quietly continues to grow. The actual level of investment has no effect on this. The recession will impair investments, but that is not fed back to the productive capacity. To put it another way: the income effect of investments is picked up by the model; the capacity effect is not. The autonomous nature of the productivity trend is of course highly unsatisfactory, assuming that one wishes to understand the sluggish growth in Britain!

Next, this production function is not used to grasp capacity, but the other way round: to derive employment from a given output and a given length of the working week. That is thus the Keynesian order of things; capacity is only a constraint. By adding a further relation that writes the supply of labour as a function of demographic development, unemployment is determined. The tale about the production function therefore serves to reply to the question of how much unemployment is to be expected.

In conclusion, a strange point is that in Britain the development of capacity is taken as given. The exogenous growth of production in manufacturing implied in the model is 3·8 per cent a year. This is surprisingly high, for the actual figure for the period 1955–73 was 3·2 per cent a year, and this period included the prosperous sixties. The high estimate for the future may seem optimistic, but in the set-up of the model the opposite is the case. For production is derived from demand; the high productivity figure simply leads to more unemployment! The Treasury Model, with its 3·8 per cent, incorporates a sombre view of the labour market.

This rendering of a few relationships may show that I am rather critical of these equations. In actual fact the same applies here that I find of the Stone model: the crisis of the seventies is not properly described by the Treasury Model. The influence of the profit squeeze is hardly recognizable. High taxes play only a Keynesian role; they reduce demand, while the financial incentives remain what they are. The hyperclassical view that taxes are fatal to enterprise and investment cannot be refuted or confirmed by the Treasury – the whole relationship hardly occurs in the model. Wage inflation hardly has any influence on employment. The accelerated scrapping of old vintages is not contained in the model. The growth of productivity, which was notoriously slow, is autonomous and is not explained. There is much between' heaven and earth of which this model knows nothing.

Now this criticism is easy. The Treasury Model has been set up to solve Keynesian problems of the sixties: constant overspending within a sluggishly developing capacity, as a result of which the balance of payments is upset. The moot point is whether the problems of the seventies are in fact of Keynesian origin. I may moreover be open to the retort that the things that I want to have quantified are so slippery that they evade the grasp of the econometricians. The following section is concerned with this.

4 · STRONG AND WEAK LINKS

The reader may perhaps have acquired the feeling that quantitative economics is worthless. But that is too gloomy a view. Some relationships can be determined quite well, others cannot. The question is what causes the difference.

Econometrics has a good case in the quantification of large flows that display a stable relationship. Total consumption depends on disposable income. Imports depend on total production (and stockbuilding, which can change in the short term). In the midst of tempestuous developments the flows of international trade display remarkable firmness. Inputs and outputs of branches of industry also belong quite systematically together – inter-industry analysis is based on this.* Other reasonably strong links are the relationships between some impulses and their effect – the Keynesian multiplier is an example of something which is not a hard and fast parameter, but nevertheless the fluctuations are limited. And the capital-output ratio is a classic example of a very sluggish quantity. I am therefore opposed to the view that the search for constants is doomed to failure, since people are after all people and therefore subject to change. Constants can quite definitely be spotted in human behaviour. The models are full of reasonable, stable equations.

But human decisions can in fact sometimes disturb the fixed nature of relationships. That is above all the case when it is a matter of increasing and reducing stocks. The stocks themselves – the number of homes in a country, the number of cars, the stock of capital goods, the population – are sluggish quantities. However, the change in them – that is, what we designate by Δ – may fluctuate strongly. Thus consumers are capable of shifting the purchase of consumer durables in time – that makes a massive difference to the sales of those goods. Consequently someone like G. Katona (*The Powerful Consumer*, 1960) does not have the slightest confidence in Keynesian economics. As stated above, this is not too bad if we examine a longer series of years, but in the short term the relation of the sales of durables to income is as soft as butter. In the short run employment can be better or worse than expected. Stockpiling can also occur in commerce;

*Started by Wassily Leontief, *The Structure of the American Economy*, 1943. The idea is that a distinction is made between various sectors (for instance three: primary production, manufacturing, services; or two hundred) that all supply one another. The inputs and outputs are related to one another by fixed coefficients. Leontief wanted to get to know these coefficients. This knowledge can be useful when we want to investigate the effect of a strike in the steel industry, or an oil crisis. One difficulty with input-output analysis is that the coefficients do not always prove to be fixed; but sometimes they vary in a systematic manner. Thus the energy sector has increased strongly, not only in absolute but also in relative terms; today many more oil equivalents are required per unit of product than in the 1950s. In Leontief's terminology (see the title of his book above) this is a structural change.

this affects the balance of payments above all. Here too it is a matter of fairly short-lived deviations from an in itself fairly hard and fast relationship, namely that between imports and total spending.

The most striking case of stockpiling, which has long worried empirical economics, is that of investments. Here not only unreliable regression coefficients turn up, but also fundamental differences of opinion in the variables that have to be included by way of explanation. We have repeatedly seen above that the great disagreement between the classicists, the Keynesians and the monetarists boils down above all to a difference of opinion about the investment equation. The classicists want above all savings (or the interest rate) included as an independent variable; the Keynesians prefer sales, perhaps even the increase in sales (accelerator). The monetary school points to the money supply (and, in connection with that, the interest rate). Moreover, profits play an uncertain role. There have to be profits, if businesses are to be prepared to invest, but how much profit leads to how much investment depends on the situation – in other words, the parameter is not a fixed one.

A second group of unreliable elements in the model is to be found in the *balances*: differences between quantities that move independently of one another. They are more difficult to grasp as they are smaller but essential differences between larger variables. Here we encounter not only an econometric but also a theoretical crux: are the variables that are being balanced really independent of one another? Or is an equilibrium mechanism at work?

The examples are there for the picking: the deficit (or surplus) on the balance of payments, the deficit (or surplus) on the Budget. The component parts often develop independently of each other; this is a typical Keynesian, unclassical point of view. Exports are determined by quite different factors from imports. The rate of exchange is not an establisher of equilibrium. Government expenditure is determined by factors other than government receipts (even though the Chancellor of the Exchequer establishes a certain connection between the two sides of his Budget; the extent of the budgetary deficit does not leave him as cold as the orthodox Keynesians might desire). As soon as we write these balances as dependent variables, we find unstable parameters.

Now if we moreover feed the balances back into the model, the whole set-up becomes particularly uncertain. And yet this feedback is highly desirable with regard to the deficit on the balance of payments and the deficit of the Treasury. For the balance of payments determines the changes in the stock of foreign exchange and thus in part the creation of money; the Treasury deficit determines the government's financing requirement and thus likewise the creation of money. It is therefore not pleasant that precisely these variables are among the weak points of the model. With the feedback of the uncertain balances we have, I think, put a finger on one of the main reasons why macro-economics is such an uncertain science.

Unfortunately, there are still more of these strategic balances. Unemployment is one. Here too there is a limited difference between two very extensive quantities that develop fairly independently of one another: the total supply of labour and total employment. The classical theory links these two variables together via the wage rate – but, since Keynes, we no longer put very much faith in that mechanism. Unemployment is politically of extreme importance, and it can change quickly: in 1972 registered unemployment was at 4·5 per cent, which is too much; in 1973 it was at less than 3 per cent. There were then complaints about unfilled vacancies. This balance is sometimes fed back into the model, namely in the wage equation and in unemployment benefit, in the difference between possible and actual output. Between 1968 and 1978 British unemployment rose from 2 per cent of the working population to 6 per cent. If, say, three-quarters of this increase is explained by the model, one can at first sight call that a fairly satisfactory scientific result. But the additional 1 per cent of unemployment that remains unexplained will still give economics a bad name as a science.*

*In another sense, too, unemployment is a balance. Every weekday people register at the labour exchange; every day people find a job. Inflow and outflow are a multiple of the pool itself. The newspapers report on

From an intellectual and political point of view there is another very questionable case of a balance that is difficult to explain. That is profit: the difference between proceeds and costs. Moreover, macro-profit conceals the presence of losses in some firms – it is in this double respect a balance. True, in this case we may not say that the two big variables, i.e. costs and proceeds, are entirely independent of one another, and that profit is only a passive residue. There are quite definitely forces at work that try to keep profit at its normal level. The entrepreneur does his best to achieve that. So does the internal resistance of private enterprise. Alfred Marshall thought that there was something like a 'normal' profit per branch of industry. It is quite conceivable that, macro-economically, there is a kind of normal profit level. But that does not alter the fact that varying proceeds in combination with rather inflexible costs have long made profit a vulnerable quantity.

In the last few decades that vulnerability has been increased by the continuing wage inflation and the increasing burden of taxation. Moreover, a shift in international competitive relations has been going on: the textile industry is moving to the developing countries. Japan is taking over shipbuilding. As a result of all these things the 'profit squeeze' that we have discussed in Chapter IX occurred. It would be going too far to say that economics understands nothing at all of this phenomenon. In every manual we can find a short list of factors determining the size of profit. Such a book refers to F. Knight (reward for risk-taking), J. Schumpeter (bonus for taking the lead), A. Lerner (degree of monopoly). Theoretically that is instructive, but a list of this kind is not a regression equation. We have to admit that we do not have a quantitative profit theory. Constant parameters have not yet been found in this field. In every model profit is a very weak point.

And that then avenges itself once more, because profit must most definitely be fed back. We may suspect that business activity depends on it, certainly as far as investments are concerned.

---

dismissals – not on people who find a job – and thus suggest that soon not a single Briton will have a job.

But we do not know to what extent. The investment equation is in any case a shaky element, and that is not improved by the absence of a reliable profit equation. If anywhere, here is a fine field for research.*

All these uncertainties together, and especially those with respect to unemployment and profit, are a disappointment to people who had considered economics to be a very secure science. Perhaps they were misled by the precision with which the text-books present their simulation models. Perhaps too the general self-assurance, not to say self-complacency, of many economists had led to overestimation of the profession. The disappointment assumes serious forms in times when unemployment is on the increase and the word Depression is on everybody's lips. That was the situation in the mid seventies. Then bitter complaints were heard such as: economics doesn't understand anything about it! The economists have been kidding us! They said that they could prevent unemployment and, now that the chips are down, they don't want to know how to do it! These complaints and reproaches are worth considering in more detail, which we shall go on to do now.

5·THE CRISIS OF THE SEVENTIES EXPLAINED?

Can economists explain the crisis of the seventies? Some bitter observers say no – because otherwise they would have done something about it. This view mixes up explaining and combating.

---

*There is of course a considerable amount of literature on profits, but this is almost entirely of a speculative or reflective nature (the latter particularly in F. H. Knight, *Risk, Uncertainty and Profit*, 1921). Quantitative macro-economic research is scarce. There is a fine article by W. Nordhaus, 'The Falling Share of Profits', *Brookings Papers on Economic Activity*, 1974, in which he asks in surprise how the American economy can keep going on so little profit. Nordhaus also tries to explain the fluctuations in profit; successfully where Keynesian fluctuations are concerned, unsuccessfully where the longer-term movement is concerned. An interesting book is A. Woods, *A Theory of Profits*, 1975. He links the *required* profit to the *required* growth rate and to the requirements that firms make of self-financing. This argument is more normative than explanatory. It brings us without fail to the idea that profits in Britain are too low.

Whether inflation and unemployment can be suppressed is a political matter, which will be discussed in the following chapter. Here we are concerned with *understanding* the remarkable combination of considerable price increases, low growth and unemployment that afflicts Britain in particular. Now we have enough consistent views of this problem to maintain that our insight into the historical situation leaves absolutely nothing to be desired. There are theories galore:

(1) *The complacent long-term view*. Its adherents ask: what crisis? Economic growth always goes by fits and starts. Sometimes, as in the sixties, the growth rates are so high that they need a special explanation, and then, of course, things go somewhat more slowly. In an occasional year growth may prove to be negative (1975) – no wonder, with that oil crisis. After the shock of rising import prices, things get going again. In 1977 the national product was 10 per cent higher than in 1970. However, the awkward thing is that productivity grows more reluctantly than sales, and the result is unemployment. The growth of productivity in Britain is somewhat lower than in other countries, but so what? We can't all head the field. If productivity were to increase more quickly then, given the limited sales, there would be more unemployment. This is not a dramatic increase: registered unemployment grew from 2·5 per cent in 1970 to 6 per cent in 1978. That is of course unpleasant for its victims. However, part of this unemployment is voluntary. This comes about because unemployment benefit in Britain is rather generous. As a result, the mobility of labour is less. We thus see that unemployment and unfilled vacancies exist side by side.* Real income continues to rise, though slowly, and we may say that Britain is becoming

*According to one calculation, J. Taylor, 'The Unemployment Gap in Britain's Production Sector, 1953–1973', in G. D. N. Worswick (ed.), *The Concept and Measurement of Involuntary Unemployment*, 1976, the increase in unemployment over two decades is entirely due to friction, i.e. the existence side by side of unemployment and unfilled vacancies. In the fifties frictional unemployment was almost nil. In 1973 total unemployment was almost 3 per cent; of this, 2·3 per cent was caused by friction. If the trend that Taylor calculates for the period 1953–73 also applied to 1978, less than half of the 6 per cent unemployment would have to be explained by a deficiency of demand.

richer from year to year. Every year it is again true to say that you never had it so good.

(2) *The Keynesian view.* The crisis came about through the instability of spending, leading to a deficiency of demand for goods and services. Wage inflation has little to do with this – otherwise considerable unemployment would have occurred in the sixties. Balanced growth requires that production moves along a precisely determined growth path *à la* Harrod-Domar. In the seventies the British rate of growth fell below this percentage. This was due above all to the stagnation in world trade. If this stagnation is taken as given, a deflationary impulse follows from it. This propagates itself via the multiplier in domestic sales, and above all in investments. An accelerator acts on these investments, i.e. a fall in growth from 4 to 2 per cent halves the investments. This hard blow again makes itself felt through the whole system via the multiplier.

This analysis is formalized in weakened form by the Stone model and the Treasury Model. The parameters of the Treasury Model are such that the result more or less tallies with reality. What more do you want? In actual fact the real Keynesian should be grateful that the crisis does not spread much more virulently. By stepping up the multiplier and the accelerator to some extent a Keynesian model easily generates a violent depression. After the stagnation year 1975 expansion investments would have to disappear entirely. Paradoxically, the Keynesians are faced with the task of explaining why the crisis is not worse than it is. After all, there still is some growth: a recession, not a real depression.

In my personal opinion the Keynesian view contains an obvious nucleus of truth – 'Keynes is dead' is nonsense – but it does not represent the whole truth.

(3) *The monetarist view.* The crisis was caused by the disruption of the international monetary system. The dollar has become increasingly plentiful and has fallen dramatically. The oil countries have taken possession of an enormous part of the world supply of money and they are unable to spend all that money. Speculation drags the world from crisis to crisis. In such an unstable environment no country can flourish, and that applies in

particular to Britain, with its many overseas ramifications. As a result the pound keeps on falling, though this does not help to improve Britain's competitive position, since the wage-price spiral immediately swallows up every advantage of the depreciation. The monetary authorities see no possibility of putting a stop to the excessive money supply and so inflation continues, while at the same time the real quantities (above all exports and investments) suffer. Slumpflation is everywhere.

This monetary view, too, detached from all others, can explain what is going on, but it easily gives an over-explanation. And here again I think that it is exaggerated. There are countries (the United States, Germany) where growth still continued quite considerably. And so the monetary crisis is not all that frightening.

(4) *The classical view.* Britain suffers from two ills: wage inflation and a rapidly increasing tax burden. Of course world trade is also disappointing, but such causes operate in the background. Wage inflation is reflected in increases in money wages that far exceed productivity. A free-enterprise system can stand that for a while, but not long. This disease has been going on in Britain for decades now. Firms try to absorb the wage increase by forced substitution of capital for labour. This often takes place by the accelerated scrapping of old vintages, as a result of which many jobs are lost. The new vintages are good for productivity but create insufficient jobs. On top of this there is the impossibility of passing on the wage push year after year. A decrease in the rate of return thus occurs, which finally erodes business. As a result investments are not enough to replace the scrapped old machines. In that case both productivity and employment suffer: the typical phenomenon of the seventies. In addition no money is left for technical innovation.

The second cause of slumpflation is the increase in taxation – this comes on top of the effect of the wage push and has exactly the same effect. The incentive to invest slackens. So does the entrepreneurial incentive. Moreover, everyone tries to pass on the tax burden to his neighbour, by which the vicious circle of inflation is stimulated and regular profits are squeezed even more. Only speculators in houses and land, and some obscure figures, earn a lot of money, but they don't spend it productively (the latter is a variant of Ricardo). Britain is going to the dogs. Anyone who harps at some length on that theme must be surprised that production is still growing.*

(5) *The long wave mystical view.* Economic life is subject to long waves, called kondratieffs after one of the first people to describe them. The cycle covers some thirty years. At the beginning of the seventies we were at a peak, so now we are inevitably going down. Moreover, shorter waves are also operating, of, for instance, seven years (known as juglars). And there is nothing we can do about them: these are historical laws.

(6) *The Marxist view.* Capitalism is doomed to perish; that the end is near is heralded by the fact that one crisis follows another with increasing speed. Moreover, they become deeper, and they increasingly spread on a world-wide scale. Marx predicted what would happen with profits: the Law of the Decreasing Rate of Profit. The statistics that would lead us to believe that real disposable income in most capitalist countries is steadily increasing have been faked by the lackeys of the ruling class.

(7) *The synthetic view.* (This has my personal preference.) Why shouldn't we combine the usable elements from the above theories? The classical, the Keynesian and the monetary approaches do not exclude one another: there are synthetic models, such as that of Hickman and Coen (see section 2). And anyone who wants to can toss in long wave mysticism and fashionable Marxism. Moreover, in the seventies – as in every other decade since Adam and Eve – a number of specific historical causes have been in operation. A shift is going on in the international division of labour at the expense of the old industries, and within Britain

*It is quite feasible to explain the increase in unemployment entirely by a neo-classical mechanism with a Cobb-Douglas production function containing three ingredients: a wage push, as in fact occurred in the seventies; a low passing-on elasticity, i.e. a limited reaction of prices to the wage push and a high share of labour of 0·8. I have performed this calculation for the Netherlands. By setting the passing-on elasticity at 0·5 we already get an overprediction of unemployment, and then no tax increases have been taken into account. The figures may be found in J. Pen, 'Wages, Profits and Employment in the Mid-Seventies: the Controversial Case of the Netherlands', in *Pioneering Economics* (Festschrift for Professor Demaria, ed. T. Bagliotti, 1978).

too some regions are on the decline. Everybody knows that the working climate in the U.K. is not as favourable as might be desired; strikes and opposition to technical innovation have been discussed *ad nauseam*. Anyone who has simply studied the history of the port of London is not surprised that the growth of the British national product leaves something to be desired. By combining macro-economics with detailed studies of British economic life we can understand everything. We can explain to every jobless person between Falmouth and Thurso why he or she is out of work. Not a price has risen or we can sort out why. Not a firm goes bankrupt or we can explain why it did. There is nothing mysterious about these things – that is in fact my sincere, personal opinion.

Is there then nothing wrong with the explanatory power of economic theory? No, dear reader, the whole point of this book is that such a historical explanation of a unique situation is not real economic science. After the event we can understand everything; that is what economic historians try to do. I cannot forbid anyone to be satisfied with such an approach. I don't look down on historians. But anyone who is serious about the requirements of modern science demands a little bit more.

That little bit more is the search for the structure, the constant in change. I'm not satisfied until I know the values of strategic parameters. For instance, we have to know how much unemployment has to be ascribed to the one cause – too little spending – and how much to the other – too high wages – and how much to yet another – the increasing burden of taxation. How much delay in growth is imported and how much is of domestic origin? How much profit squeeze is due to the unions? Such closely specified quantitative knowledge is constantly sought. That is what is respectable about economic science. But unwavering results are not available, certainly not as regards the British economy.

Why do I insist on this methodological question? For three reasons. In the first place because we cannot now sufficiently make out which of the above explanations is the best one. Of course, Marxist ideology or the mystic wave 'theory' can be refuted by pointing to some simple evidence. But the Keynesian, monetary and classical views remain too much *views* – that is to say the subject of endless debate. If everything were in order science ought to be able to intervene in such broad debates and say: *that's how it is.* If an argument breaks out in the pub about the speed of sound you can ring up a physicist. If the argument is about the income velocity of money the economist does not give a hard and fast answer. We continue to take part in a general discussion on causes and effects, which is very fine, but it is not the same as science.

In the second place a properly specified model is required for predicting the consequences of external shocks. A new oil boycott cannot be predicted by economists – that is not our trade. But the consequences of such a boycott have to be mapped. It must be possible to calculate the balance of payments, investments, unemployment for different values of the exogenous variables. That leaves something to be desired. I am afraid the operation cannot be performed by the actual British models. A given shift in international trade will have its effect on the British economy. This, too, must be predicted by economics – it is very much a question of whether that can be done accurately. It must be possible to calculate the effect of a given increase in the burden of taxation on investments, production and growth. That cannot be done in the Treasury Model. This kind of conditional forecast requires more knowledge than that embodied in the British models now available.

This brings me to the third reason why I am attached to real economic science. Only with hard and fast parameters can we economists be of service to the politicians. That comes up for discussion in the following chapter.

CHAPTER XII

Economic Steersmanship

1 · THE AWKWARD RELATIONSHIP
BETWEEN THEORY AND POLICY

Many people think that it is hardly necessary to make a distinction between economic theory and economic policy – that is splitting hairs. I am of the opposite opinion. Economics tries to understand the world, politics tries to control it, and these are two different things. But at the same time it is true that theories have been devised to change the world. The economist and the politician are combined in one human being.

The Keynesian theory is a case in point. The *General Theory* wanted to explain the unemployment of the thirties but at the same time remedy it. The theory pointed in the direction of more public expenditure, and that choice seemed perfectly clear and imperative. But later Keynesians realized that a depression can also be remedied by reducing taxes. The choice between more public expenditure and less tax is not an easy one and certainly does not follow from a simple macro-economic theory. The relative size of the collective sector is at stake – a controversial matter that arouses political emotions. Keynesian theory cannot make any choice at all here – such a choice requires value judgements that the theory does not contain.

There is tremendous discussion on these value judgements and their role in science. My opinion is as follows: there is nothing wrong with value judgements, but there is nothing 'scientific' about them either – because they can't be proved, verified or falsified. They are assertions along the lines of: 'I don't like Brahms', 'I like Edna O'Brien's books' – to which possible answers are: 'Oh, is that so', or 'In that case, I don't like you'. The matter comes to a head because economic policy does not have just one aim (full employment), but many: economic growth, better distribution, less inflation, a cleaner environment, spreading of activities over the country – and if we take a close look there are still many more. The corner shop must stay. Work in the port of London may not decrease. We have to have quite different homes and new radiant cities. Existing rules of law and freedoms must be respected, or exactly the opposite.

Such value judgements come into effect with every policy measure, since some interests are always fostered and others harmed in such a case. Devaluation is good for exporters; it is bad for importers and for consumers with fixed incomes. High wages for the one group are bad for other groups. More goods can be bad for the environment. The politician can choose only because he prefers the one to the other. The theory does not know which side it must choose.* Does this mean that the theory is of no use to policy?

No, there is hope. The clear-cut solution has long been that the politicians say what objectives they wish to achieve and science says what instruments they can use to do so. As Tinbergen has shown, models can help in this. In such cases the sequence of the reasoning that has been used in this book is inverted. We used the model to explain endogenous variables (national income, employment) if the exogenous or autonomous variables are given (growth of world trade, government expenditure, tax burden). But we can also introduce given target variables, such as 3 per cent unemployment, into the model and then calculate what value the variables must assume which the government can influence: government expenditure, tax burden, money wages. These are the instrument variables. If the model is used in this way it is called a decision model. The distinction between target variables and instrument variables means that politicians and economists retain their own responsibility and yet can enter into a pleasant and useful relationship.

Of course the separation between ends and means presents many difficulties. Politicians are not accustomed to formulating

---

*I do not claim that the theory is for this reason always free from value judgements. On the contrary, they always creep in, especially if the theory takes the shape of a *vision*. That is a danger if we are not aware of it, but by paying close attention to it we can almost avert the danger. Vision is not prohibited, but it is not the same as science.

what they want in quantitative terms. They say: we want full employment, without it always being clear whether they have in mind 0 per cent or 3 per cent (William Beveridge in *Full Employment in a Free Society*, 1944) or 5 per cent (high frictional unemployment). In that case the economist can ask for an explanation. As a rule he will be given a whole series of different answers, depending on the politician he is speaking to. But the government must ultimately manage to acquire a point of view and the economist can urge this.

In another respect too the role of the economist in the discussion need not be a passive one. He can demonstrate that the politicians want too much at once – a not unusual state of affairs. If the model is in order, this inconsistency is unerringly exposed by the computer. For instance, overspending emerges. What must the economist do if he finds this? Shrug his shoulders and give up?

The answer is no. He still has a task in trying to elucidate the possible combination of policy instruments. There are two different approaches to this. One is associated with Tinbergen's name;* the other with that of H. Theil.†

Tinbergen's starting point is the well-known proposition that the number of equations must equal the number of dependent variables. In terms of a decision model: the number of instrument variables must equal the number of target variables. If a policy problem cannot be solved (because the goals seem to conflict) additional instruments must be devised. The example mentioned above calls attention to three goals: full employment, price stability and balance of payments equilibrium. Suppose we consider two instruments: budgetary policy and the rate of exchange. It is easy to see that the government can ensure the True Equilibrium along Keynesian lines, and with the help of the rate of exchange a sufficient volume of exports; sufficient in the sense that exports match the imports that correspond to the optimal national income. Mind you, we suppose that the rate of exchange is indeed fixed at this favourable level; if it is too high and the government does not want to lower it because it fears that devaluation is considered as a political defeat, this instrument

* *On the Theory of Economic Policy*, 2nd edn, 1952.
† *Economic Forecasts and Policy*, 1961.

is blocked and even the two targets cannot be realized. Full employment leads to a deficit on the balance of payments. But even if we have equilibrium on the balance of payments and full employment without an inflationary gap we may encounter a wage-price spiral; our model shows that wages may drive up prices and prices drive up wages, even without an inflationary gap. To stop this rot we need an additional instrument: a wage policy, or a price policy, or the combination of both in an incomes policy. Indeed, the idea of an incomes policy came to the fore as a way out of this dilemma. The sad point is, however, that this particular instrument so often fails to win popular support. People reject the idea of tying their incomes to productivity increases because they fear that other groups ('they') will succeed in avoiding or breaking the rules. This is a weakness of the Tinbergen approach: instruments are never 'neutral' in a political sense. As economists we may deplore this, but the fact remains.

In a situation where instruments are inapplicable the Theil approach becomes helpful. Here target variables are 'traded off' against each other. The economist says to the politician: now that you don't accept additional instruments you can't have it both ways, and all I can do for you is show you the price of reaching one objective in terms of another objective. The most striking example of this is, of course, the Phillips curve: the inverse relationship between unemployment and the wage level. If the model shows that the unemployment figures are really relevant to the spiral, the economist may show the unemployment it takes to suppress the spiral. He may draw up a numerical table from which the politicians can make their choice. Generally speaking, the Theil method is somewhat more cynical than the Tinbergen method; others would call it more realistic. But the Tinbergen approach reminds us of our duties: it is the task of the inventive economist (in his capacity as a citizen) to look for new instruments of economic policy.

2 · EQUILIBRIUM POLICY AND POLITICS

In the preceding section it was mentioned *en passant* that, in a community, forces may be active which can frustrate economic policy. It is worth while to apply this idea to the various elements of neo-Keynesian policy. It is as well to realize that this policy must be conducted in a complex force field, which deserves closer study. It is not my intention to elaborate this theory, in which elements of sociology and political science are combined, but a few remarks may serve to show what is involved. The clearest examples are in the field of public finance.

Some adherents of modern budget manipulation have made it appear too much as if government expenditure and taxes could be adjusted without more ado to the level set by the needs of the income flow. This tends to ignore the fact that the original function of government expenditure is quite different from that ascribed to it by the Keynesians; primarily, the items of expenditure on the budget have appeared on the scene to serve a specific purpose: the issue of passports, the arresting and trying of burglars, the education of young people. The structure of government expenditure is built up politically. There are voters and newspapers with a lively interest in these specific objectives; there are also separate pressure groups at work, advocating specific expenditure. All these views and preferences are considered to find expression via parliamentary procedure. The budget of a Western country is a law or a collection of laws enacted by the legislature. The political realization forms a game with very special rules, in which public opinion, the interested parties, Members of Parliament, ministers, civil servants, scientists, the press, and anybody else who wants to, take part. All these groups exert a certain force.

Now in this force field the macro-economic objectives must be brought to bear. This is in itself no mean task – it implies a constant rowing against the tide. Moreover, the statesman comes up against customs, procedures, theories which go back for centuries and which come into being with intentions quite different from those of Functional Finance. The historical origin of these rules of play lies in the wish to protect the people against the arbitrary power of a spendthrift or warlike ruler. The protection of the citizen against a domineering government demands a different technique of budget manipulation from the rapid and flexible adjustment of budget items desired by modern macro-economics.

Constant difficulties arise out of this misalignment between the traditional procedure and traditional objective on the one hand and the desiderata of anti-cyclical policy on the other hand.

However, these difficulties are minor compared to those proceeding from democracy. This form of society accentuates the direct, visible interests. But if total expenditure is too high the Keynesian advocates unpopular measures. Taxes have to be raised, something that nobody likes. The growth of spending has to be checked; this is a direct infringement of some interests. One of the characteristics of a democracy is that everything that is unpopular is loudly criticized. Another characteristic is that a government must try to remain in power. A Keynesian policy is therefore an unsuitable means. The dangers evoked by overspending are not directly and personally felt by a single group in society. In Britain these dangers manifested themselves in the fifties and the sixties as permanent difficulties with the balance of payments. The British were not unaware of these difficulties – on the contrary, they were featured for so long on the front pages that the balance of payments had become a kind of collective migraine which you never get used to but which you assume that you can if necessary learn to live with. The connection between balance of payments and slight overspending was repeatedly made, and forgotten again and again. This forgetfulness was encouraged by the fact that different current causes of the balance of payments crisis kept on emerging, and still do: speculative movements of capital, violent fluctuations on the international money markets. It is forgotten that fundamental, slow-acting forces are in operation. One of them is the slow drift of the government along with overspending: the inflationary infection.

This infection is active both on the tax side and public expenditure. In a boom tax proceeds exceed expectations – the Chancellor of the Exchequer receives more than he had thought every year, and the temptation to spend the extra is great. The Keynesian view advises against this, but the recommendation is unpopular. On the expenditure side too there is a tendency towards rapid growth in good times (in bad times too, come to that, but for other reasons). Many budget items relate to provisions complementary to those of business and households. In a boom there are lots of cars on the roads; perhaps the roads are not designed to carry this heavy traffic. A corresponding budget item is increased. Long queues form at crossroads; fly-over junctions are required; pressure groups do their best to get contracts for these large-scale projects. Business requires more energy; the government is obliged to make investments on behalf of power supplies.

There is still more, much more. Thus, as the households earn more, a large number of their children will study. Educational capacity may then prove too small within a short time; and so school buildings have to be constructed, teachers appointed, laboratories fitted out, libraries extended. People visit the theatre and the concert hall more often, since their incomes, swollen by the boom, allow them to do so; and every encouragement of cultural activity costs the government money. Ultimately the stage is reached in which everything seems possible. Members of Parliament advocate new provisions on the strength of the fact that additional expenditure in other sectors has already been permitted by the Chancellor of the Exchequer. 'If that expenditure was justified, this certainly is.' Parliament is then no longer the watchdog of the level of expenditure; it pushes up government expenditure. The fact that the larger parliamentary parties have their specialists in agriculture, transport, education, public health, etc., contributes to this forcing up of expenditure, for the specialists argue in favour of their own sector and may often be regarded as extensions of pressure groups.* The financial specialists of the parliamentary parties then come and tell the government afterwards that total government expediture and taxation are too high. In a boom in particular this makes correct management difficult. In government finance cumulation occurs, without compensation.

In this political force field one can often observe as an additional complication the division of government bodies into national and local, such as Federal, state, and county. The local authorities often are not very conscious of anti-cyclical policy, to put it mildly. Nor is this implicit in their function. But they play

*Attention has been drawn to this in particular by W. Drees, Jr, *On the Level of Government Expenditures in the Netherlands after the War*, 1955.

a prominent part in a general encouragment of expenditure. They cannot help this; their expenditure is certainly justified in the sense that it relates to fine and useful things. But through this division of responsibility, little sometimes comes of anti-cyclical policy.

The inflationary infection of governments has certainly contributed to the constant tendency towards overspending that characterized the fifties and sixties. It occurred in every country. In most countries too the disadvantages were not particularly dangerous. Prices rose, but that need not be a particularly serious phenomenon in itself. Money wages rose even more strongly – and this would not have been a disaster either, if a slow grinding-down of profits had not occurred. In the course of time business became increasingly vulnerable. This erosion was due more to the wage-price spiral than to the overspending, though the two elements cannot be properly separated from each other. Moreover, the growing tax burden played a part in the process, and this causal factor too cannot, unfortunately, be precisely separated by science from the others. But, all in all, the overspending of the fifties and sixties was not a destructive occurrence; I would be prepared to defend the proposition that in most countries it did more good than bad. It led to a somewhat faster growth of real incomes.

But note, this opinion holds for most countries, but probably not for Britain. There the slight overspending did great harm. The cause is in the balance of payments, and above all in the influence that this had on the policy of the British government. That influence was very bad and, strangely enough, that was so because the various British governments tried to put the Keynesian lessons into practice.

This seems paradoxical. But the point is that the balance of payments fluctuates – the British balance of payments too displays short waves on top of an underlying unfavourable trend. Exports and imports are great variables, with an appreciable difference. The British government has allowed itself to be led too much by the short fluctuations and too little by the underlying trend. The result is a nervous policy, which first encourages an upswing and then roughly checks it. The growth spurts were always short ones. This is known as stop-go. It is the degeneration of Keynesian policy.*

We can also put it another way. A Keynesian policy is in any case unsuitable for suppressing short fluctuations, since the multiplier requires time. Even if the government itself should react immediately – which is not so in the democratic game – even then waves of, say, three years could not be properly remedied. If a government nevertheless tried to do that, it runs a considerable risk of destabilizing the economy. Every time that the recession begins, the authorities apply the brakes.

That this is not a theoretical possibility but grim reality is demonstrated by an investigation made by a group of economists under the auspices of the Organization for Economic Cooperation and Development, Paris, into the effectiveness of cyclical policy in various OECD countries. The group, under the direction of B. Hansen,† studied the period 1955–65. Their conclusion was that the stabilization policy had contributed in most countries to a steady growth to some extent. The great exception was Britain. British policy had, overall, aggravated the difficulties. In my opinion that is not because the country has such poor rulers or such poor economists. The cause lies in the fundamental difficulties with the balance of payments brought about by the war and the disintegration of the Empire (everybody knows the story, but tells it in his own way). There was not an adequate reaction to these changes in the form of a somewhat slower growth of consumption. As a result growth had to be slowed down forcibly and jerkily every time the panic about the balance of payments reached a climax.

But the sad story of stop-go does raise the question of whether a Keynesian policy alone would have been strong enough to solve the balance of payments problem in the longer term. The answer is no. The support of an incomes policy is required. The latter should have laid the permanent basis for suppressing the spiral, strengthening the export position, creating room for growth of productivity. On that basis a Keynesian policy could

*See M. Shanks, *Planning and Politics, the British Experience, 1960–76*, 1977.

†B. Hansen, *Fiscal Policy in Seven Countries*, 1969.

have been successful. We therefore come to the key question of why this incomes policy did not get started.

Before we discuss that, it is as well to bear in mind that too high a level of spending is a problem of the fifties and the sixties. The characteristic trouble of the seventies is the opposite: unemployment, unutilized productive capacity, minimum growth. It looks as if this is the classic example of a disease that Keynesian therapy can cure. The reader is right if he or she thinks that the recession of the seventies presents a test case for the practicability of Keynesian policy. But apparently something has gone wrong here too – to investigate this I have devised the following dialogue.

3 · BETWEEN THE READER AND THE AUTHOR, ON KEYNESIAN POLICY IN A RECESSION

READER: I'm a British subject with a political objective: unemployment, which threatens to exceed 6 per cent at the end of the seventies (it is now 1978), must go down. I have understood from the preceding pages that it is difficult to deal with short fluctuations; however, what we're going through now is no short fluctuation, but a long and nasty recession. I have further gathered that there are decision models that offer me, as a citizen, a choice between policy measures for achieving my aims. Now, you're a model-builder –

AUTHOR: Model-user –

R: And you can perhaps answer my questions. Do you happen to have a decision model for the United Kingdom handy?

A: Yes, indeed. In 1975 H. P. Evans and C. J. Riley, economic advisers to the Treasury, published an article on 'Simulations with the Treasury Model'.* They produced computer runs indicating the consequences of policy measures – very interesting material for what it gives and doesn't give – very interesting indeed...

R: I thought that you weren't so crazy about the Treasury Model?

---

*In G. A. Renton, *Modelling the Economy*, 1975. The collection also contains policy simulations with the London Business School Model. The results are not essentially different from those of Evans and Riley.

A: Yes, it's exclusively Keynesian, but now we're talking about a Keynesian policy for combating the unemployment of the seventies and so it's a good model to start with – not to finish with. But now, according to the rules, you must first specify your objective.

R: As I've already said, unemployment has got to go down – from 6 to 0 per cent.

A: Shall we send all the unemployed to Australia?

R: Are you serious?

A: No, but I suspect that you have more than one objective. I can also suggest to you that all the ugly high-rise flats that were built in the fifties and sixties be demolished within a year and straight-away rebuilt, but on a small scale – small is beautiful – in the countryside. While this is going on we'll house the occupants in tents. We'll force the unemployed to take part in the project. If that doesn't entirely meet your objective, we'll demolish the rest of London as well.

R: Right then. I don't want any rough stuff – we're not living in Cambodia. Let's keep it to macro-economic measures, in other words budgetary manipulation, because that's what this book is about. Or wouldn't that help? You have a worried look.

A: Well, part of the unemployment is to be found in firms and industries that have hardly anything to expect from increase in demand. They are outdated or the victims of shifts in the international division of labour. If we push up the domestic demand to eliminate this unemployment, we create overspending. Here we encounter difficulty, greatly underrated by simple textbooks, of establishing the productive capacity. You can't say: there is 6 per cent unemployment, and therefore the capacity is 6 per cent greater than production. Part of that 6 per cent does not relate to capacity, unless people are first retrained and relocated – no small task.

R: Do Riley and Evans [to be referred to further as R and E] tell us how many people are involved?

A: No, but if we may believe Jim Taylor [see Chapter XI, section 5] and extrapolate a bit to the end of the seventies, we certainly arrive at 3 per cent frictional unemployment.

R: You don't mean to say that there's nothing to be done about it?

A: No, but it's a matter of retraining and relocating – also relocating the work to the people – regional policy. That's difficult, and it only works if the total demand is high enough. But not too high, because overspending restrains mobility. The macro-models are silent about these subtle matters. Let's say that we eliminate 3 per cent unemployment by creating demand à la Keynes. Would you approve of that?

R: If you say so. Should it presently prove that we can easily achieve that 3 per cent increase in production I'd like to come back to that concession. What policy measures can you offer?

A: R and E have worked out the effects of three typical Keynesian instruments: additional government expenditure (more specifically government consumption, such as the hiring of additional teachers and policemen), a reduction in income tax and a reduction in purchase tax.* Which do you prefer?

R: Well, that depends. I know a few public services that don't give enough service – the police are undermanned ... But what kind of reduction of income tax did you have in mind?

A: R and E performed their exercise with an increase in the personal tax allowance.

R: I'm in favour of that. And VAT is so high as well ... May I opt for all three measures at the same time?

A: Certainly. We can for instance make a package of £400 million

---

*R and E have also made computer runs for something else: an increase in national insurance grants completely covered by an increase in contributions. The model predicts a highly favourable effect on production. I suggest that this measure be kept out of the discussion because I do not trust the model on this point. The additional grants lead to more consumption, that I'm prepared to accept, but the contributions have to be paid by somebody. In so far as these are employed persons, only the propensity to save between employed persons and recipients of grants can increase the net demand – not a very impressive something. In so far as employers pay the extra contributions, and there is no passing-on, profits become smaller. The latter seems rather probable in today's Britain. An intensification of the profit squeeze will hardly be suitable for pushing up production. The Treasury Model here predicts something that does not proceed from the Keynesian view and that is at variance with the classical view.

a year of increased expenditure, the same amount of income tax reduction and the same amount of purchase tax reduction. That's £1,200 million, in 1972 prices.

R: Why precisely those amounts?

A: Because R and E put them into their model. We can then see how far we get.

R: Go ahead then. How far do we get?

A: According to R and E this increased expenditure leads to 0·83 per cent increase in production. Income tax reduction leads to 0·71 per cent, purchase tax reduction to 1·05 per cent. These effects take some time; the multiplier has to do its work, and the accelerator. Price effects are also involved, especially in the case of purchase tax, which in turn affect exports. After about four years the impulse will have more or less spent itself, but even before then quite considerable income effects are visible. The percentages that I quoted apply after four years.

R: I've meanwhile been adding up what the programme yields. I get 2·59 per cent. Since we have to have 3 per cent, I suggest that the operation be raised from £1,200 million to £1,400 million. In 1972 prices. That seems an awful lot of money to me. May I ask whether you have an idea of the size of national income in 1972?

A: Something like £55,000 million.

R: In other words, an injection of 2·6 per cent to attain an effect of 3 per cent? That seems an improbably poor result to me. It's quite different from what Keynesian theory would have us believe – high multipliers . . .

A: Well, that depends on which books or parts of books you read. In earlier chapters of this book you've been able to pick up something about $s+t+m$ or – a more complicated formula – $l-c+ct+m$. For Britain such multipliers don't work out much higher than one. And yet that also surprises me a little, because the relation between the 3 per cent effect and 2·6 per cent impulse is no ordinary multiplier. It is the result of a model, in which the operation of the accelerator has also been included, together with price effects that work via exports in the case of purchase tax. R and E therefore speak of a 'dynamic multiplier', in which all these reactions are thus firmly embedded. They have calculated this parameter for the three policy instruments. After sixteen quarters it is 1·33 for government expenditure, 1·34 for purchase tax and 1·12 for income tax. Yes, it really is very low. The Treasury Model is Keynesian all right, but in a subdued, very subdued form. On the one hand that's a good thing, because otherwise the British economy would have tumbled into a depression through the external shocks of the seventies. But on the other hand the British economy also reacts much more sluggishly to deliberate impulses. We shall have to take drastic measures to get out of this impasse.

R: How are things exactly with the effect on employment? We keep on talking about an additional production of 3 per cent, but does that also give 3 per cent more jobs?

A: Well, in principle production and work run parallel to one another in the Treasury Model. True, there are time lags among these, but let's just forget them. Unemployment, on the other hand, reacts very weakly – however that comes about . . .

R: Don't R and E say why?

A: Yes, it may have something to do with the registration of applicants for work – but if we start to take that into account we get odd figures. The effect on unemployment is only half that on production. In that case the necessary impulse becomes twice as great – no, we'd better forget it.

R: I don't like that. These uncertainties – I thought that these models were so accurate? But we've a long way to go yet, because we have to extrapolate the results of the model to the end of the seventies. Let's say 1978, because it is to be hoped that we have figures on that year. What does our employment programme look like in terms of 1978?

: The required impulse becomes greater. Prices have about \ubled and productivity has also increased again. The simplest \ng is to express everything in national income. If we put the \ulse at 2·6 per cent again we arrive at a sum of £3,600 million \978.

\at seems an awfully large amount to me. It's charged against \get – of how much?

\nething like £56,000 million, if we take all expenditure. At first sight we have to relate the programme to the budgetary deficit; that's some £4,000 million, and so it looks as if we have to nearly double the deficit. But according to the Keynesians that calculation is wrong.

R: I figured that too. As a result of our operation national income, sales, everything increases; and tax is levied on that. What do R and E say about this?

A: Nothing. Their model does not contain an endogenous calculation for tax proceeds and so the computer has nothing to say. Strange, when you come to think of it. After all, it's a Treasury Model.

R: Perhaps the Treasury finds tax proceeds too delicate a matter to entrust to computers. Can we estimate something ourselves?

A: Of course. The tax rate, including national insurance contributions, is about 50 per cent. Moreover, a reduction in unemployment leads to a reduction in benefit paid to the unemployed. A large part of the money – let's say half – returns to the Exchequer. So the operation costs the Exchequer some £1,800 million net. Which therefore means an increase in the national debt.

R: Is that a problem?

A: That's up to you. I thought that you'd given high priority to one objective – employment.

R: Agreed. After all, you tell me the debt is not a burden on our children and you keep berating me for not believing you. But now the balance of payments, for I have the feeling that that's where the shoe is going to pinch.

A: Certainly. R and E give precise information on this. The package of £1,400 million would have yielded a balance of payments effect of minus £300 million in 1972, or over 20 per cent of the total programme. That includes the attracting of imports, but also the encouragement of exports by the lower prices via purchase tax. The simplest thing would be to transplant this 20 per cent plus to 1978, but that's not permitted, because import prices have risen more strongly than the average price level. I suggest that we put the balance of payments effect at one-third.

R: Rough and ready methods . . .

A: Yes, but we can also take a quarter. It does not matter much, for in either case the result is rather discouraging. Whether a deterioration in the balance of payments works out at £1,200 million or £800 million – in both cases it's a figure that is much higher than the hard-won surpluses on current account in 1977 and 1978.

R: I must say that that alarms me. All the time in the seventies we've had those deficits – in 1975 £1,700 million, in 1976 £1,400 million. Not until 1977 was there a surplus – of £300 million. For 1978 a surplus of £400 million is expected, and the government is rather proud of that. That programme of ours – Britain can't afford it. Can't you think of something?

A: We can shift between the three types of measures. Reduction of purchase tax ultimately encourages exports. According to R and E that makes a net difference on the balance of payments of 10 per cent or so. Special measures for the building trade yield more jobs and fewer balance of payments effects than general injections.

R: But that's all small stuff; it doesn't help to solve the problem. Must we conclude that a Keynesian policy is absolutely impossible?

A: That's too sweeping. In 1977 the British Government announced a programme for budgetary 1978–9 of the order of magnitude of £2,000 million. It looks a bit like ours. It's nearly half the size, but still . . .

: Would that programme eliminate half of our 3 per cent unemployment, then?

That's difficult to say. Look, the tax reductions announced by Chancellor of the Exchequer are in part not genuine ones. I an this: as a result of the wage–price spiral the burden of a gressive tax automatically increases. They call it the tax drag. cancel that out the rates have occasionally to be reduced or, this case, the personal allowances raised. That's a pleasant age that the Chancellor has for the nation, but it is slightly tive. The figures that R and E give us are genuine reductions, ductions in respect of what the econometricians call the un – what comes out of the computer if the burden of n is unchanged.

R: If I understand you correctly, it is rather meaningless for the government to perform such a programme – it has to be compared with what would have happened without tax drag. Moreover, our £3,600 million is quite a lot higher than the government's £2,000 million. I continue to feel that Britain is not following a large-scale Keynesian policy –

A: I have that feeling too.

R: And that it perhaps is unable to do so. But then it becomes time for the creative economist to indicate new solutions – I read that somewhere.

A: Yes, that was about the Tinbergen approach, and about incomes policy. The latter is warmly recommended, only it never got off the ground . . .

R: But surely we've had voluntary limits since 1975? First of all we had Stage I and Stage II and then Pay Guidelines, didn't we?

A: Yes, but the British wage–price spiral remained the strongest in all of Europe. An incomes policy is nice to talk about, but as the result counts this pudding is not a very tasty one. Could it not perhaps be that Britain cannot afford a Keynesian policy because there is no incomes policy?

R: Your question is a leading one. You evidently think so.

A: Yes, in fact I do. And I also felt – see the previous section – that overspending in Britain could not be properly combated without an incomes policy. Now it seems to me that the same applies to combating the recession.

R: In other words, a key problem. I'd like to know why, according to you, Britain doesn't have such a policy.

A: On to the next section for that.

4 · THE SEVEN DIFFICULTIES WITH AN INCOMES POLICY

An incomes policy tries to depress the wage–price spiral to 0 per cent, or 3 per cent or, if need be, to 5 per cent. To find out what this basic recipe means we need no decision model. Constant prices mean that the increase in the level of wages must be equal to the rise in labour productivity – and the latter is 2, 3 or 4 per cent but never 8 per cent or 10 per cent. The increase in profit margins must be nil; in other words profits may grow only in breadth, not in depth. Variations can be applied to this basic recipe: some wages may be increased because they were lagging behind the others; in times of squeezed profits it is necessary for profits to recover and prices have to go up; rising import prices have to be passed on, otherwise profits are reduced; and if we accept a price increase greater than nil we must also accept that money wages increase more strongly than productivity. Such variations can supersede the basic receipe. In practice they spoil the dish. This is the first reason why an incomes policy fails.

An incomes policy does not demand sacrifices of the nation. True, money incomes are prevented from rising, but real incomes go their usual way – perhaps they will become a little higher through the incomes policy. The growth of real incomes is determined by the growth of productivity, and the spiral has a bad effect on that growth – if only because the spiral hampers a Keynesian policy (see the last two sections). Owing to the fact that practically everybody – the government, the unions, the journalists – depicts incomes policy as making a sacrifice a firm basis is laid for non-cooperation. Talk about sacrifices makes people shy off, and every group starts to think: after you. Misunderstanding rules. This is the second reason why incomes policy can't succeed.

The refusal to participate (or the condition that *all others* participate, which amounts to a refusal) is not just stupidity. For every group – teachers, miners – it is true to say that the ideal incomes policy is as follows: everyone joins in except us. The secretive pursuit of this goal causes the policy to fail and everyone is worse off than before – the spiral continues. You can call this a breakdown in communication, or a built-in tendency towards irrational behaviour. Games theoreticians call it the Prisoner's Dilemma.* It is the third stumbling block.

---

*It often happens: armaments race, forcing up advertising budgets, some cases of cut-throat competition, ever-faster aircraft. And all because another does it too.

An incomes policy requires compulsion. That is unpleasant for whoever is subject to that compulsion, but also for the authorities who have to do the compelling. They are depicted as tyrants. Supervisory machinery has to be created. The police have to catch offenders. The one offender is caught and the other is not – this is certain to lead to bitterness. Politicians are quick to see this and switch to voluntary restraint. However, that is not enough. (Or they play the temporary game, which is worse than nothing, as we shall see later.) Liberals cannot follow a strong incomes policy, Conservatives don't want one and Labour comes to grief on the unions. That is the fourth reason.

The fifth difficulty is that incomes policy takes away the greatest part of the tasks of the unions: bargaining for wage increases. Under a 3 per cent policy little success remains to be gained. Union leadership is exposed to severe criticism if it takes part in this. Even voluntary restraint (15 per cent instead of 16 per cent) will constantly be used as a weapon by radical members. In the world of fiction, imaginary wage reductions become powerful arguments with which to pursue harassed union officials. The unions consequently do not participate permanently. Nor does the Labour Party, and the same applies to the Conservatives since, once they are in power, they will have to do business with the unions.

Sixthly, an incomes policy that is sometimes depicted as very fine and just always proves in practice to be rough and unfair. Justice beckons far in the background – where the wage-price spiral has been suppressed and the pressure groups live together like lambs. In the foreground unpleasant things are occurring. The authorities are bearing down on those they can catch; the latter are workers who come under a collective agreement. Others, usually free professions, escape. A price policy is a necessary complement to an incomes policy, for even under a profit squeeze some businessmen manage to secure very palatable price increases. But everybody knows that such price control works badly in the case of individual products, repairs and changes of quality. Equal cases are dealt with unequally. Jurists condemn that.*

*See G. P. Schultz and R. Z. Aliber, *Guidelines, Informal Controls and*

The seventh difficulty is that an incomes policy, if it is to work, must be a consistent long-term policy. In reality it is always something that is introduced by way of an emergency measure, then gives rise to blazing rows and is soon abolished again. During the short time that the policy more or less has an effect tension is built up which discharges afterwards. The wage-price spiral makes up its arrears like mad. A pessimist might think that the short-lived attempts that Britain has experienced in the last decade have strengthened the wage-price spiral rather than damped it down. In this cynical reasoning purely verbal attempts at an incomes policy even have a negative effect. They further disputes and thus inflation, and are worse than laissez-faire. But opposed to this is a different view, which seems to me kinder and more realistic, namely that an incomes policy is at least a method for making employers, unions and government communicate. Where people get together to talk, a few problems might perhaps be solved.

The list above of stumbling blocks and traps is a long one, and that is a pity, especially for Britain. Other countries do not need an incomes policy as much because they have other built-in methods of damping down the spiral (Switzerland, the Federal Republic of Germany), or because they have fewer balance of payments problems (the Netherlands) or because they have a stronger growth potential (the United States) or because they have abandoned or have never known full employment and are quite chaotic anyway (Italy, Latin America). An incomes policy is a civilized method of mastering an uncivilized event, namely the senseless wage-price spiral, and thus making room for a full-employment policy. Britain needs an expansionist Keynesian policy and we have seen that such a policy cannot succeed if the balance of payments does not allow it to do so. And that will continue to be the case as long as the wage-price spiral in Britain is stronger than elsewhere in Europe. If this connection penetrates public opinion, there may perhaps still be some hope. It is not a

---

the Market Place, 1966. This is concerned with policy in the United States – and it is not flattering to that policy. Economists and lawyers jointly hammered it, and they really were not all Friedmanians.

good thing in politics to assume the absolute unattainability of something that nevertheless seems a civilized idea.

5 · THE LONG VIEW

Nobody doubts that the seventies form a difficult period. A modicum of despair can do no harm, but we must not exaggerate. With reference to 1972 Michael Shanks wrote that the British economy was in a desperate state* – and that was just the start, for then came the oil crisis, the violent increase in import prices, the blazing inflation, the stagnation of 1975, the ever-deeper fall of the pound, the ever-increasing rise in unemployment. These events should surely have summoned up complete collapse – but that is not the way things went. The national product grew, stagnated, grew again. At the end of the seventies it was over 10 per cent higher than in 1970. Real personal disposable income per head was even 20 per cent higher. All kinds of forms of comfort did what they had already been doing for years – increase. The percentage of households with a telephone rose from 38 in 1970 to 53 in 1976. For central heating the percentages were 32 and 47.† It is not that the telephone and central heating determine human happiness, but they are small signs of economic progress. The view that this kind of progress is now finished is based on the speaker's mood, not on facts.

It is, however, true that economic policy is faced with a number of heavy tasks. The first is of an international nature: the worldwide monetary system has to be improved. This is no small thing, since it means that the dollar has to be put on a sound basis again, that oil money has to be recycled, that exchange rates have to be stabilized, that the financing requirements of the developing countries have to be met – and all that in a world full of conflicting interests and political disputes. The citizen economist can give only three simple recommendations. Countries with strong balances of payments must combat domestic recessions by in-

* *Planning and Politics, The British Experience 1960–1976* (1977). The theme of this book is that politics drags itself from failure to crisis and from crisis to failure.

† *United Kingdom in Figures 1977* (Government Statistical Service).

creased spending, otherwise they drag other countries down with them. Countries with domestic recessions may not take refuge in protectionist measures, otherwise total international trade shrinks even more. And countries with strong balances of payments must help the weak ones. To summarize all three recommendations in one: a Keynesian, expansive policy remains the solution and a restrictive national solution makes matters worse. If the countries keep to this, we must hope that world trade will continue to grow.

Within this context a second problem looms up. It is quite feasible that the growth of productivity within a number of Western countries remains on the high side compared with the growth of sales. In itself that is by no means a new or alarming phenomenon. On the contrary, it opens up possibilities for a shorter working day, a shorter working week, longer holidays, earlier retirement. This is a form of progress of civilization that has already been going on for a century. Only the difficulty is that the process of labour-saving does not run smoothly. In some sectors it goes too quickly, and summons up unemployment. Other branches of industry where profits are too small cannot tolerate shorter working hours and shake labour out roughly – possibly via bankruptcy. In the coming decades considerable political inventiveness will be required in order to strike a balance between gradual and civilized contraction of working hours on the one hand and rough reduction of the number of employed persons on the other. Employment policy will have to be partly directed towards increasing the demand for finished products, but also partly towards re-allocation, mobility and more leisure time.

A tricky problem here is how the costs of such operations have to be distributed. There will have to be government subsidies, but on what scale? The danger threatens that the burden of subsidies, via taxes, comes to weigh too heavily on the sectors in which money is still earned, with the result that these too get into financial difficulties. One possible answer to this is moderation of the money incomes of employed persons. Here we encounter an additional argument for an incomes policy. Others will say that labour-saving technical progress gives us a reason for a new type of collective bargaining – employers offer guarantees of employment in exchange for lower wage claims. These things will come up in the future in different institutional variants.

The lower growth rate of production that is to be expected – that is to say lower than the high figures of the sixties – creates in addition to the danger of unemployment the following (third) problem, namely that of the size of the collective sector. Many countries, including Britain, have become used to a rapid growth in government spending. Various mechanisms, described in section 2 of this chapter, operate in this direction. Now relative growth of the public sector can quite easily be absorbed within a growing economy – although, above all in Britain, the complaint is heard that the burden of taxation is already too high now to maintain a flourishing private sector. This complaint cannot be properly verified by economic theory; we have seen that model-building makes inadequate allowance for the effect of taxes on investments and incentives. But one thing that is certain is that a further growth of the public sector, given a slower growth of the national product, will encounter great political difficulties. The growth of real disposable income – which was still present in the mid seventies – may in the long run work out to be too small to give people satisfaction. Little else will remain other than that governments take a very critical look at the allocation of new public activities. Thereby constant reference will have to be made to the bad times, but the latter will foster the general atmosphere of depression and crisis. It is the inevitable fate of democracy that unpopular measures are attainable only by first explaining to people that an emergency is occurring. But this practice may defeat its own goals.

The fourth problem is that of the environment and energy. In the long term it will probably be the most drastic one. Within the growth of production strict selection will have to take place. Everything that pollutes impermissibly, wastes scarce natural resources impermissibly and consumes energy impermissibly will have to be halted by the government. The price mechanism (charges: the polluter must pay) and physical measures will have to be used side by side. Extremely unpopular steps will have to be taken, such as a restriction of air traffic. (Present growth rates of this activity will prove to be absolutely destructive.) That a very strict policy is necessary follows from the fact that even under such restrictive policy a number of dangerous developments can hardly be checked. The pollution of the sea by oil will continue even with the best policy; shipwrecks and illegal discharges will attend to that. The depletion of sources of energy will at most go more slowly, but it will be impossible to prevent it. Which is a reason to take the most effective measures possible to halt it where this is still possible.

Of all the problems that this entails, I shall mention only one. Is it necessary that we switch forthwith to zero growth? If so, how can that be reconciled with the desirability of maintaining the growth in world trade? If not, how can we save the remnants of natural landscapes and the last beautiful beaches?

My personal view is this. Postulating zero growth is no help, for even at the present level of production pollution is much too high. Come to that, zero growth is easy to achieve, as British experience in the mid seventies showed. By large deflationary tax increases production could quite well be stopped from growing further. But we wouldn't like it. The result could be unemployment, general despair and a very dirty environment. For in a depression not a single authority will be prepared to close a stinking factory – in the name of employment we would have to allow everything that creates work, however dirty it is.

My recipe is the other way round. The economy must flourish – a high level of investment, attractive profits, full employment. In that climate the authorities must lay down strict criteria. Everything that pollutes and wastes must be countered. New factories that demand considerable energy do not get planning permission. No new airfields. No impairment of any part of nature whatever. Such a strict selective policy may very well lead to zero growth, or even to negative growth. But then the growth of labour productivity is halted at once. What remains is automatically more labour-intensive. I admit that this seems a contradictory recipe, something like vegetarian soup containing lots of meat. I also recognize that it demands heroic efforts on the part of the authorities – they have to row against the stream of many interests, those of both employers and workers. This policy calls for compulsion and intervention, and will meet with tremendous criticism. The country must be ruled in the name of the long term, with short-term objectives sacrificed. The prospects are at best uncertain.

The fifth problem concerns the controllability of society. It looks as if the government is going to be faced with difficult tasks in the coming decades – there has to be more intervention than before, and that calls for an obliging attitude on the part of the citizens. Even now some feel that the limits of compliance have been reached: with regard to taxes, to prohibitions, in traffic. The failure of an incomes policy in practically every country illustrates the fact that citizens are not always prepared to cede their traditional rights. There is no doubt that in the future income restraint will be called for in order to follow the Keynesian policy which is necessary for employment and which is at the same time required for distributing work among people. If we want to expand the collective sector a further moderation of private claims is necessary. Entrepreneurs must accept the fact that the authorities forbid those investments that are not up to standard. Consumers may perhaps be faced by rationing (camping, air travel). It is easy to understand that this leads to protest, unruliness and aggressiveness. Especially when the traditional conflicts about income distribution are constantly emphasized and people are made to believe that inequality is increasing, there is the chance of political instability that blocks the long-term solutions. Some sombre observers are therefore of the opinion that democracy cannot stand up to the new tasks and that the struggle for future economic policy will almost certainly be lost.*

It cannot be predicted whether these gloomy prophets will be proved right. It is, however, clear which argument political economy must advance against this uncontrollability. It is difficult to list them without lapsing into the unctuousness and sermonizing that usually mar such recommendations, but they

---

*Along these gloomy lines, Robert L. Heilbroner, *Inquiry into the Human Prospect*, 1974.

amount to tolerance and complaisance and awareness of the long term as opposed to short-term self-interest. It is really too silly to write, but it is after all true: the economist, as a citizen, has the task of bringing forward this kind of reasonable argument.

Is Macro-Economics a Science?

An answer in seven parts.

(1) Yes, of course it is. Anyone who wants to ponder national income will have to have concepts available. These can be found in macro-economic literature. We have to know what an inflationary gap is, and monetary equilibrium, and the multiplier. Anyone who talks about economic growth and then thinks that economics only has the construction of increasingly polluting factories in mind gets confused. Macro-economics is therefore an indispensable science for the citizen.

Against this answer it may be adduced that here 'science' does not mean much more than 'language'. And in fact nobody can practise macro-economics without having learnt the corresponding language. This book is therefore in part a grammar. Anyone who has read it can have his say. But in itself that says nothing about the content of the assertions.

(2) Of course macro-economics is a science because it orders one's mind. Thus a little thought soon makes it clear that micro-economic propositions lose their validity in macro-economics or operate the other way round. That is because things in macro-economics have two or more sides to them. Prices are incomes and incomes are prices. The creation of national debt means that our children inherit debts, but they also inherit claims. The simple marshalling of thoughts also includes the utilization of available data. Figures can immediately refute popular opinions – for instance that in the seventies Britain went downhill (real national income grew almost constantly). In this modest sense macro-economics has definitely scientific qualities. But there is a more ambitious view of what constitutes a science.

(3) There is no such thing as macro-economics, for the central concepts from this so-called science cannot stand up to elementary criticism. Real national income is a fiction; with a changing package of goods and new products, not only can it not be measured, it cannot even be defined. The stock of capital goods

cannot be reduced to one common denominator and so does not exist either. There is no such thing as a price level. Productive capacity is altogether an absolutely incomprehensible pseudo-quantity.

I can understand this scepticism without sharing it. If people want to follow it, that is up to them, but in that case there can be no further question of argument about wage increases, the burden of taxation, unemployment. Deep silence falls.

(4) Macro-economics certainly exists, because grandiose views of society exist. Adam Smith, David Ricardo, Karl Marx and John Maynard Keynes have one by one drawn a macro-economic social picture – their ideas have wielded power over people and in particular over statesmen. Marx considered his own socialism eminently scientific.

I won't argue with the bit about the grandiose view, but I doubt whether it's a science. I would prefer to interpret science as meaning a closely connected whole of verifiable and provisionally verified or at least not falsified hypotheses. There is certainly connection in the grandiose theories of the great economists, but the hypotheses are in many cases vaguely formulated, and the verification has often not taken place. In addition whole chunks of the theory have been falsified (particularly in the case of Ricardo and Marx). What cannot be verified is ideology, not science. Ideologies are necessary too; they have a fructifying effect on all kinds of things, and also on theory-forming. This is *par excellence* the field of creativity. But real science comes after that.

(5) Macro-economics is an exact science that arrives at razor-sharp conclusions which in addition are highly elegant. The books are full of them. National income will assume that value at which it generates as much expenditure as corresponds to its own size. In well-defined circumstances an equal increase in government expenditure and taxes causes national income to increase to the same extent as the budget. The deficit on the national budget in a self-contained country is equal to the surplus on the capital market. If the elasticity of substitution between labour and capital is less than one, the share in national income of the most rapidly growing factor of production falls. The growth

rate is the quotient of the propensity to save and the capital coefficient. The share of labour in national income is equal to the labour elasticity of production. The increase in labour productivity in steady growth is equal to technical progress divided by the share of labour. Striking propositions, aren't they?

Yes, I agree, but it is and remains formal theory, a twin sister of mathematics. I am not trying to disparage this way of practising economics – on the contrary, this technique yields striking results. In this way we build consistent ideas. As you may have noticed these ideas are more or less explained in this book. The nice thing is that some of them are so surprising.

However, the unpleasant side of the formal theory is that it says little about the real world in which we live, and above all that it gives some scholars the idea that they have the world in their pocket. Students and prospective economists also sometimes derive from the formal theory a kind of euphoria which they take for a grasp of economic events. In reality they have only practised algebra and drawn graphs. Sometimes they have produced numerical examples – excellent, as long as we do not think that things have also to go the same way in reality. We do not have to regard them as real verifiable hypotheses. Anyone who believes that $M.V = P.T$ or $Y = k(C_o + I_o)$ are results of genuine economic science is mistaken. Part of the self-conceit of economists is due to this kind of mistake.

(6) Macro-economics hardly exists as a real science. I share this strict judgement. We may have coherent systems of hypotheses, cast in quantitative form – so-called models – but when it is a matter of verification the results are occasionally disappointing. I make the requirement that we have to get to know the structure: the constant in change or, to put it more exactly, the form of the model and the numerical value of its parameters. That is real, structuralist macro-economics. Such models explain the past, predict the future and offer a basis for deriving the value of the instrument variables for the value of the targets fixed by the politicians.

Interpreted in this way macro-economics (or rather econometrics) has achieved a few things, but no more than that. Admittedly, it is not yet fifty years old and progress has been made.

But the parameters often melt in our hands, and in the course of turbulent events the model is sometimes rather unreliable. The investment equation is notoriously weak. Profits form a slippery and at the same time highly strategic variable. The feedback of profits to investments and employment makes the model undependable. As a result, prediction remains uncertain. The strictest methodological requirement is: only what has been predicted has been understood. Tested against this, macro-economics is in a weak position.

But there is hope. Research technique is making progress, new hypotheses are being repeatedly adduced, and research workers are checking one another. All this effort would be in vain if there were no structures, that is, if the human mind were not able to impose regularity on macro-economic events. Some deny this possibility, and in that case no science is possible. I am not as sceptical as that. I remain a structuralist.

(7) Macro-economics is not acceptable as a science, some say, because that greatly overrated subject cannot give any solid policy recommendations. Evidently the economists cannot put a stop to inflation and unemployment.

I do not agree with this view. It is based on an accumulation of misunderstandings. The main one of these is the mixture of insight and therapy; science explains how the world fits together, but this does not mean that there are any remedies available. Understanding is somewhat different from controlling. A second misunderstanding: science does not carry on its banner full employment and price stability as objectives – those are politicians' objectives. The latter can come and seek the advice of macro-economics, and science then consults the decision model in its turn. It gives advice of a conditional nature.

I personally have the impression that unemployment could be eliminated, together with the wage-price spiral, if politicians were really to give the highest priority to those objectives; but at the same time I have the impression that they will not do that, because the public – that is all of us together – would not approve of it. In that sense unemployment and inflation are voluntary. The same holds good for environmental pollution and waste of energy. Although these (political) pronouncements may be disputed, I remain convinced that science cannot be blamed for the failure of politics.

It proves that the reader cannot get away from deciding on his own view of macro-economics. There is ample choice: a non-existent subject full of chimeras; the presumptuous trade of the charlatan; the self-conceit of schoolmasters; the grandiose view that dominates the world; a series of elegant and exact propositions, some of which are most surprising; a common-sense approach to the struggle for one's daily bread, suitable for eliminating widespread misunderstandings and demonstrating eminently practical connections; a hesitant, groping science, seeking the strategic parameters of a changing reality. It is in any case a subject full of discoveries, full of temptation and tumult – a fascinating subject. A subject with a future, for it does not seem that the problems with which this book is concerned will evaporate in the coming decades.

A Short Glossary

BALANCE OF PAYMENTS: a list of all transactions which a country has engaged in with other countries in the course of a year.

BEARS: investors who do not trust share prices and therefore prefer to stay liquid.

BUDGET: a list of government income and expenditure.

BULLS: the opposite of bears; see the latter.

CIRCULATION: The movement of money and goods between firms, households, the government, and foreign countries; that is, the creation and spending of income.

CONSUMPTION FUNCTION: the relation between consumption and national income.

COST INFLATION: a rise in money costs.

DECISION MODEL: a model used for calculating what values of the instrument variables match the desired values of the target variables. See model, target variable, variable.

DEFICIENCY OF DEMAND: see deflationary gap.

DEFLATION: presence of a deflationary gap; see the latter.

DEFLATIONARY GAP: the difference between expenditure that leads to full employment and actual expenditure.

DEVALUATION: increase in the price of foreign currencies; not to be confused with deflation.

DISINFLATION: reduction of the inflationary gap; see the latter.

EXPENDITURE: what consumers, investors, and the government spend on goods and services.

FUNCTIONAL FINANCE: Keynesian budgetary policy aimed at banishing inflation and deflation.

GROWTH FUNCTION: relationship between the percentage increase in production and the percentage increases in labour and capital.

HAYEK SITUATION: strained national economy, scarcity of

factors of production on the market, a struggle for the means of production.

HOARDING: holding back money, increasing cash holdings.

INFLATION: presence of an inflationary gap; see the latter.

INFLATIONARY GAP: the difference between actual expenditure and the expenditure that leads exactly to full employment.

INVESTMENT: expanding the machinery of production; also the buying of securities.

LABOUR PRODUCTIVITY: volume of production divided by employment.

LEAK: reduction in total expenditure as a result of saving, importing, or paying taxes.

MODEL: depiction of reality (in our case the money and goods flow) by means of a system of connections (equations) between measurable quantities (variables).

MULTIPLIER: relation between the extra national income proceeding from extra expenditure and that extra expenditure itself.

NATIONAL BOOKKEEPING: statistical registration of incomes and expenditure.

NATIONAL INCOME: the sum of all wages, profits, rents, and interest.

NATIONAL PRODUCT: the total flow of goods produced by a national economy; also known as the real national income.

PLANNING: method of calculation using models, aimed at rationalization of economic policy.

PRICE INFLATION: general rise in prices.

PRODUCTION FUNCTION: the way in which the level of output depends upon the inputs of productive factors.

PRODUCTIVITY: the volume of production divided by the quantity of factors of production (output divided by the total of all inputs).

PROPENSITY TO CONSUME: consumption divided by national income.

PROPENSITY TO IMPORT: imports divided by national income.

PROPENSITY TO SAVE: that part of income that is saved; savings divided by national income.

QUANTITY THEORY: theory of the value of money, starting from the quantity of money.

RATE OF EXCHANGE: price of foreign currency in terms of the currency of one's own country.

REFLATION: reducing the deflationary gap; see the latter.

REGRESSION COEFFICIENT: number expressing the extent to which a variable influences the dependent variable.

REGRESSION EQUATION: connection between a quantity (the dependent variable) and a number of others influencing it (independent variables).

REVALUATION: reducing the price of foreign currency; not to be confused with reflation.

SHEEP: investors who are neither bulls nor bears, and who therefore believe that shares will remain at their current prices.

TARGET VARIABLE: the quantity in a model which the government aims at giving a certain value by influencing another variable (the instrument variable).

TAX BURDEN: tax revenue divided by national income. It is not a real burden, however strange this may seem.

TOTAL EXPENDITURE FUNCTION: the connection between total expenditure and national income.

VARIABLE: quantity which changes, e.g. national income, prices, consumption.

VELOCITY OF CIRCULATION OF MONEY: the number of times money changes hands per unit of time.

Note on Further Reading

For a first textbook on economics, I suggest you try Paul A. Samuelson's *Economics, An Introductory Analysis* (1948; tenth edition 1976); you will be in the company of at least three million other readers all over the world. If you are intrigued by the mathematical aspects of the subject, you will find Stephen Glaister's elegant *Mathematical Methods for Economists* (1972; second edition 1978) rewarding. If your vocabulary in the subject is rather limited, consult *The Penguin Dictionary of Economics* by G. Bannock, R. E. Baxter and R. Rees (1972; second edition 1978). It is not simply a dictionary but a textbook arranged alphabetically.

When you are ready to tackle a solid, general book on macro-economics, there is a wide choice. I recommend W. H. Branson's *Macro-Economic Theory and Policy* (1972; second edition 1979), or *Macro-Economic Analysis and Stabilization Policy* by S. J. Turnovsky (1977).

Special aspects of the subject are well represented. On Keynes, there is *The Life of John Maynard Keynes* by Roy Harrod (1951; Pelican 1972). On money, John Kenneth Galbraith has told part of its fascinating story in *Money, Whence It Came, Where It Went* (1975). *The Economics of Inequality* by A. B. Atkinson (1975) is an excellent guide to the subject of income distribution; for the more theoretical side, try Jan Tinbergen's *Income Distribution* (1971).

If you are tired of the fashionable type of growth pessimism, Wilfred Beckerman's *In Defence of Economic Growth* (1974) will provide you with all the counter-arguments.

Suppose you feel ready to tackle a really impressive exercise in neo-classical theory, difficult but rewarding: if you can work your way through *The Growing Economy* by James E. Meade (1968), and if you can understand most of it, then you can consider yourself a real economist.

Index of Names

MORE ABOUT PENGUINS
AND PELICANS

For further information about books available from Penguins please write to Dept EP, Penguin Books Ltd, Harmondsworth, Middlesex UB7 0DA.

In the U.S.A.: For a complete list of books available from Penguins in the United States write to Dept CS, Penguin Books, 625 Madison Avenue, New York, New York 10022.

In Canada: For a complete list of books available from Penguins in Canada write to Penguin Books Canada Ltd, 2801 John Street, Markham, Ontario L3R 1B4.

In Australia: For a complete list of books available from Penguins in Australia write to the Marketing Department, Penguin Books Australia Ltd, P.O. Box 257, Ringwood, Victoria 3134.

'This momentous book will rank as the contemporary successor to the classic works of Booth and Rowntree; its case histories alone should put paid to those who still assert that there is no longer poverty in Britain' – Barbara Wooton

POVERTY IN THE UNITED KINGDOM
A survey of household resources and standards of living
Peter Townsend

'The chief conclusion of this report is that poverty is more extensive than is generally or officially believed, and has to be understood not only as an inevitable feature of severe social inequality but also as a particular consequence of actions by the rich to preserve and enhance their wealth and so deny it to others ... The extremely unequal distribution of wealth is perhaps the single most notable feature of social conditions in the United Kingdom.'

Professor Townsend's massive and controversial survey is the most comprehensive investigation into poverty and wealth in Britain ever undertaken. It has virtually the scope and prestige of a Royal Commission, and will stand as the seminal work on the subject for years to come.

'Not only presents the results of the most extensive survey of poverty carried out in Britain, but also brings together Townsend's thinking over the last 25 years on the subject of poverty, the position of social minorities, and the role of social institutions. It is a veritable tour de force' – *Guardian*

'The contribution to knowledge and understanding is great indeed, and covers so many topics and correlations that it will provide material for discussion for years to come' – *New Society*